The Complete Ketogenic Guide for Women Over 50

600 Healthy and Delicious Recipes to Eat Well Every Day, Lose Weight, and Regain Confidence in your Body. 30 Days Meal Plan Included.

Emma Wilson

Table of Contents

Introduction

As women grow older, there are a variety of changes occurring within their bodies. Having a great deal of impact, estrogen reduction often causes weight gain and a slower metabolism. The keto diet, with adjustments for the particular requirements of women over fifty years old, is a beautiful way to lose weight while relieving some of the aches and pains experienced as the lack of estrogen takes hold.

The ketogenic diet can be beneficial in more ways than just weight loss. Follow the principles of food choices suggested by studies performed around the world and reap the benefits of this popular diet. Ease into ketosis with the plan outlined, and you will find a smoother transition to a low-carbohydrate lifestyle. Use the tips and tricks to smooth over rough spots and use the food list to try new foods.

While on the Keto diet, you are building up energy stores for your body to utilize. This means that you should be feeling a necessary boost in your energy levels and the ability to get through each moment of each day without struggling. You can say goodbye to the sluggish feeling that often accompanies other diet plans.

When you are on Keto, you should only be experiencing the benefits of additional energy and unlimited potential. Your diet isn't going to always feel like a diet. After some time, you will realize that you enjoy eating a Keto menu very much. Because your body will be switching the way it metabolizes, it will also be switching what it craves. Don't be surprised if you end up craving fats and proteins as you progress on the Keto diet — this is what your body will eventually want.

Keto diet helps control blood sugar and improve nutrition, which in turn not only improves insulin response and resistance but also protects against memory loss, which is often a part of aging. You have the tools to reach success in losing weight on the keto diet. In the end, the weight loss will be a very generous reward you will enjoy.

How Keto Works

The ketogenic diet is a perfect combination of an equal number of macros essential for the human body's perfect and healthy functioning. This diet is mostly focused on foods that are rich in fats, while carbohydrates are considerably lowered. How was the ketogenic diet discovered? Although this diet may have only recently become popular, it is not new at all. It is almost a century old. The ketogenic diet was used mainly to lower the incidence of seizures in epileptic children. People wanted to check out how the keto diet would work with an entirely healthy person as things usually go.

This diet makes the body burn fats much faster than it does carbohydrates. The carbohydrates that we take in through food arc turned into glucose, one of the leading "brain foods." So, once you start following the keto diet, food with reduced carbohydrates is forcing the liver to turn all the fats into fatty acids and ketone bodies. The ketones go to the brain and take the place of glucose, becoming the primary energy source. This is how your body turns towards the next best energy source to function correctly. This diet's primary purpose is to make your body switch from the way it used to function to an entirely new way of creating energy, keeping you healthy and alive.

Once you start following the ketogenic diet, you will notice that things are changing, first and foremost, in your mind. Before, carbohydrates were your main body 'fuel' and were used to create glucose so that your brain could function. Now you no longer feed yourself with them. In the beginning, most people feel odd because their natural food is off the table. When your menu consists of more fats and proteins, it is natural to feel that something is missing. Your brain alarms you that you haven't eaten enough and sends you signals that you are hungry. It is literally "panicking" and telling you that you are starving, which is not correct. You get to eat, and you get to eat plenty of good food, but not carbs. This condition usually arises during the first day or two. Afterward, people get used to their new eating habits.

Once the brain "realizes" that carbs are no longer an option, it will focus on "finding" another abundant energy source: in this case, fats. Not only is your food rich in fats, but your body contains stored fats in large amounts. As you consume more fats and fewer carbs, your body "runs" on the fats, both consumed and stored. The best thing is that, as the fats are used for energy, they are burned. This is how you get a double gain from this diet. Usually, it will take a few days of consuming low-carb meals before you start seeing visible weight loss results. You will not even have to check your weight because the fat layers will be visibly reduced.

For most people, this transition from a regular carb-rich diet can be quite a challenge. Most people are used to eating bread, pasta, rice, dairy products, sweets, soda, alcohol, and fruits, so quitting all these foods might be challenging. However, this is all in your head. If you manage to win the "battle" with your mind and endure the diet for a few days, you will see that you no longer have cravings as time goes by.

Plus, the weight loss and the fat burn will be a great motivation to continue with this diet. Many people who don't truly need to lose weight and are completely healthy still choose to follow the keto diet because it is a great way to keep their meals balanced. Also, it is the perfect way to cleanse the body of toxins, processed foods, sugars, and unnecessary carbs. The combination of these things is usually the main reason for heart failure, some cancers, diabetes, cholesterol, or obesity. If you ask a nutritionist about this diet, they will recommend it without a doubt. The keto diet can be followed forever and has no side effects. It does not restrict you from following it for a few weeks or a month. Once you get your body to keto foods, you will not think about going back to the old ways of eating your meals.

Benefits for Women over 50

When the entire ketogenic lifestyle is followed along with dietary changes, it results in the following known benefits:

1. Accelerates Metabolism

As a person ages, it is the rate of metabolism that slows down with time. Metabolism is the sum total of all the processes that are carried out in the body. It consists of the building of new cells and elements, as well as the breaking of the existing agents into other elements. The fat-sourced high energy and release of ketones accelerate the rate of metabolism in the body.

2. Hormones Production

It is said that a woman's body is particularly more sensitive to dietary changes than the male body. It is mainly because there are several hormones that are at play in a woman's body. With a slight change in dietary habits and lifestyle, women can harness more benefits out of their fasting regime. Hormones in women's bodies are not only responsible for regulating the mood and internal body processes, but they also affect other systems in the body. Controlled release of energy and a healthy diet is responsible for maintaining the balance of estrogen and progesterone in the body.

3. PCOS

Polycystic ovarian syndrome is another common disorder that is prevalent among women of all ages, especially those over 50. PCOS cases are often the result of consistently high levels of insulin in the blood. Therefore, the ketogenic diet, due to its lowering of insulin effect, can treat or prevent PCOS to some extent. It can also control and counter the negative effects of PCOS in women.

4. Diabetes

Insulin resistance is a condition in which the body resists producing insulin. When the body fails to produce insulin, the pancreatic cells produce more insulin to lower the blood glucose levels. Excessive insulin production over a longer period of time ultimately wears out the pancreatic cells, and they lose the ability to produce necessary insulin levels, thus leading to diabetes. Since intermittent fasting can prevent insulin resistance by naturally lowering blood glucose levels, it also reduces the risks of diabetes. The ketogenic diet controls the insulin levels in the blood, thus prevents the risks of insulin resistance and diabetes.

5. Oxidative Stress

There are various chemical reactions that are occurring within the human body as a result of metabolism. These reactions produce millions of products and byproducts. Some chemical reactions produce free radicals, which are highly reactive in nature. When these radicals are left in the body for a longer duration of time, they can oxidize other elements in the cells and mingle with the natural cell cycle, ultimately leading to cell death. The cumulative effect of those free radicals is termed oxidative stress. When this stress increases, it can negatively affect human health. Ketones produced through ketosis work as antioxidants, which remove the free radicals and toxins from the body.

6. Cures Cancer

The ketogenic diet also improves the immune system, which helps patients to fight against all sorts of diseases, especially cancer. When the body undergoes ketosis, there is an increased production of lymphocytes that kills the pathogens or agents that may lead to cancer. Several cancer treatments also use this natural immune system to fight against cancerous cells.

7. Inflammation

Inflammation is the swelling of body tissues and organs for any practical reason. In women over the age of 50, inflammation can result from hormonal or electrolyte imbalance. Accumulation of uric acid and high sugar and cholesterol levels may also cause inflammation. Diseases like osteoporosis, or arthritis, which are common among women, also cause inflammation. Similarly, inflammation can also occur in the brain due to Alzheimer's or dementia. In any case, inflammation is always painful and health-damaging. Ketosis can help the body fight against the agents, causing inflammation. It promotes the immune system to increase its productivity. The damaged cells, which cause inflammation in the neighboring area, are then actively removed through autophagy to clean the body and repair it.

8. Weight Loss

Finally, weight loss is the most promising and obvious advantage of the ketogenic diet. Women over 50 years of age actively seek the keto diet to lose weight. It can reduce two to three pounds of weight within a week.

BREAKFAST RECIPES

Keto Low Carb Crepe

Preparation Time: 5 minutes | **Cooking Time:** 8 minutes | **Servings:** 4 | **Calories:** 118

Ingredients: 2 eggs | 1 white egg | 1 tbsp unsalted butter | 1-1/3 tbsp cream cheese
2/3 tbsp psyllium husk

Directions: Prepare the batter and for this, put all the ingredients in a bowl, except for butter, and then whisk by using a stick blender until smooth and very liquid. Bring out a skillet pan, put it over medium heat, add ½ tbsp butter and when it melts, pour in half of the batter, spread evenly, and cook until the top has firmed. Carefully flip the crepe, then continue cooking for 2 minutes until cooked and then move it to a plate. Add remaining butter and when it melts, cook another crepe in the same manner and then serve.

Keto Chewy Chaffle

Preparation Time: 5 minutes | **Cooking Time:** 5 minutes | **Servings:** 2 | **Calories**: 142

Ingredients: ½ cup shredded mozzarella cheese full-fat | 1 egg, pasteurized | 2 tsp coconut flour

Directions: Turn on a mini waffle maker and let it preheat for 5 minutes. In the meantime, bring out a medium bowl, put all the ingredients in it, and then mix by using a blender until smooth. Scoop the batter evenly into the waffle maker, shut with lid, and let it cook for 3 to 4 minutes until firm and golden brown.

Keto Creamy Bacon Dish

Preparation Time: 5 minutes | **Cooking Time:** 7 minutes | **Servings:** 2 | **Calories**: 150

Ingredients: ½ tsp dried basil | ½ tsp minced garlic | ½ tsp tomato paste | 3 slices of bacon, chopped
2 oz unsalted butter, softened

Directions: Bring out a skillet pan, put it over medium heat, add 1 tbsp butter and when it starts to melt, add chopped bacon and cook for 5 minutes. Then remove the pan from heat, add remaining butter, along with basil and tomato paste, season with salt and black pepper and stir. Move bacon butter into an airtight container, cover with the lid, and refrigerate for 1 hour until solid.

Chia Breakfast Bowl

Preparation Time: 10 minutes | **Cooking Time:** 0 minutes | **Servings:** 2 | **Calories**: 298

Ingredients: ¼ cup whole chia seeds | 2 cups almond milk, unsweetened | 1 tsp. vanilla extract
2 tbsp. sugar-free maple syrup | Toppings: cinnamon and extra maple syrup | nuts and berries

Directions: Combine the syrup, milk, chia seeds, and vanilla extract in a bowl and stir to mix. Let stand for 30 minutes, then whisk. Transfer to an airtight container. Cover and refrigerate overnight. Serve.

Cheesy Breakfast Muffins

Preparation Time: 15 minutes | **Cooking Time:** 12 minutes | **Servings:** 6 | **Calories**: 214

Ingredients: 4 tablespoons melted butter | 3/4 tablespoon baking powder | 1 cup almond flour
2 large eggs, lightly beaten | 2 ounces cream cheese mixed with 2 tablespoons heavy whipping cream
handful of shredded Mexican blend cheese

Directions: Preheat the oven to 400°F. Grease 6 muffin tin cups with melted butter and set aside. Combine the baking powder and almond flour in a bowl. Stir well and set aside. Stir together four tablespoons melted butter, eggs, shredded cheese, and cream cheese in a separate bowl. The egg and the dry mixture must be combined using a hand mixer to beat until it is creamy and well blended. The mixture must be scooped into the greased muffin cups evenly.

Eggs and Cheddar Breakfast Burritos

Preparation Time: 15 minutes | **Cooking Time:** 6 minutes | **Servings:** 4 | **Calories**: 478

Ingredients: 4 low-carb soft tortillas | 3 tbsp butter | 2 small yellow onions, chopped
½ medium orange bell pepper, deseeded and chopped | 10 eggs, beaten | salt and black pepper, to taste
8 tbsp grated cheddar cheese (white and sharp) | 2 tbsp chopped fresh scallions | hot sauce for serving

Directions: Melt the butter in a skillet over medium heat and stir-fry the onions and bell pepper for 3 minutes or until softened. Pour the eggs into the pan, let set for 15 seconds and then, scramble. Season with salt, black pepper, and stir in the cheddar cheese. Cook until the cheese melts. Lay out the tortillas, divide the eggs on top, and sprinkle some scallions and hot sauce on top. Fold two edges of each tortilla in and tightly roll the other ends over the filling. Slice into halves and enjoy the burritos.

Spinach, Mushroom, and Goat Cheese Frittata

Preparation Time: 15 minutes | **Cooking Time:** 20 minutes | **Servings:** 5 | **Calories**: 265

Ingredients: 1 cup fresh mushrooms, sliced | 6 bacon slices, cooked and chopped | 10 large eggs, beaten
1 cup spinach, shredded | 1/2 cup goat cheese, crumbled | 2 tablespoons olive oil | pepper and salt

Directions: Preheat the oven to 350°F. Heat oil and add the mushrooms and fry for 3 minutes until they start to brown, stirring frequently. Fold in the bacon and spinach and cook for about 1 to 2 minutes, or until the spinach is wilted. Slowly pour in the beaten eggs and cook for 3 to 4 minutes. Making use of a spatula, lift the edges for allowing uncooked egg to flow underneath. Top with the goat cheese, then sprinkle the salt and pepper to season. Bake in the preheated oven for about 15 minutes until lightly golden brown around the edges.

Vegan Breakfast Skillet

Preparation Time: 3 minutes | **Cooking Time:** 5 minutes | **Servings:** 4 | **Calories**: 275

Ingredients: 400 g firm tofu, drained and crumbled | 20 g chickpeas | 100 g spinach | 3 tbsp. olive oil
1 tbsp. garlic powder | 1 tsp paprika | ½ tsp turmeric powder | ¼ tsp salt | ¼ tsp pepper

Directions: Heat olive oil in a skillet. Add crumbled tofu and stir for 2-3 minutes. Stir in all the spices. Add chickpeas and spinach — sauté for another minute. Serve hot.

Yogurt Waffles

Preparation Time: 15 minutes | **Cooking Time:** 25 minutes | **Servings:** 5 | **Calories**: 265

Ingredients: 1/2 cup golden flax seeds meal | 1/2 cup plus 3 tablespoons almond flour
1-1/2 tablespoons granulated erythritol | 1 tablespoon unsweetened vanilla whey protein powder
¼ teaspoon baking soda | 1/2 teaspoon organic baking powder | 1/4 teaspoon xanthan gum
1 large organic egg, white and yolk separated | 1 organic whole egg | 3 ounces plain Greek yogurt
2 tablespoons unsweetened almond milk | 1-1/2 tablespoons unsalted butter | salt, as required

Directions: Preheat the waffle iron and then grease it. In a large bowl, add the flour, erythritol, protein powder, baking soda, baking powder, xanthan gum, salt, and mix until well combined. In another bowl or container, put in the egg white and beat until stiff peaks form. In a third bowl, add two egg yolks, whole egg, almond milk, butter, yogurt, and beat until well combined. Place egg mixture into the bowl of the flour mixture and mix until well combined. Gently, fold in the beaten egg whites. Place 1/4 cup of the mixture into preheated waffle iron and cook for about 4–5 minutes or until golden brown. Repeat with the remaining mixture. Serve warm.

Green Vegetable Quiche

Preparation Time: 20 minutes | **Cooking Time:** 20 minutes | **Servings:** 4 | **Calories:** 298

Ingredients: 6 organic eggs | 1/2 cup unsweetened almond milk | 2 cups fresh baby spinach, chopped
1/2 cup green bell pepper, seeded and chopped | 1 scallion, chopped | 1/4 cup fresh cilantro, chopped
1 tablespoon fresh chives, minced | 3 tablespoons mozzarella cheese, grated | salt & ground black pepper

Directions: Preheat your oven to 400°F. Lightly grease a pie dish. In a bowl, add eggs, almond milk, salt, and black pepper, and beat until well combined. Set aside. In another bowl, add the vegetables and herbs and mix well. At the bottom of the prepared pie dish, place the veggie mixture evenly and top with the egg mixture. Let the quiche bake for about 20 minutes. Remove the pie dish from the oven and immediately sprinkle with the Parmesan cheese. Set aside for about 5 minutes before slicing. Cut into desired sized wedges and serve warm.

Keto Mushroom Sausage Skillet

Preparation Time: 5 minutes | **Cooking Time:** 25 minutes | **Servings:** 5 | **Calories**: 357

Ingredients: sixteen ounces of cremini mushroom | sixteen ounces of pork sausage
one cup of mozzarella cheese, grated | two tablespoons of olive oil | two medium green onions, for garnish

Directions: Collect all ingredients and cook them. To heat it, switch on the oven to broil. Load half the olive oil into a cast iron skillet and switch on medium heat on the stovetop. Wash the mushrooms, dry them well with a paper towel, and cut them into strips. Cook the sausages in the cast iron skillet on the stovetop over medium to high heat until they are golden and thoroughly fried. Remove the sausages from the pan until they are thoroughly cooked and arrange them on a cutting board. Add the remaining olive oil to the skillet, add the mushrooms and cook until the mushrooms are golden brown. Chop up the pork sausage on a cutting board while the mushrooms are frying, with a diagonal break. Add the sliced pork sausage to the skillet and scatter with mozzarella cheese as soon as the mushrooms are thoroughly cooked. Place it on a grill inside the oven until the cheese begins to melt. Look closely at the microwave. The cheese melts quickly! Remove and garnish with green onions from the oven.

Cheddar Scramble

Preparation Time: 10 minutes| **Cooking Time:** 8 minutes | **Servings:** 2 | **Calories**: 264

Ingredients: 1 small yellow onion, chopped finely | 12 large organic eggs, beaten lightly
salt and ground black pepper, as required | 4 ounces cheddar cheese, shredded | 2 tablespoons olive oil

Directions: In a large wok, heat oil over medium heat and sauté the onion for about 4–5 minutes. Add the eggs, salt, and black pepper and cook for about 3 minutes, stirring continuously. Remove from the heat and immediately, stir in the cheese. Serve immediately.

Ricotta Omelet with Swiss Chard

Preparation Time: 10 minutes | **Cooking Time:** 15 minutes | **Servings:** 2 | **Calories**: 693

Ingredients: 6 eggs | 2 tbsp. almond milk | ½ tsp. kosher salt | ½ tsp. ground black pepper
6 tbsp. unsalted butter, divided | 2 bunch Swiss chard, cleaned and stemmed | 2/3 cup ricotta

Directions: Add the eggs, and milk. Season with salt and pepper then whisk. Set aside. In a skillet, melt 4 tbsp. butter. Add the veggie leaves and sauté until just wilted. Remove from pan. Set aside. Now melt 1 tbsp. butter in the skillet. Add half of the egg mixture. Spread the mixture. Cook for about 2 minutes. Add half of the ricotta when the edges are firm, but the center is still a bit runny. Bend 1/3 of the omelet over the ricotta filling. Transfer to a plate. Repeat with the remaining butter and egg mixture. Serve with Swiss chard.

Omelet with Goat Cheese and Herb

Preparation Time: 5 minutes | **Cooking Time:** 12 minutes | **Servings:** 2 | **Calories**: 523

Ingredients: 6 eggs, beaten | 2 tbsp. chopped herbs (basil, parsley or cilantro) | 4 oz. fresh goat cheese
kosher salt and black pepper to taste | 2 tbsp. unsalted butter

Directions: Whisk together the eggs, herbs, salt, and pepper. Melt 1 tbsp. butter in a skillet. Put half of the egg mixture and cook for 4 to 5 minutes, or until just set. Crumble half the goat cheese over the eggs and fold in half. Cook for 1 minute, or until cheese is melted. Transfer to a plate. Repeat process with the remaining butter, egg mixture, and goat cheese. Serve.

Bacon and Zucchini Egg Breakfast

Preparation Time: 10 minutes | **Cooking Time:** 10 minutes | **Servings:** 2 | **Calories**: 242

Ingredients: 2 cups zucchini noodles | 2 slices of raw bacon | ¼ cup grated Asiago cheese | 2 eggs
salt and pepper, to taste

Directions: Cut the bacon slices into ¼ inch thick strips. Cook the bacon in a pan for 3 minutes. Add the zucchini and mix well. Season with salt and pepper. Flatten slightly with a spatula and make 2 depressions for the eggs. Sprinkle with the cheese. Break one egg into each dent. Cook 3 minutes more, then cover and cook for 2 to 4 minutes, or until the eggs are cooked. Serve.

Berry Chocolate Breakfast Bowl

Preparation Time: 10 minutes | **Cooking Time:** 0 minutes | **Servings:** 2 | **Calories**: 287

Ingredients: 1/2 cup strawberries, fresh or frozen | 1/2 cup blueberries, fresh or frozen
1 cup unsweetened almond milk | sugar-free maple syrup to taste | 2 tbsp. unsweetened cocoa powder
1 tbsp. cashew nuts (for topping)

Directions: The berries must be divided into four bowls, pour on the almond milk. Drizzle with the maple syrup and sprinkle the cocoa powder on top, a tablespoon per bowl. Top with the cashew nuts and enjoy immediately.

Breakfast Skillet

Preparation Time: 10 minutes | **Cooking Time:** 15 minutes | **Servings:** 2 | **Calories**: 556

Ingredients: 1 lb. organic ground turkey/grass-fed beef | 6 eggs | 1 cup Keto-friendly salsa of choice

Directions: Warm the skillet using oil (medium heat). Add the turkey and simmer until the pink is gone. Fold in the salsa and simmer for two to three minutes. Crack the eggs and add to the top of the turkey base. Place a lid on the pot and cook for seven minutes until the whites of the eggs are opaque. Note: the cooking time will vary depending on how you like the eggs prepared.

Bagels with Cheese

Preparation Time: 10 minutes | **Cooking Time:** 15 minutes | **Servings:** 6 | **Calories**: 374

Ingredients: 2.5 cups mozzarella cheese | 1 tsp. baking powder | 3 oz cream cheese | 2 eggs
1.5 cups almond flour

Directions: Shred the mozzarella and combine with the flour, baking powder, and cream cheese in a mixing container. Pop into the microwave for about one minute. Mix well. Let the mixture cool and add the eggs. Break apart into six sections and shape into round bagels. Note: You can also sprinkle with a seasoning of your choice or pinch of salt if desired. Bake them for approximately 12 to 15 minutes. Serve.

Bacon & Avocado Omelet

Preparation Time: 5 minutes | **Cooking Time:** 5 minutes | **Servings:** 1 | **Calories**: 719

Ingredients: 1 slice crispy bacon | 2 large organic eggs | half of 1 small avocado
5 cup freshly grated Parmesan cheese | 2 tbsp ghee or coconut oil or butter

Directions: Prepare the bacon to your liking and set aside. Combine the eggs, parmesan cheese, and your choice of finely chopped herbs. Warm a skillet and add the butter/ghee to melt using the medium-high heat setting. When the pan is hot, whisk and add the eggs. Prepare the omelet working it towards the middle of the pan for about 30 seconds. When firm, flip, and cook it for another 30 seconds. Arrange the omelet on a plate and garnish with the crunched bacon bits. Serve with sliced avocado.

Bacon Omelet

Preparation Time: 10 minutes| **Cooking Time:** 15 minutes | **Servings:** 3 | **Calories**: 427

Ingredients: 4 large organic eggs | 1 tablespoon fresh chives, minced | | 1 tablespoon unsalted butter
4 bacon slices | salt and ground black pepper, as required | 2 ounces cheddar cheese, shredded

Directions: In a bowl, add the eggs, chives, salt, and black pepper, and beat until well combined. Heat a non-stick frying pan over medium-high heat and cook the bacon slices for about 8–10 minutes. Place the bacon onto a paper towel-lined plate to drain. Then chop the bacon slices. With paper towels, wipe out the frying pan. In the same frying pan, melt butter over medium-low heat and cook the egg mixture for about 2 minutes. Carefully, flip the omelet and top with chopped bacon. Cook for 1–2 minutes or until desired doneness of eggs. Remove from heat and immediately, place the cheese in the center of omelet. Fold the edges of omelet over cheese and cut into 2 portions. Serve immediately.

Green Veggies Quiche

Preparation Time: 20 minutes | **Cooking Time:** 20 minutes | **Servings:** 5 | **Calories**: 176

Ingredients: 6 organic eggs | ½ cup unsweetened almond milk | 2 cups fresh baby spinach, chopped
½ cup green bell pepper, seeded and chopped | 3 tablespoons mozzarella cheese, grated
1 scallion, chopped | ¼ cup fresh cilantro, chopped | 1 tablespoon fresh chives, minced
salt and ground black pepper, as required | Parmesan cheese, to taste

Directions: Preheat your oven to 400°F. Lightly grease a pie dish. In a bowl, add eggs, almond milk, salt, and black pepper, and beat until well combined. Set aside. In another bowl, add the vegetables and herbs and mix well. In the bottom of prepared pie dish, place the veggie mixture evenly and top with the egg mixture. Bake for about 20 minutes or until a wooden skewer inserted in the center comes out clean. Remove pie dish from the oven and immediately sprinkle with the Parmesan cheese. Set aside for about 5 minutes before slicing. Cut into desired sized wedges and serve warm.

Chicken & Asparagus Frittata

Preparation Time: 15 minutes | **Cooking Time:** 12 minutes | **Servings:** 4 | **Calories**: 158

Ingredients: ½ cup grass-fed cooked chicken breast, chopped | 1/3 cup Parmesan cheese, grated
1/3 cup boiled asparagus, chopped | ¼ cup cherry tomatoes, halved | ¼ cup mozzarella cheese, shredded
6 organic eggs, beaten lightly | salt and ground black pepper, as required

Directions: Preheat the broiler of oven. In a bowl, add the Parmesan cheese, eggs, salt, and black pepper, and beat until well combined. In a large ovenproof wok, melt butter over medium-high heat and cook the chicken and asparagus for about 2–3 minutes. Add the egg mixture and tomatoes and stir to combine. Cook for about 4–5 minutes. Remove from the heat and sprinkle with the Parmesan cheese. Now, transfer the wok under broiler and broil for about 3–4 minutes or until slightly puffed. Cut into desired sized wedges and serve immediately.

Baked Apples

Preparation Time: 10 minutes | **Cooking Time:** 1 hour | **Servings:** 4 | **Calories**: 175

Ingredients: 4 tsp Keto-friendly sweetener | 0.75 tsp cinnamon | 0.25 cup chopped pecans
4 large granny smith apples

Directions: Set the oven temperature at 375° F. Mix the sweetener with the cinnamon and pecans. Core the apple and add the prepared stuffing. Add enough water into the baking dish to cover the bottom of the apple. Bake them for about 45 minutes to 1 hour.

Baked Eggs in the Avocado

Preparation Time: 10 minutes | **Cooking Time:** 20 minutes | **Servings:** 1 | **Calories:** 452

Ingredients: half of 1 avocado | 1 egg | 1 tbsp olive oil | half cup shredded cheddar cheese

Directions: Heat the oven to reach 425°F. Discard the avocado pit and remove just enough of the 'insides' to add the egg. Drizzle with oil and break the egg into the shell. Sprinkle with cheese and bake them for 15 to 16 minutes until the egg is the way you prefer. Serve.

Banana Pancakes

Preparation Time: 10 minutes | **Cooking Time:** 15 minutes | **Servings:** 3 | **Calories**: 157

Ingredients: butter | 2 bananas | 4 eggs | 1 tsp cinnamon | 1 tsp baking powder (optional)

Directions: Combine each of the fixings. Melt a portion of butter in a skillet using the medium temperature setting. Prepare the pancakes 1-2 minutes per side. Cook them with the lid on for the first part of the cooking cycle for a fluffier pancake. Serve plain or with your favorite garnishes such as a dollop of coconut cream or fresh berries.

Bacon & Cheese Frittata

Preparation Time: 5 minutes | **Cooking Time:** 5 minutes | **Servings:** 6 | **Calories:** 320

Ingredients: 1 cup heavy cream | 6 eggs | 5 crispy slices of bacon | 2 chopped green onions
4 oz cheddar cheese | Also needed: 1 pie plate

Directions: Warm the oven temperature to reach 350° Fahrenheit. Whisk the eggs and seasonings. Empty into the pie pan and top off with the remainder of the fixings. Bake 30-35 minutes. Wait for a few minutes before serving for the best results.

Spinach-Blueberry Smoothie

Preparation Time: 5 minutes | **Cooking Time:** 0 minutes | **Servings:** 2 | **Calories:** 353

Ingredients: 1 cup of coconut milk | 1 cup spinach | ½ English cucumber, chopped | ½ cup blueberries
1 scoop plain protein powder | 2 tablespoons coconut oil | 4 ice cubes | mint sprigs, for garnish

Directions: Put the coconut milk, spinach, cucumber, blueberries, protein powder, coconut oil, and ice in a blender and blend until smooth. Pour into 2 glasses, garnish each with the mint, and serve.

Creamy Cinnamon Smoothie

Preparation Time: 5 minutes | **Cooking Time:** 0 minutes | **Servings:** 2 | **Calories**: 492

Ingredients: 2 cups of coconut milk | 1 scoop vanilla protein powder | 5 drops liquid stevia
1 teaspoon ground cinnamon | ½ teaspoon alcohol-free vanilla extract

Directions: Put the coconut milk, protein powder, stevia, cinnamon, and vanilla in a blender and blend until smooth. Pour into 2 glasses and serve immediately.

Bacon & Egg Breakfast Muffins

Preparation Time: 15 minutes | **Cooking Time:** 30 minutes | **Servings:** 12 | **Calories:** 69

Ingredients: 8 large eggs | 8 slices bacon | 66 cup green onion

Directions: Warm the oven at 350° Fahrenheit. Spritz the muffin tin wells using a cooking oil spray. Chop the onions and set aside. Prepare a large skillet using the medium temperature setting. Fry the bacon until it's crispy and place on a layer of paper towels to drain the grease. Chop it into small pieces after it has cooled. Whisk the eggs, bacon, and green onions, mixing well until all of the fixings are incorporated. Dump the egg mixture into the muffin tin (halfway full). Bake it for about 20 to 25 minutes. Cool slightly and serve.

Creamy Almond and Cheese Mix

Preparation Time: 10 minutes | **Cooking Time:** 20 minutes | **Servings:** 6 | **Calories:** 231

Ingredients: 1 cup almond milk | cooking spray | 9 ounces cream cheese, soft | 6 eggs, whisked
1 cup cheddar cheese, shredded | 6 spring onions, chopped | salt and black pepper, to taste

Directions: Heat up your air fryer with the oil at 350 degrees F and grease it with cooking spray. In a bowl, put and mixed the eggs with the rest of the ingredients, whisk well, pour and spread into the air fryer and cook everything for 20 minutes. Divide everything between plates and serve.

Chai Waffles

Preparation Time: 15 minutes | **Cooking Time:** 20 minutes | **Servings:** 4 | **Calories:** 286

Ingredients: 4 eggs, separated | 3 tablespoons coconut flour | 3 tablespoons powdered erythritol
1 -1/4 teaspoon baking powder | 1 teaspoon vanilla extract | 1/2 teaspoon ground cinnamon
1/4 teaspoon ground ginger | pinch ground cloves | pinch ground cardamom
3 tablespoons coconut oil, melted | 3 tablespoons unsweetened almond milk

Directions: Divide the eggs into two separate mixing bowls. Whip the whites until stiff peaks develop and then set aside. Whisk the egg yolks into the other bowl with the coconut flour, Erythritol, baking powder, cocoa, cinnamon, cardamom, and cloves. Pour the melted coconut oil and the almond milk into the second bowl and whisk. Fold softly in the whites of the egg until you have just combined. Preheat waffle iron with cooking spray and grease. Spoon into the iron for about 1/2 cup of batter. Cook the waffle according to directions from the maker. Move the waffle to a plate and repeat with the batter leftover.

Keto Fruit Cereal

Preparation Time: 20 minutes | **Cooking Time:** 5 minutes | **Servings:** 3 | **Calories**: 201

Ingredients: 1 cup of coconut flakes | ½ cup of sliced strawberries | ¼ cup of sliced raspberries

Directions: Preheat oven to 300 degrees F. Prepare a baking tray with parchment paper. Slice the berries into small bits. Spread the coconut flakes on the tray, bake for 5 minutes until brown from the edges. Take out the baked coconut cereals, let it cool. Then, add in sliced raspberries and strawberries. Enjoy with almond milk.

Bacon Hash

Preparation Time: 5 minutes | **Cooking Time:** 10 minutes | **Servings:** 2 | **Calories**: 366

Ingredients: 1 small green pepper | 2 jalapenos | 1 small onion | 4 eggs | 6 bacon slices

Directions: Chop the bacon into chunks using a food processor. Set aside for now. Slice the onions and peppers into thin strips. Dice the jalapenos as small as possible. Heat a skillet and fry the veggies. Once browned, combine the fixings and cook until crispy. Place on a serving dish with the eggs.

Easy Boiled Eggs

Preparation Time: 5 minutes | **Cooking Time:** 5 minutes | **Servings:** 2 | **Calories:** 151

Ingredients: ¼ tsp ground black pepper | ¼ tsp salt | ½ of a medium avocado | 2 eggs

Directions: Put a medium pot over medium heat, fill it half full with water and bring it to boil. Then carefully Put the eggs in the boiling water and boil the eggs for 5 minutes until soft-boiled, 8 minutes for medium-boiled, and 10 minutes for hard-boiled. When eggs have boiled, move them to a bowl containing chilled water and let them rest for 5 minutes. Then crack the eggs with a spoon and peel them. Cut each egg into slices, season with salt and black pepper, and serve with diced avocado.

Goat Cheese Frittata

Preparation Time: 15 minutes | **Cooking Time:** 15 minutes | **Servings:** 4 | **Calories**: 412

Ingredients: 1 tbsp. avocado oil for frying | 2 oz. bacon slices, chopped | 1 small yellow onion, chopped 2 scallions, chopped | 1 tbsp. chopped fresh chives | salt and black pepper, to taste | 8 eggs, beaten 1 tbsp. unsweetened almond milk |1 tbsp. chopped fresh parsley | 3-1/2 oz. (100 g) goat cheese, divided 3/4 oz. (20 g) grated Parmesan cheese | 1 red bell pepper

Directions: Let the oven preheat to 350°F/175°C. Heat the avocado oil in a medium cast-iron pan and cook the bacon for 5 minutes or golden brown. Stir in the bell pepper, onion, scallions, and chives. Cook for 3 to 4 minutes or until the vegetables soften. Season with salt and black pepper. In a bowl or container, the eggs must be beaten with the almond milk and parsley. Pour the mixture over the vegetables, stirring to spread out nicely. Share half of the goat cheese on top. Once the eggs start to set, divide the remaining goat cheese on top, season with salt, black pepper, and place the pan in the oven— Bake for 5 to 6 minutes or until the eggs set all around. Take out the pan, scatter the Parmesan cheese on top, slice, and serve warm.

Creamy Bacon Eggs

Preparation Time: 10 minutes | **Cooking Time:** 10 minutes | **Servings:** 4 | **Calories:** 387

Ingredients: 6 oz. bacon | 4 eggs | 5 tablespoons heavy cream | 1 tablespoon butter | 1 teaspoon paprika ½ teaspoon nutmeg | 1 teaspoon salt | 1 teaspoon ground black pepper

Directions: Chop the bacon into small pieces and sprinkle it with salt. Mix to combine and put in the air fryer basket. Preheat the air fryer to 360°F and cook the bacon for 5 minutes. Meanwhile, crack the eggs in a bowl and whisk them using a hand whisker. Sprinkle the egg mixture with paprika, nutmeg, and ground black pepper. Whisk egg mixture gently. Toss the butter into the bacon and pour the egg mixture. Add the heavy cream and cook for 2 minutes. Stir the mixture with a spatula until you get scrambled eggs and cook for 3 minutes more. Transfer onto serving plates.

Cheddar Bacon Hash

Preparation Time: 8 minutes | **Cooking Time:** 8 minutes | **Servings:** 4 | **Calories:** 445

Ingredients: 1 zucchini | 7 oz. bacon, cooked | 4 oz. cheddar cheese | 2 tablespoon butter | 1 tsp salt 1 teaspoon ground black pepper | 1 teaspoon paprika | 1 teaspoon cilantro | 1 teaspoon ground thyme

Directions: Chop the zucchini into the small cubes and sprinkle it with salt, ground black pepper, paprika, cilantro, and ground thyme. Preheat the air fryer to 400°F and toss the butter into the air fryer basket tray. Melt it and add the zucchini cubes. Cook the zucchini for 5 minutes. Meanwhile, shred Cheddar cheese. Shake the zucchini cubes carefully and add the cooked bacon. Sprinkle the zucchini mixture with the shredded cheese and cook it for 3 minutes more. Transfer the breakfast hash in the serving bowls and stir.

Asparagus with Bacon and Eggs

Preparation Time: 5 minutes | **Cooking Time:** 8 minutes | **Servings:** 2 | **Calories**: 179

Ingredients: ¼ tsp salt | 1 egg | 1/8 tsp ground black pepper | 2 slices of bacon, diced | 4 oz asparagus

Directions: Bring out a skillet pan, put it over medium heat, add bacon, and cook for 4 minutes until crispy. Move cooked bacon to a plate, then add asparagus into the pan and cook for 5 minutes until tender-crisp. Crack the egg over the cooked asparagus, season with salt and black pepper, then switch heat to medium-low level and cook for 2 minutes until egg white has set. Chop the cooked bacon slices, sprinkle over egg and asparagus and serve.

Cheesy Brussels Sprouts and Eggs

Preparation Time: 5 minutes | **Cooking Time:** 20 minutes | **Servings:** 4 | **Calories**: 242

Ingredients: 1 tablespoon olive oil | 1 pound Brussels sprouts, shredded | 1 tablespoon chives, chopped ½ cup coconut cream | salt and black pepper (taste) | 4 eggs, whisked | ¼ cup cheddar cheese, shredded

Directions: Preheat the Air Fryer at 360 degrees F and grease it with the oil. Spread the Brussels sprouts on the bottom of the fryer, then add the eggs mixed with the rest of the ingredients, toss a bit and cook for 20 minutes. Divide between plates and serve.

Pesto Scramble

Preparation Time: 5 minutes | **Cooking Time:** 5 minutes | **Servings:** 2 | **Calories**: 160

Ingredients: 1 tbsp basil pesto | 1 tbsp unsalted butter | 1/8 tsp ground black pepper | 1/8 tsp salt 2 eggs | 2 tbsp grated cheddar cheese

Directions: Crack eggs in a bowl, add cheese, black pepper, salt, and pesto and whisk until combined. Bring out a skillet pan, put it over medium heat, add butter and when it melts, pour in the egg mixture, and cook for 3 to 5 minutes until eggs have scrambled to the desired level.

Keto Parmesan Frittata

Preparation Time: 10 minutes | **Cooking Time:** 15 minutes | **Servings:** 6 | **Calories**: 202

Ingredients: 6 eggs | 1/3 cup heavy cream | 1 tomato | 5 oz. chive stems | 1 tablespoon butter 1 teaspoon salt | 1 tablespoon dried oregano | 6 oz. Parmesan | 1 teaspoon chili pepper

Directions: Crack the eggs into the air fryer basket tray and whisk them with a hand whisker. Chop the tomato and dice the chives. Add the vegetables to the egg mixture. Pour the heavy cream. Sprinkle the liquid mixture with the butter, salt, dried oregano, and chili pepper. Shred Parmesan cheese and add it to the mixture too. Sprinkle the mixture with a silicone spatula. Preheat the air fryer to 375°F and cook the frittata for 15 minutes.

Avocado Salad Dish

Preparation Time: 8 minutes | **Cooking Time:** 5 minutes | **Servings:** 2 | **Calories**: 104

Ingredients: ½ of a medium avocado, sliced | 1 tbsp apple cider vinegar | 4 slices of bacon, chopped 4 oz chopped lettuce | 1 tbsp olive oil

Directions: Prepare bacon and for this, put a skillet pan over medium heat and when hot, add chopped bacon and cook for 5 to 8 minutes until golden brown. Then distribute lettuce and avocado between two plates, top with bacon, drizzle with olive oil and apple cider and serve.

Eggplant Omelet

Preparation Time: 5 minutes | **Cooking Time:** 10 minutes | **Servings:** 2 | **Calories:** 184

Ingredients: 1 large eggplant | 1 tbsp coconut oil, melted | 1 tsp unsalted butter | 2 eggs
2 tbsp chopped green onions

Directions: Set the grill and let it preheat at the high setting. In the meantime, prepare the eggplant, and for this, cut two slices from eggplant, about 1-inch thick, and reserve the remaining eggplant for later use. Brush slices of eggplant with oil, season with salt on both sides, then put the slices on grill and cook for 3 to 4 minutes per side. Move grilled eggplant to a cutting board, let it cool for 5 minutes and then make a home in the center of each slice by using a cookie cutter. Bring out a frying pan, put it over medium heat, add butter and when it melts, add eggplant slices in it and crack an egg into its each hole. Let the eggs cook for 3 to 4 minutes, then carefully flip the eggplant sliced and continue cooking for 3 minutes until the egg has thoroughly cooked. Season egg with salt and black pepper, move them to a plate, then garnish with green onions and serve.

Sausage Styled Rolled Omelet

Preparation Time: 5 minutes | **Cooking Time:** 8 minutes | **Servings:** 2 | **Calories**: 126

Ingredients: 1 tbsp chopped spinach | 1 tbsp whipped topping | 2 eggs | 2 oz ground turkey
2 tbsp grated mozzarella cheese

Directions: Bring out a skillet pan, put it over medium heat, add ground turkey and cook for 5 minutes until cooked through. In the meantime, crack eggs in a bowl, add whipped topping and spinach and whisk until combined. When the meat is cooked, move it to a plate, then switch heat to the low level and pour in the egg mixture. Cook the eggs for 3 minutes until the bottom is firm, then flip it and cook for 3 minutes until the omelet is firmed, covering the pan. Sprinkle cheese on the omelet, cook for 1 minute until cheese has melted, and then slide omelet to a plate. Spread ground meat on the omelet, roll it, then cut it in half and serve.

Tofu Egg Scramble

Preparation Time: 15 minutes | **Cooking Time:** 20 minutes | **Servings:** 5 | **Calories:** 109

Ingredients: 10 oz tofu cheese | 2 eggs | 1 teaspoon chives | 1 tablespoon apple cider vinegar
½ teaspoon salt | 1 teaspoon ground white pepper | ¼ teaspoon ground coriander

Directions: Shred the tofu and sprinkle it with the apple cider vinegar, salt, ground white pepper, and ground coriander. Mix and leave for 10 minutes to marinade. Meanwhile, preheat the air fryer to 370°F. Transfer the marinated tofu to the air fryer basket tray and cook for 13 minutes. Meanwhile, crack the eggs in a bowl and whisk them. When the tofu has cooked, pour the egg mixture in the shredded tofu cheese and stir with a spatula. When the eggs start to firm place the air fryer basket tray in the air fryer and cook the dish for 7 minutes more. Remove the cooked meal from the air fryer basket tray and serve.

Flax & Hemp Porridge

Preparation Time: 10 minutes | **Cooking Time:** 15 minutes | **Servings:** 3 | **Calories**: 196

Ingredients: 2 tablespoons flax seeds | 4 tablespoons hemp seeds | 1 tablespoon butter
¼ teaspoon salt | 1 teaspoon stevia | 7 tablespoons almond milk | ½ teaspoon ground ginger

Directions: Place the flax seeds and hemp seeds in the air fryer basket. Sprinkle the seeds with salt and ground ginger. Combine the almond milk and stevia together. Stir the liquid and pour it into the seed mixture. Add butter. Preheat the air fryer to 370°F and cook the hemp seed porridge for 15 minutes. Stir carefully after 10 minutes of cooking. Remove the hem porridge from the air fryer basket tray and chill it for 3 minutes. Transfer the porridge into serving bowls.

Power Cream with Strawberry

Preparation Time: 5 minutes | **Cooking Time:** 0 minutes | **Servings:** 2 | **Calories:** 214

Ingredients: 1 tbsp coconut oil | 2 tsp vanilla extract, unsweetened | 4 oz fresh strawberries
4 oz coconut cream, full-fat

Directions: Bring out a large bowl, put all the ingredients in it and then mix by using an immersion blender until smooth. Distribute evenly between two bowls and then serve.

Savory Keto Pancake

Preparation Time: 5 minutes | **Cooking Time:** 5 minutes | **Servings:** 2 | **Calories:** 167

Ingredients: ¼ cup almond flour | 1-½ tbsp unsalted butter | 2 eggs | 2 oz cream cheese, softened

Directions: Bring out a bowl, crack eggs in it, whisk well until fluffy, and then whisk in flour and cream cheese until well combined. Bring out a skillet pan, put it over medium heat, add butter and when it melts, drop pancake batter in four sections, spread it evenly, and cook for 2 minutes per side until brown.

Cheddar Soufflé with Herbs

Preparation Time: 10 minutes | **Cooking Time:** 8 minutes | **Servings:** 4 | **Calories:** 244

Ingredients: 5 oz. cheddar cheese, shredded | 3 eggs | 4 tablespoons heavy cream | 1 tablespoon chives
1 tablespoon dill | 1 teaspoon parsley | ½ teaspoon ground thyme

Directions: Crack the eggs into a bowl and whisk them carefully. Add the heavy cream and whisk it for 10 seconds more. Add the chives, dill, parsley, and ground thyme. Sprinkle the egg mixture with the shredded cheese and stir it. Transfer the egg mixture into 4 ramekins and place the ramekins in the air fryer basket. Preheat the air fryer to 390°F and cook the soufflé for 8 minutes. Once cooked, chill well.

Eggplant and Chives Spread

Preparation Time: 5 minutes | **Cooking Time:** 20 minutes | **Servings:** 4 | **Calories:** 190

Ingredients: 3 eggplants | salt and black pepper, to taste | 2 tablespoons chives, chopped
2 tablespoons olive oil | 2 teaspoons sweet paprika

Directions: Put the eggplants in your air fryer's basket and cook them for 20 minutes at 380 degrees F. Peel the eggplants put them in a blender, add the rest of the ingredients, pulse well, divide into bowls and serve for breakfast.

Keto Cheese Rolls

Preparation Time: 5 minutes | **Cooking Time:** 0 minutes | **Servings:** 2 | **Calories**: 166

Ingredients: 1 oz. butter, unsalted | 2 oz mozzarella cheese, sliced, full-fat

Directions: Cut cheese into slices and then cut butter into thin slices. Top each cheese slice with a slice of butter, roll it and then serve.

Zucchini Spread

Preparation Time: 5 minutes | **Cooking Time:** 15 minutes | **Servings:** 4 | **Calories**: 240

Ingredients: 4 zucchinis, roughly chopped | 1 tablespoon sweet paprika | salt and black pepper, to taste
1 tablespoon butter, melted

Directions: Grease a baking pan that fits the Air Fryer with the butter, add all the ingredients, toss, and cook at 360 degrees F for 15 minutes. Transfer to a blender, pulse well, divide into bowls and serve.

Spinach and Eggs Mix

Preparation Time: 5 minutes | **Cooking Time:** 20 minutes | **Servings:** 4 | **Calories:** 220

Ingredients: 1 tablespoon olive oil | ½ teaspoon smoked paprika | 12 eggs, whisked
3 cups baby spinach | salt and black pepper, to taste

Directions: In a bowl, mix all the ingredients except the oil and whisk them well. Heat up your air fryer at 360 degrees F, add the oil, heat it up, add the eggs and spinach mix, cover, cook for 20 minutes, divide between plates and serve.

Cheesy Turkey Bake

Preparation Time: 5 minutes | **Cooking Time:** 25 minutes | **Servings:** 4 | **Calories:** 244

Ingredients: 1 turkey breast, skinless, boneless, cut into strips and browned | 2 teaspoons olive oil
2 cups almond milk | 2 cups cheddar cheese, shredded | 2 eggs, whisked | 1 tablespoon chives, chopped
salt and black pepper, to taste

Directions: In a bowl, mix the eggs with milk, cheese, salt, pepper, and the chives and whisk well. Preheat the air fryer at 330 degrees F, add the oil, heat it up, add the turkey pieces, and spread them well. Add the eggs mixture, toss a bit, and cook for 25 minutes. Serve right away for breakfast.

Vegan Breakfast Hash

Preparation Time: 15 minutes | **Cooking Time:** 5 minutes | **Servings:** 4 | **Calories:** 135

Ingredients: 1 cup cooked quinoa | 1 cup shredded broccoli | 2 tbsp. flax seed | ½ cup coconut flour
1 tsp garlic powder | 1 tsp onion powder | 2 tbsp. coconut oil

Directions: Stir flax seeds with half a cup of water in a large mixing bowl. Leave for a few minutes. Stir in all remaining ingredients. From the mixture into patties. Heat vegetable oil in a pan. Fry the patties for 2-3 minutes per side.

Tomatoes and Eggs Mix

Preparation Time: 5 minutes | **Cooking Time:** 25 minutes | **Servings:** 4 | **Calories:** 221

Ingredients: 1 and 1/2 tablespoons olive oil | 30 ounces canned tomatoes, chopped | 6 eggs, whisked
½ pound cheddar, shredded | 2 tablespoons chives, chopped | salt and black pepper, to taste

Directions: Add the oil to your air fryer, heat it up at 350 degrees F, add the tomatoes, eggs, salt and pepper and whisk. Also, add the cheese on top and sprinkle the chives on top. Cook for 25 minutes, divide between plates and serve for breakfast.

Coconut Pancake Hash

Preparation Time: 7 minutes | **Cooking Time:** 9 minutes | **Servings:** 9 | **Calories:** 148

Ingredients: 1 teaspoon baking soda | 1 tablespoon apple cider vinegar | 1 teaspoon salt
1 teaspoon ground ginger | 1 cup coconut flour | 5 tablespoons butter | 1 egg | ¼ cup heavy cream

Directions: Combine the baking soda, salt, ground ginger, and flour in a bowl. Take a separate bowl and crack in the egg. Add butter and heavy cream. Use a hand mixer and mix well. Combine the dry and liquid mixture together and stir it until smooth. Preheat the air fryer to 400°F. Pour the pancake mixture into the air fryer basket tray. Cook the pancake hash for 4 minutes. Scramble the pancake hash well and keep cooking for 5 minutes more. Transfer to serving plates and serve hot.

Eggs and Bell Peppers

Preparation Time: 5 minutes | **Cooking Time:** 20 minutes | **Servings:** 4 | **Calories:** 229

Ingredients: 1 red bell pepper, cut into strips | 1 green bell pepper, cut into strips | 4 eggs, whisked
1 orange bell pepper, cut into strips | 2 tablespoons mozzarella, shredded | cooking spray
salt and black pepper, to taste

Directions: In a bowl, mix the eggs with all the bell peppers, salt and pepper and toss. Preheat the air fryer at 350 degrees F, grease it with cooking spray, pour the eggs mixture, spread well, sprinkle the mozzarella on top and cook for 20 minutes. Divide between plates and serve for breakfast.

Creamy Almond and Cheese Mix

Preparation Time: 10 minutes | **Cooking Time:** 20 minutes | **Servings:** 6 | **Calories:** 231

Ingredients: 1 cup almond milk | cooking spray | 9 ounces cream cheese, soft | 6 eggs, whisked
1 cup cheddar cheese, shredded | 6 spring onions, chopped | salt and black pepper, to taste

Directions: Heat up your air fryer with the oil at 350 degrees F and grease it with cooking spray. In a bowl, mix the eggs with the rest of the ingredients, whisk well, pour and spread into the air fryer and cook everything for 20 minutes. Divide everything between plates and serve.

Herbed Eggs Mix

Preparation Time: 5 minutes | **Cooking Time:** 20 minutes | **Servings:** 4 | **Calories:** 232

Ingredients: 10 eggs, whisked | ½ cup cheddar, shredded | 2 tablespoons parsley, chopped
2 tablespoons chives, chopped | 2 tablespoons basil, chopped | cooking spray | salt and black pepper

Directions: In a bowl, mix the eggs with all the ingredients except the cheese and the cooking spray and whisk well. Preheat the air fryer at 350°F, grease it with the cooking spray, and pour the eggs mixture inside. Sprinkle the cheese on top and cook for 20 minutes. Divide everything between plates and serve.

Olives Bake

Preparation Time: 5 minutes | **Cooking Time:** 20 minutes | **Servings:** 4 | **Calories:** 240

Ingredients: 2 cups black olives, pitted and chopped | 4 eggs, whisked | ¼ teaspoon sweet paprika
1 tablespoon cilantro, chopped | ½ cup cheddar, shredded | pinch of salt & black pepper | cooking spray

Directions: In a bowl, mix the eggs with the olives and all the ingredients except the cooking spray and stir well. Heat up your air fryer at 350 degrees F, grease it with cooking spray, pour the olives and eggs mixture, spread and cook for 20 minutes. Divide between plates and serve for breakfast.

Cheddar and Broccoli Bake

Preparation Time: 5 minutes | **Cooking Time:** 25 minutes | **Servings:** 4 | **Calories:** 214

Ingredients: broccoli head, florets separated and roughly chopped | 2 ounces cheddar cheese, grated
4 eggs, whisked | 1 cup almond milk | 2 teaspoons cilantro, chopped | salt and black pepper, to taste

Directions: In a bowl, mix the eggs with the milk, cilantro, salt and pepper and whisk. Put the broccoli in your air fryer, add the eggs mix over it, spread, sprinkle the cheese on top, cook 350 degrees F for 25 minutes, divide between plates and serve for breakfast.

Basil Mozzarella Eggs

Preparation Time: 5 minutes | **Cooking Time:** 20 minutes | **Servings:** 4 | **Calories**: 207

Ingredients: 2 tablespoons butter, melted | 6 teaspoons basil pesto | 1 cup mozzarella cheese, grated
6 eggs, whisked | 2 tablespoons basil, chopped | a pinch of salt and black pepper

Directions: In a bowl, mix all the ingredients except the butter and whisk them well. Preheat your Air Fryer at 360 degrees F, drizzle the butter on the bottom, spread the eggs mix, cook for 20 minutes, and serve for breakfast.

Cherry Tomatoes Omelet

Preparation Time: 5 minutes | **Cooking Time:** 20 minutes | **Servings:** 4 | **Calories**: 230

Ingredients: 4 eggs, whisked | 1 pound cherry tomatoes, halved | 1 tablespoon parsley, chopped
1 tablespoon cheddar, grated | salt and black pepper, to taste | cooking spray

Directions: Put the tomatoes in the air fryer's basket, cook at 360 degrees F for 5 minutes and transfer them to the baking pan that fits the machine greased with cooking spray. In a bowl, mix the eggs with the remaining ingredients, whisk, pour over the tomatoes and cook at 360 degrees F for 15 minutes. Serve right away for breakfast.

Tofu and Spinach Frittata

Preparation Time: 15 minutes | **Cooking Time:** 5 minutes | **Servings:** 4 | **Calories**: 236

Ingredients: 400 g firm tofu | 2 tbsp. tamari | 2 tbsp. nutritional yeast | 1 tsp turmeric |2 tbsp. oil
1 tbsp. garlic powder | 2 cups baby spinach, chopped | 1 red bell pepper, chopped

Directions: Combine tofu, tamari, nutritional yeast, turmeric, and garlic powder in a food processor. Blend until smooth. Fold in the spinach and bell pepper into the mixture. Brush an iron skillet with olive oil. Pour the mixture into the skillet. Bake for 25 minutes at 360°F.

Avocado Tofu Scramble

Preparation Time: 15 minutes | **Cooking Time:** 0 minutes | **Servings:** 1 | **Calories**: 164

Ingredients: 1 tbsp. fresh parsley, chopped | ½ medium avocado | ½ cup bell pepper, chopped
½ block firm tofu drained and crumbled | ½ cup onion, chopped | 1 tsp olive oil | 1 tbsp. water | salt
¼ tsp cumin | ¼ tsp garlic powder | ¼ tsp paprika | ¼ tsp turmeric | 1 tbsp. nutritional yeast | pepper

Directions: In a small bowl, mix nutritional yeast, water, and spices. Set aside. Heat olive oil to the pan over medium heat. Add onion and bell pepper and sauté for 5 minutes. Add crumbled tofu and nutritional yeast to the pan and sauté for 2 minutes. Top with parsley and avocado. Serve.

Almond Hemp Heart Porridge

Preparation Time: 10 minutes | **Cooking Time:** 2 minutes | **Servings:** 2 | **Calories**: 329

Ingredients: ¼ cup almond flour | ½ tsp cinnamon | ¾ tsp vanilla extract | 5 drops stevia
1 tbsp. chia seeds | 2 tbsp. ground flax seed | ½ cup hemp hearts | 1 cup unsweetened coconut milk

Directions: Add all ingredients except almond flour to a saucepan. Stir to combine. Heat over medium heat until it starts to boil lightly. Once start bubbling, then stir well and cook for 1 minute more. Remove from heat and stir in almond flour. Serve immediately and enjoy it.

Tiramisu Chia Pudding

Preparation Time: 15 minutes | **Cooking Time:** 5 minutes | **Servings:** 1 | **Calories:** 112

Ingredients: 1/4 cup chia seeds | 2 tsp instant coffee | 2 tbsp. coconut cream | 1 tsp powdered cinnamon 1 tbsp. erythritol | ¾ cup water

Directions: Combine all ingredients in a mason jar. Shake until well blended. Chill for at least 20 mins.

Fat-Bomb Frappuccino

Preparation Time: 15 minutes | **Cooking Time:** 5 minutes | **Servings:** 1 | **Calories:** 278

Ingredients: 2/3 cup brewed coffee | ¼ cup almond milk | 2 tbsp. erythritol | 1 tsp vanilla extract 2 tbsp. coconut oil | ½ cup ice cubes

Directions: Mix all ingredients in a blender until smooth.

Chocolate Strawberry Milkshake

Preparation Time: 5 minutes | **Cooking Time:** 0 minutes | **Servings:** 2 | **Calories:** 221

Ingredients: 1 cup of ice cubes | ¼ cup unsweetened cocoa powder | 2 scoops vegan protein powder 1 cup strawberries | 2 cups unsweetened coconut milk

Directions: Add all ingredients into the blender and blend until smooth and creamy. Serve immediately.

Bacon Butter Biscuits

Preparation Time: 15 minutes | **Cooking Time:** 10 minutes | **Servings:** 6 | **Calories:** 226

Ingredients: 4 oz. bacon, cooked | 1 cup almond flour | ½ teaspoon baking soda | 3 tablespoons butter 1 tablespoon apple cider vinegar | 4 tablespoons heavy cream | 1 teaspoon dried oregano | 1 egg

Directions: Crack the egg in a bowl and whisk it. Chop the cooked bacon and add it into the whisked egg. Sprinkle the mixture with baking soda and apple cider vinegar. Add the heavy cream and dried oregano. Stir. Add butter and almond flour. Mix well with a hand mixer. When you get a smooth and liquid batter – the dough is cooked. Preheat the air fryer to 400°F. Pour the batter dough into muffin molds. When the air fryer is heated put the muffin molds in the air fryer basket and cook them for 10 minutes. Chill the muffins to room temperature.

Banana Hazelnut Waffles

Preparation Time: 3 minutes | **Cooking Time:** 5 minutes | **Servings:** 2 | **Calories:** 316

Ingredients: 2 tbsp. flaxseed meal | 1/2 cup almond flour | 2 tbsp. erythritol | 1 tsp baking powder 1 tsp ground cinnamon | 2 tbsp. hazelnut butter | ½ cup coconut milk | 1 tsp banana essence

Directions: Process all ingredients in a blender until smooth. Pour into waffle iron & cook for 3-5 mins.

Keto Choco "Oats"

Preparation Time: 5 minutes | **Cooking Time:** 5 minutes | **Servings:** 2 | **Calories:** 464

Ingredients: 200 g cauliflower, riced | 1 cup coconut milk | 2 tbsp. flax seeds | 1 tbsp. erythritol 2 tbsp. cocoa powder | 1 tbsp. vanilla extract | 50 g fresh raspberries | 1 tbsp. cacao nibs

Directions: Combine cauliflower, coconut milk, flax seeds, erythritol, cocoa powder, and vanilla extract in a pot. Simmer for 3-5 minutes. Ladle into bowls and top with fresh raspberries & cacao nibs.

Vegetable Tofu Scramble

Preparation Time: 20 minutes | **Cooking Time:** 5 minutes | **Servings:** 2 | **Calories**: 159

Ingredients: 1 block firm tofu, drained and crumbled | 1 red pepper, chopped | ¼ tsp garlic powder
1 cup spinach | 1 red pepper, chopped | 10 oz. mushrooms, chopped | ½ onion, chopped | 1 tbsp. olive oil
½ tsp turmeric | pepper and salt

Directions: Heat olive oil in a large pan over medium heat. Add onion, pepper, and mushrooms and sauté until cooked. Add crumbled tofu, spices, and spinach. Stir well and cook for 3-5 minutes and serve.

Breakfast Granola

Preparation Time: 30 minutes | **Cooking Time:** 23 minutes | **Servings:** 15 | **Calories**: 208

Ingredients: 1 tsp ground ginger | 1 tsp ground cinnamon | ¼ cup coconut oil, melted | ½ cup flaxseeds
1 cup walnuts, chopped | 2/3 cup pumpkin seeds | 2/3 cup sunflower seeds | 3 cups desiccated coconut

Directions: Add all ingredients into the large bowl and toss well. Spread the granola mixture on a baking tray and bake at 350°F/180°C for 20 minutes. Turn granola mixture with a spoon after every 3 minutes. Allow to cool completely and serve.

Grain-Free Overnight Oats

Preparation Time: 10 minutes | **Cooking Time:** 0 minutes | **Servings:** 1 | **Calories**: 378

Ingredients: 2/3 cup unsweetened coconut milk | 2 tsp chia seeds | 2 tbsp. vanilla protein powder
½ tbsp. coconut flour | 3 tbsp. hemp hearts

Directions: Add all ingredients into the glass jar and stir to combine. Close jar with lid and place in the refrigerator overnight. Top with fresh berries and serve.

Almond Coconut Porridge

Preparation Time: 10 minutes | **Cooking Time:** 2 minutes | **Servings:** 2 | **Calories**: 197

Ingredients: ¾ cup unsweetened almond milk | ½ tsp vanilla extra | 1-½ tbsp. ground flaxseed
3 tbsp. ground almonds | 6 tbsp. unsweetened shredded coconut | pinch of sea salt

Directions: Add almond milk in microwave-safe bowl and microwave for 2 minutes.
Add remaining ingredients and stir well and cook for 1 minute. Top with fresh berries and serve.

Easy Chia Seed Pudding

Preparation Time: 10 minutes | **Cooking Time:** 0 minutes | **Servings:** 4 | **Calories**: 347

Ingredients: ¼ tsp cinnamon | 15 drops liquid stevia | ½ tsp vanilla extract | ½ cup chia seeds
2 cups unsweetened coconut milk

Directions: Add all ingredients into the glass jar and mix well. Close jar with lid and place in the refrigerator for 4 hours. Serve chilled and enjoy.

Cinnamon Muffins

Preparation Time: 25 minutes | **Cooking Time:** 15 minutes | **Servings:** 20 | **Calories**: 80

Ingredients: ½ cup coconut oil, melted | ½ cup pumpkin puree | ½ cup almond butter
1 tbsp. cinnamon | 1 tsp baking powder | 2 scoops vanilla protein powder | ½ cup almond flour

Directions: Preheat the oven to 180°C/350°F. Spray a muffin tray with cooking spray and set aside. Add all dry ingredients into the large bowl and mix well. Add wet ingredients and mix until well combined. Pour batter into the prepared muffin tray and bake in preheated oven for 15 minutes. Serve and enjoy.

Keto Porridge

Preparation Time: 10 minutes | **Cooking Time:** 5 minutes | **Servings:** 1 | **Calories**: 370

Ingredients: ½ tsp vanilla extract | ¼ tsp granulated stevia | 1 tbsp. chia seeds | 1 tbsp. flaxseed meal
2 tbsp. unsweetened shredded coconut | 2 tbsp. almond flour | 2 tbsp. hemp hearts | ½ cup of water
pinch of salt

Directions: Add all ingredients except vanilla extract to a saucepan and heat over low heat until thickened. Stir well and serve warm.

The Asian Chickpea Pancake

Preparation Time: 5 minutes | **Cooking Time:** 10 minutes | **Servings:** 1 | **Calories**: 227

Ingredients: 34 grams green onion, chopped | 34 grams red pepper, thinly sliced | 1.5 g salt
70 grams chickpea powder | 1.5 grams, garlic powder | 1.25 grams, baking powder | 0.25 g, chili flakes

Directions: This chickpea pancake is super easy. All you have to do is take your vegetables, prep them, and then mix everything else, starting from the chickpea flour to the chili flakes in a bowl. Whisk until you see air bubbles, just like you would for a normal pancake. Add the chopped veggies and after one final stir, add the mixture to a preheated skillet, and allow it to spread evenly over the pan for about 5 minutes. Once the underside is cooked through, flip and let it cook for an additional 5 minutes, and once you are done, simply plate and serve.

Matcha Avocado Pancakes

Preparation Time: 10 minutes | **Cooking Time:** 5 minutes | **Servings:** 6 | **Calories:** 179

Ingredients: 1 cup almond flour | 1 medium-sized avocado, mashed | 1 cup coconut milk
1 tbsp. matcha powder | ½ tsp baking soda | ¼ tsp salt

Directions: Mix all ingredients into a batter. Add water, a tablespoon at a time, to thin out the mixture if needed. Lightly oil a non-stick pan. Ladle approximately 1/3 cup of the batter and cook over medium heat until bubbly on the surface (about 2-3 minutes). Flip the pancake over and cook for another minute.

Coconut Crepes

Preparation Time: 10 minutes | **Cooking Time:** 8 minutes | **Servings:** 3 | **Calories**: 137

Ingredients: 15 grams virgin coconut oil | ¼ cup, almond milk | ¼ cup, coconut milk
¼ grams, vanilla essence | 30 grams, coconut flour | 15 grams, almond meal | 1 cup applesauce

Directions: Coconut crepes, in addition to being super delicious, also happen to be very easy to whip up. Dump all of your ingredients into one large bowl and whisk until smooth. Then set aside for ten minutes to allow the liquid to absorb into the flour. In the meantime, lightly oil a frying pan on the stove, and pour in the batter and spread until the pan is coated with a thin layer. Cook for a couple minutes until the crepe starts to get crispy, and flip. Another minute on the stove and you are ready to serve, alongside your toppings of choice or course.

Low-Carb Breakfast "Couscous"

Preparation Time: 10 minutes | **Cooking Time:** 2 minutes | **Servings:** 4 | **Calories:** 190

Ingredients: 200 grams cauliflower, riced | 30 grams strawberries | 20 grams almonds
20 grams flax seeds | 60 grams mandarin segments | 1 cup coconut milk | 1 tbsp. erythritol
¼ tsp. cinnamon powder | 3 tbsp. rose water

Directions: Combine all ingredients in a microwave safe bowl. Cook for 2 mins at 30-second intervals.

Overnight Oat Bowl

Preparation Time: 10 minutes | **Cooking Time:** 10 minutes | **Servings:** 2 | **Calories:** 634

Ingredients: 15 grams chia seeds | 75 grams hemp hearts | 14 grams sweetener | 2/3 cup coconut milk ¼ grams vanilla extract/vanilla bean | 1.25 grams of salt

Directions: As always, overnight oats are one of the easiest meals to make, only without actual oats we keto-vegans can in a bit of a pickle. Luckily, hemp hearts are a great substitute! For best results, you'll want to thoroughly mix in all of your ingredients and allow the bowl to sit overnight in a covered container to avoid evaporation. You want the oats to sit for at least 8 hours, so if you have a long night ahead of you, plan accordingly.

Vegan Breakfast Muffins

Preparation Time: 5 minutes | **Cooking Time:** 3 minutes | **Servings:** 3 | **Calories:** 194

Ingredients: 2 tbsp. almond flour | ½ tsp baking powder | ½ tsp salt | 2 tbsp. ground flax seeds ¼ cup coconut milk | 3 tbsp. avocado oil

Directions: Whisk together almond flour, ground flax, baking powder, and salt in a bowl. Stir in coconut milk. Heat avocado oil in a non-stick pan. Ladle in the batter and cook for 2-3 minutes per side.

No-Bread Avocado Sandwich

Preparation Time: 10 minutes | **Cooking Time:** 0 minutes | **Servings:** 2 | **Calories:** 143

Ingredients: 2 oz. little gem lettuce, 2 leaves extracted | ½ oz. vegan butter 1 oz. sliced vegan cheese 1 avocado, pitted, peeled, and sliced | 1 large red tomato, sliced | chopped fresh parsley to garnish

Directions: Rinse and pat dry the lettuce leave. Arrange on a flat plate (with inner side facing you) to serve as the base of the sandwich. Spread some butter on each leaf, top with the cheese, avocado, and tomato. Garnish with some parsley and serve the sandwich immediately.

Vegan Southwestern Breakfast

Preparation Time: 10 minutes | **Cooking Time:** 5 minutes | **Servings:** 6 | **Calories:** 174

Ingredients: 1 small white onion, diced | 1 bell pepper, diced | 150 g mushrooms, sliced | 2 tbsp olive oil 400 grams firm tofu, crumbled | 1 tsp turmeric powder | 1 tbsp. garlic powder | 2 tbsp. nutritional yeast ¼ cup chopped green onions | 2 cups fresh spinach | 1 cup cherry tomatoes | 2 cups baked beans

Directions: Sautee onions, bell peppers, and mushrooms until onions are translucent. Add in the tofu. Stir in the turmeric, garlic powder, and nutritional yeast. Add green onions and spinach. Sautee for 1-2 minutes. Serve with baked beans and cherry tomatoes.

Vegan Breakfast Biscuits

Preparation Time: 10 minutes | **Cooking Time:** 10 minutes | **Servings:** 6 | **Calories:** 306

Ingredients: 1.5 cups almond flour | 1 tbsp. baking powder | ½ tsp onion powder | ½ cup coconut milk ¼ cup nutritional yeast | 2 tbsp. ground flax seeds | ¼ cup olive oil | ¼ tsp salt

Directions: Preheat oven to 450°F. Whisk together all ingredients in a bowl. Divide the batter into a pre-greased muffin tin. Bake for 10 minutes.

Vegan Breakfast Sausages

Preparation Time: 15 minutes | **Cooking Time:** 12 minutes | **Servings:** 4 | **Calories**: 271

Ingredients: 200 grams Portobella mushrooms | 150 grams walnuts | 1 tbsp. tomato paste | 1 tsp salt 75 grams Panko | 1 tsp paprika | 1 tsp dried sage | ½ tsp black pepper

Directions: Blend all ingredients in a food processor. Divide mixture into serving-sized portions and shape into sausages. Bake for 12 minutes at 375°F.

Quick Breakfast Yogurt

Preparation Time: 2 minutes | **Cooking Time:** 8 minutes | **Servings:** 6 | **Calories**: 186

Ingredients: 4 cups full-fat coconut milk | 2 tbsp. coconut milk powder | 100 g strawberries, serving

Directions: Whisk together coconut milk and milk powder in a microwave safe bowl. Heat on high for 8-9 minutes. Top with fresh strawberries and choice of sweetener to serve.

Avocado Mug Bread

Preparation Time: 2 minutes | **Cooking Time:** 2 minutes | **Servings:** 1 | **Calories**: 317

Ingredients: ¼ cup almond flour | ½ tsp baking powder | ¼ tsp salt | ¼ cup mashed avocados 1 tbsp. coconut oil

Directions: Mix all ingredients in a microwave-safe mug. Microwave for 90 sec. Cool for 2 minutes.

Meat-Free Breakfast Chili

Preparation Time: 10 minutes | **Cooking Time:** 20 minutes | **Servings:** 4 | **Calories**: 174

Ingredients: 400 grams textured-vegetable protein | ¼ cup red kidney beans | 1 tsp chili powder ½ cup canned diced tomatoes | 1 large bell pepper, diced | 1 large white onion, diced | 1 tsp paprika 1 tsp cumin powder | 1 tsp garlic powder | ½ tsp dried oregano | 2 cups water

Directions: Combine all ingredients in a pot. Simmer for 20 minutes. Serve with your favorite bread or some slices of fresh avocado.

Strawberry Chia Matcha Pudding

Preparation Time: 10 minutes | **Cooking Time:** 0 minutes | **Servings:** 1 | **Calories**: 93

Ingredients: 5 drops liquid stevia | 2 strawberries, diced | ¾ cup unsweetened coconut milk ½ tsp matcha powder | 1-½ tbsp. chia seeds

Directions: Add all ingredients except strawberries into the glass jar and mix well. Close jar with lid and place in the refrigerator for 4 hours. Add strawberries into the pudding and mix well. Serve and enjoy.

Avocado Chocó Cinnamon Smoothie

Preparation Time: 5 minutes | **Cooking Time:** 0 minutes | **Servings:** 1 | **Calories**: 95

Ingredients: ½ tsp coconut oil | 5 drops liquid stevia | ¼ tsp vanilla extract | 1 tsp ground cinnamon 2 tsp unsweetened cocoa powder | ½ avocado | ¾ cup unsweetened coconut milk

Directions: Add all ingredients into the blender and blend until smooth and creamy. Serve immediately and enjoy it.

Avocado Breakfast Smoothie

Preparation Time: 5 minutes | **Cooking Time:** 0 minutes | **Servings:** 2 | **Calories**: 131

Ingredients: 5 drops liquid stevia | ¼ cup of ice cubes | ½ avocado | 1 tsp vanilla extract
1 cup unsweetened coconut milk

Directions: Add all ingredients into the blender and blend until smooth and creamy. Serve immediately.

Apple Avocado Coconut Smoothie

Preparation Time: 5 minutes | **Cooking Time:** 0 minutes | **Servings:** 2 | **Calories**: 262

Ingredients: 1 tsp coconut oil | 1 tbsp. collagen powder | ½ cup unsweetened coconut milk
¼ apple, slice | 1 avocado | 1 tbsp. fresh lime juice

Directions: Add all ingredients into the blender and blend until smooth and creamy. Serve and enjoy.

Healthy Spinach Green Smoothie

Preparation Time: 5 minutes | **Cooking Time:** 0 minutes | **Servings:** 1 | **Calories**: 167

Ingredients: 1 cup ice cubes | 2/3 cup water | ½ cup unsweetened almond milk | 5 drops liquid stevia
½ tsp matcha powder | 1 tsp vanilla extract | 1 tbsp. MCT oil | ½ avocado | 2/3 cup spinach

Directions: Add all ingredients into the blender and blend until smooth and creamy. Serve immediately and enjoy it.

Berry Acai Breakfast Smoothie

Preparation Time: 2 minutes | **Cooking Time:** 0 minutes | **Servings:** 1 | **Calories**: 266

Ingredients: 1 cup silk tofu | 2 tbsp. coconut cream | 1 cup ice cubes | ¼ cup raspberries
2 tbsp. acai powder | 3 tbsp. soy protein powder (vanilla-flavored)

Directions: Combine all ingredients in a blender. Blend until smooth.

Chia Cinnamon Smoothie

Preparation Time: 5 minutes | **Cooking Time:** 0 minutes | **Servings:** 1 | **Calories**: 397

Ingredients: 2 scoops vanilla protein powder | 1 tbsp. chia seeds | ½ tsp cinnamon | 1 tbsp. coconut oil
½ cup of water | ½ cup unsweetened coconut milk

Directions: Add all ingredients into the blender and blend until smooth and creamy. Serve immediately.

Gingerbread-Spiced Breakfast Smoothie

Preparation Time: 2 minutes | **Cooking Time:** 0 minutes | **Servings:** 2 | **Calories**: 449

Ingredients: 1 cup coconut milk | 1 bag tea | ¼ tsp cinnamon powder | 1/8 tsp nutmeg powder
1/8 tsp powdered cloves | 1/3 cup chia seeds | 2 tbsp. flax seeds

Directions: Put the teabag in a mug and pour in a cup of hot water. Allow to steep for a few minutes. Pour the tea into a blender together with the rest of the ingredients. Process until smooth.

Cheese Stuffed Mushrooms

Preparation Time: 10 minutes | **Cooking Time:** 20 minutes | **Servings:** 4 | **Calories**: 139

Ingredients: 4 Portobello mushrooms | 1 tsp fresh thyme, chopped | 1 cup blue cheese, crumbled | salt

Directions: At 350 degrees F, preheat your oven. Clean the mushrooms and cut the stems from the caps. Place the mushroom caps in a greased baking sheet. Thoroughly mix blue cheese with salt and thyme in a mixing bowl. Stuff each mushroom cap with ¼ cup of blue cheese mixture. Bake the stuffed mushroom caps for 20 minutes. Garnish as desired. Serve warm and fresh.

Avocado Fries

Preparation Time: 15 minutes | **Cooking Time:** 30 minutes | **Servings:** 4 | **Calories:** 123

Ingredients: 1 teaspoon Italian seasoning | 1 large ripe peeled avocado, cut in chunks
3/4 cup Parmesan, grated | black pepper and salt, to taste

Directions: At 325 degrees F, preheat your oven. Layer a baking sheet with parchment paper. Add avocado pieces to a bowl and stir in parmesan cheese, Italian seasoning, black pepper, and salt. Mix these ingredients together to coat the avocado then spread it on a baking sheet. Bake these chips for 30 minutes in the preheated oven. Serve warm and crispy.

Cheese Crisps

Preparation Time: 10 minutes | **Cooking Time:** 40 minutes | **Servings:** 6 | **Calories:** 72

Ingredients: 2 teaspoons taco seasoning | 1 package cheddar slices (8-oz.)

Directions: At 250 degrees F, preheat your oven. Layer a baking sheet with parchment paper. Cut each cheddar slice into 9 squares and then place them in the baking sheet. Keep a 1-2 inches gap between each piece of cheese. Drizzle taco seasoning over the cheese slices. Bake them for 40 minutes in the preheated oven. Allow them to cool for 10 minutes. Serve fresh and crispy.

Mix Veggie Fritters

Preparation Time: 5 minutes | **Cooking Time:** 7 minutes | **Servings:** 2 | **Calories:** 191

Ingredients: ½ tsp nutritional yeast | 1 oz chopped broccoli | 1 zucchini, grated, squeezed
2 eggs | 2 tbsp almond flour

Directions: Wrap grated zucchini in a cheesecloth, twist it well to remove excess moisture, and then Put zucchini in a bowl. Add remaining ingredients, except for oil, and then whisk well until combined. Bring out a skillet pan, put it over medium heat, add oil and when hot, drop zucchini mixture in four portions, shape them into flat patties and cook for 4 minutes per side until thoroughly cooked.

Bacon Asparagus Rolls

Preparation Time: 15 minutes | **Cooking Time:** 14 minutes | **Servings:** 9 | **Calories:** 129

Ingredients: 1 garlic clove, minced | 6 bacon slices, cut into thirds | black pepper and salt, to taste
5 oz. cream cheese, softened | 9 asparagus spears, blanched, cut into half

Directions: At 400°F, preheat your oven. Layer a medium-sized baking sheet with parchment paper. Add bacon to a skillet and cook until crispy. Transfer the crispy cooked bacon to a plate lined with a paper towel. Mix garlic with cream cheese, black pepper, and salt in a suitable mixing bowl. Spread ½ tablespoon of cream cheese mixture over each bacon strip. Place one asparagus spear at the center and wrap the bacon around it. Place the wrapped asparagus in the baking sheet and bake for 5 min. Serve warm & fresh.

Creamy Avocado Dip

Preparation Time: 11 minutes | **Cooking Time:** 0 minutes | **Servings:** 7 | **Calories**: 130

Ingredients: 1/2 cup plain Greek yogurt | juice of 1 lime | 2 ripe avocados, peeled and pitted
2 garlic cloves, minced | kosher salt and black pepper, to taste

Directions: Take a suitable medium bowl, add avocados and mash it with a fork. Add yogurt, lime juice, and garlic then mix well. Adjust seasoning by adding black pepper and salt. Mix well and serve.

Burger Fat Bombs

Preparation Time: 13 minutes | **Cooking Time:** 15 minutes | **Servings:** 10 | **Calories**: 115

Ingredients: 2 oz. cheddar cheese, cut into 20 cubes | 1 lb. ground beef | 1/2 teaspoon garlic powder
2 tablespoons cold butter, diced into 20 pieces | salt and black pepper, to taste

Directions: At 375 degrees F, preheat your oven. Take two mini-muffin trays and grease it with cooking spray. Add beef, salt, black pepper, and garlic powder to a suitable mixing bowl. Now add a teaspoonful of beef mixture into each muffin cup. Press the beef against the bottom of each cup. Add one-piece butter and one piece of cheddar in the beef cup. Now cover the butter and cheddar by folding the edges of the beef mixture over them. Press the beef mixture in all the muffin cups to make meatballs. Bake beef fat bombs for 15 minutes in the preheated oven. Serve warm and fresh.

Jalapeño Popper Cups

Preparation Time: 15 minutes | **Cooking Time:** 20 minutes | **Servings:** 10 | **Calories**: 93

Ingredients: 2 jalapeños, sliced | 1 cup mozzarella cheese, shredded | 1/4 cup sour cream | 10 large eggs

Directions: At 375 degrees F, preheat your oven. Beat eggs with sour cream, jalapenos, mozzarella, and sour cream. Take a suitable muffin tray and grease it with cooking spray. Divide the egg mixture into the muffin cups. Bake the poppers for 20 minutes in the preheated oven until golden brown from top. Serve warm and fresh.

Roasted Cauliflower with Prosciutto, Capers, and Almonds.

Preparation Time: 10 minutes | **Cooking Time:** 25 minutes | **Servings:** 2 | **Calories:** 288

Ingredients: 12 oz. cauliflower florets | 2 tablespoons leftover bacon grease, or olive oil
pink Himalayan salt | freshly ground black pepper | 2 ounces sliced prosciutto, torn into small pieces
¼ cup slivered almonds | 2 tablespoons capers | 2 tablespoons grated Parmesan cheese

Directions: Preheat the oven to 400°F. Line a baking pan with a silicone baking mat or parchment paper. Put the cauliflower florets in the prepared baking pan with the bacon grease, and season with pink Himalayan salt and pepper. Or if you are using olive oil instead, drizzle the cauliflower with olive oil and season with pink Himalayan salt and pepper. Roast the cauliflower for 15 minutes. Stir the cauliflower so all sides are coated with the bacon grease. Distribute the prosciutto pieces in the pan. Then add the slivered almonds and capers. Stir to combine. Sprinkle the Parmesan cheese on top, and roast for 10 minutes more. Divide between two plates, using a slotted spoon so you don't get excess grease in the plates, and serve.

Cheese Fries

Preparation Time: 5 minutes | **Cooking Time:** 4 minutes | **Servings:** 4 | **Calories:** 200

Ingredients: 8 oz. Halloumi cheese, sliced into fries | 2 oz. tallow | 1 serving marinara sauce, low carb

Directions: Heat the tallow in a pan over medium heat. Gently place halloumi pieces in the pan. Cook halloumi fries for 2 minutes on each side or until lightly golden brown. Serve with marinara sauce & enjoy

Seed Crackers

Preparation Time: 12 minutes | **Cooking Time:** 15 minutes | **Servings:** 6 | **Calories:** 136

Ingredients: 3 large eggs | 2-½ cups unblanched almond flour | 1/2 cup mixed seeds, chopped
1 tablespoon extra-virgin olive oil

Directions: At 325 degrees F, preheat your oven. Layer a baking sheet with parchment paper. Add almond flour and salt to a mixing bowl. Beat eggs with oil in a separate bowl. Stir in almond flour mixture and mix well to make a rough dough. Roll the dough into ¼ inches thick sheet and cut it into squares. Place all the squares in the baking sheet and bake them for 15 in the preheated oven. Serve fresh.

Roasted Almonds

Preparation Time: 5 minutes | **Cooking Time:** 5 minutes | **Servings:** 4 | **Calories:** 342

Ingredients: 2 cups almonds, blanched | 2 tablespoons rosemary | 2 tablespoons olive oil
1 teaspoon paprika | 1 teaspoon salt

Directions: In a pan over medium-high, heat add almonds and heat until toasted. Reduce heat to medium-low and add salt, paprika, and rosemary. Cook almonds for another 3 min and serve.

Zoodles Side Dish

Preparation Time: 10 minutes | **Cooking Time:** 0 minutes | **Servings:** 4 | **Calories**: 188

Ingredients: 4 zucchinis, cut with a spiralizer | 2 tablespoons olive oil | a pinch of salt and black pepper
1 cup mozzarella, shredded | 2 cups cherry tomatoes, halved | ¼ cup basil, torn | 2 tbsp. balsamic vinegar
Directions: In a bowl, combine the zucchini noodles with salt, pepper and the oil, toss and leave aside for 10 minutes. Add mozzarella, tomatoes, basil and vinegar, toss, divide between plates and serve as a side dish.

Coconut Cauliflower Mash

Preparation Time: 10 minutes | **Cooking Time:** 10 minutes | **Servings:** 6 | **Calories**: 200

Ingredients: 2 cauliflower heads, florets separated | 1/3 cup coconut cream | 1/3 cup coconut milk
1 tablespoon chives, chopped | a pinch of salt and black pepper

Directions: Put some water in a pot, bring to a boil over medium-high heat, add cauliflower florets, cook them for 10 minutes, drain them well, mash using a potato masher and stir. Add the cream, the coconut milk, salt, pepper and chives, stir well, divide between plates and serve as a side dish.

Coconut Brussels Sprouts

Preparation Time: 10 minutes | **Cooking Time:** 30 minutes | **Servings:** 6 | **Calories:** 271

Ingredients: 2 pounds Brussels sprouts, halved | 2 tablespoons olive oil | pinch of salt and black pepper
1 teaspoon sesame oil | 2 garlic cloves, minced | ½ cup coconut amino | 2 teaspoons apple cider vinegar
1 tablespoon stevia | 2 teaspoons garlic chili sauce | pinch of red pepper flakes | ½ cup water

Directions: Spread the sprouts on a lined baking sheet, season them with salt and pepper, drizzle the olive oil, toss them, bake them in the oven at 425 degrees F for 20 minutes and transfer them to a bowl. Heat up a pan with the sesame oil over medium heat, add garlic, stir and cook for 1 minute. Add coconut amino, water, vinegar, stevia, chili paste, salt, pepper and pepper flakes, stir, bring to a simmer and cook for 3 minutes. Add the sprouts, toss, introduce the pan in preheated broil over medium-high heat, broil them for 6 minutes, divide between plates and serve as a side dish.

Parmesan Brussels Sprouts

Preparation Time: 10 minutes | **Cooking Time:** 30 minutes | **Servings:** 4 | **Calories**: 222

Ingredients: 1 pound Brussels sprouts, halved | 1 teaspoon oregano, dried | 1 tablespoon olive oil
3 garlic cloves, minced | ½ teaspoon hot paprika | 2 tablespoons keto ranch dressing
1 tablespoon Parmesan, grated | a pinch of salt and black pepper

Directions: Spread the sprouts on a lined baking sheet, add oregano, oil, garlic, paprika, salt and pepper, toss, bake them in the oven at 425 degrees F for 30 minutes, add parmesan and keto ranch dressing, toss well, divide between plates and serve as a side dish.

Crunchy Parmesan Crisps

Preparation Time: 5 minutes | **Cooking Time:** 3 minutes | **Servings:** 12 | **Calories**: 64

Ingredients: 12 tablespoons Parmesan cheese, shredded

Directions: Preheat your oven to 400° Fahrenheit. Spray a baking tray with cooking spray. Place each tablespoon of cheese on a baking tray. Bake in preheated oven for 3 minutes or until lightly brown. Allow cooling time, serve, and enjoy!

Fried Cauliflower Rice

Preparation Time: 10 minutes | **Cooking Time:** 15 minutes | **Servings:** 4 | **Calories:** 200

Ingredients: 1 tablespoon ghee, melted | 1 small yellow onion, chopped | 2 hot dogs, sliced
1 tablespoon avocado oil | 1 garlic clove, minced | 2 and ½ cups cauliflower rice, steamed
2 eggs, whisked | 2 tablespoons coconut amino | 2 scallions, sliced

Directions: Heat up a pan with the ghee over medium-high heat, add onion, garlic and hot dogs, stir and cook for 5 minutes. Add cauliflower rice and avocado oil, stir and cook for 5 minutes more. Add the eggs, toss everything, cook for 5 more minutes until the eggs are scrambled, add the amino and the scallions, toss, divide between plates and serve as a side dish.

Cheesy Asparagus Dish

Preparation Time: 10 minutes | **Cooking Time:** 30 minutes | **Servings:** 6 | **Calories:** 200

Ingredients: 3 garlic cloves, minced | ¾ cup coconut cream | 2 pounds asparagus, trimmed
1 cup Parmesan, grated | a pinch of salt and black pepper | 1 cup mozzarella, shredded

Directions: In a baking dish, combine the asparagus with the garlic, cream, salt, pepper, mozzarella and top with the parmesan, introduce in the oven and bake at 400 degrees F for 30 minutes. Divide between plates and serve as a side dish.

Wholesome Keto Avo-Burgers

Preparation Time: 5 minutes | **Cooking Time:** 5 minutes | **Servings:** 2 | **Calories:** 205

Ingredients: 2 avocados | 2 eggs | 2 tbsp chopped lettuce | 2 tbsp mayonnaise | 4 strips of bacon

Directions: Bring out a skillet pan, put it over medium heat and when hot, add bacon strips and cook for 5 minutes until crispy. Move bacon to a plate lined with paper towels, crack an egg into the pan, and cook for 2 to 4 minutes or until fried to the desired level; fry remaining egg in the same manner. Prepare sandwiches and for this, cut each avocado in half widthwise, remove the pit, and scoop out the flesh. Fill the hollow of two avocado halves with mayonnaise, then top each half with 1 tbsp of chopped lettuce, 2 bacon strips, and a fried egg, and then cover with the second half of avocado. Sprinkle sesame seeds on avocados and serve.

Green Shakshuka

Preparation Time: 15 minutes | **Cooking Time:** 10 minutes | **Servings:** 4 | **Calories**: 322

Ingredients: 1/2 medium green bell pepper, deseeded and chopped | 1 celery stalk, chopped
1/4 cup green beans, chopped | 1 garlic clove, minced | 2 tbsp. fresh mint leaves | 1/2 cup baby kale
3 tbsp. fresh parsley leaves | 1/4 tsp. plain vinegar | salt and black pepper, to taste | 4 eggs
1/4 tsp. nutmeg powder | 7 oz. Feta cheese, divided | 1 tbsp. olive oil | 2 tbsp. almond oil

Directions: Heat the olive oil and almond oil in a medium frying pan over medium heat. Add the bell pepper, celery, green beans, and sauté for 5 minutes or until the vegetables soften. Stir in the garlic, mint leaves, two tablespoons of parsley, and cook until fragrant, 1 minute. Add the kale, vinegar, and mix. Once the kale starts wilting, season with salt, black pepper, nutmeg powder, and stir in half of the feta cheese—Cook for 1 to 2 minutes. After, use the spatula to create four holes in the food and crack an egg into each hole. Cook until the egg whites set still running. Season the eggs with salt and black pepper. Turn the heat off and scatter the remaining feta cheese on top. Garnish with the remaining parsley and serve the shakshuka immediately.

Avo-Tacos

Preparation Time: 15 minutes | **Cooking Time:** 5 minutes | **Servings:** 4 | **Calories**: 179

Ingredients: 30 ml avocado oil | 60 g cauliflower rice | 58 grams, walnuts or pecans, crushed
14 grams, chipotle chili, chopped | 14 grams, jalapeno pepper, minced | 20 grams onions, chopped
2.5 grams cumin | 2.5 grams salt, sea salt preferred | 100 grams, tomato, ripe and diced | 15 ml lime juice

Directions: The Avo-Taco is so easy to make that you'll want to do this every week. Start by grabbing a bowl and putting the salsa ingredients together; in a small bowl, you'll need the diced tomatoes, jalapeno, the onion and half of the lime. If you want, you can add in a bit of cilantro to give it a bit more freshness, and don't forget to add the salt! Once you're done, put a frying pan on medium heat and add the avocado oil and let it heat. In the meantime, you can get together the rest of the ingredients, including the cauli-rice (which you can totally make at home if you want--it's a 5-minute blend job), and toss in everything but the avocado, and cook on low to medium heat for about 5 minutes. Add the mixture to the avocado halves and top with salsa and munch away!

Chipotle Jicama Hash

Preparation Time: 5 minutes | **Cooking Time:** 10 minutes | **Servings:** 5 | **Calories**: 175

Ingredients: 4 slices bacon, chopped | 12 oz. jicama, peeled and diced | 4 oz. purple onion, chopped
1 oz. green bell pepper, seeded and chopped | 4 tbsp. Chipotle mayonnaise

Directions: Using a skillet, brown the bacon on a high heat. Remove and place on a towel to drain the grease. Use the remaining grease to fry the onions and jicama until brown. When ready, add the bell pepper and cook the hash until tender. Transfer the hash onto two plates and serve each plate with 4 tablespoons of Chipotle mayonnaise.

Brussels Sprout Chips

Preparation Time: 6 minutes | **Cooking Time:** 20 minutes | **Servings:** 4 | **Calories**: 102

Ingredients: 1 teaspoon garlic powder | 1/2 lb. brussels sprouts, sliced thinly | black pepper, to taste
1 tablespoon extra-virgin olive oil | 2 tablespoons Parmesan, grated | Kosher salt, to taste

Directions: At 400 degrees F, preheat your oven. Toss brussels sprouts with parmesan, garlic powder, oil, black pepper, and salt. Spread the brussels sprouts in the baking sheet in a single layer. Bake them for 10 minutes in the preheated oven. Toss them well, then bake again for 10 minutes until crispy. Serve warm and crispy.

Fried Queso Blanco

Preparation Time: 20 m.+2 h. freezing time | **Cooking Time:** 30 min | **Servings:** 4 | **Calories**: 282

Ingredients: 5 oz queso Blanco | 1 ½ tbsp. olive oil | 3 oz. cheese | 2 oz. olives |1 pinch red pepper flakes

Directions: Cube some cheese and freeze it for 1-2 hours. Pour the oil in a skillet and heat to boil over a medium temperature. Add the cheese cubes and heat till brown. Combine the cheese together using a spatula and flatten. Cook the cheese on both sides, flipping regularly. While flipping, fold the cheese into itself to form crispy layers. Use a spatula to roll it into a block. Remove it from the pan, allow it to cool, cut it into small cubes, and serve.

Spinach with Bacon & Shallots

Preparation Time: 5 minutes | **Cooking Time:** 25 minutes | **Servings:** 4 | **Calories**: 361

Ingredients: 16 oz. raw spinach | ½ cup chopped white onion | ½ cup chopped shallot | 2 tbsp. butter
½ pound raw bacon slices

Directions: Slice the bacon strips into small narrow pieces. In a skillet, heat the butter and add the chopped onion, shallots, and bacon. Sauté for 15-20 minutes or until the onions start to caramelize, and the bacon is cooked. Add the spinach and sauté on medium heat. Stir frequently to ensure the leaves touch the skillet while cooking. Cover and steam for around 5 mins, stir and continue until wilted. Serve!

Spicy Roasted Pecans

Preparation Time: 5 minutes | **Cooking Time:** 10 minutes | **Servings:** 9 | **Calories**: 189

Ingredients: 1 teaspoon salt | 8 oz. pecans | 1 tablespoon coconut oil | 1 teaspoon paprika powder

Directions: At 325 degrees F, preheat your oven. Toss pecans with salt, coconut oil, and paprika powder in a suitable bowl. Spread the pecan in a baking sheet. Roast the spicy pecans for 10 minutes in the preheated oven. Toss the pecans when cooked halfway through. Serve and enjoy.

Mediterranean Side Salad

Preparation Time: 10 minutes | **Cooking Time:** 0 minutes | **Servings:** 4 | **Calories**: 200

Ingredients: 1 pint cherry tomatoes, halved | 1 cup kalamata olives, pitted and sliced | ¼ cup olive oil
1 cucumber, sliced | ½ red onion, sliced | 1 cup Feta cheese, crumbled | juice of ½ lemon
2 tablespoons red vinegar | a pinch of salt and black pepper | 1 teaspoon oregano, dried

Directions: In a salad bowl, combine the tomatoes with the olives, cucumber and onion. In a separate bowl, combine the lemon juice with the vinegar, salt, pepper, oregano and oil and whisk well. Pour this over your salad, toss, sprinkle cheese at the end and serve as a side dish.

Mozzarella Brussels Sprouts

Preparation Time: 10 minutes | **Cooking Time:** 30 minutes | **Servings:** 6 | **Calories:** 288

Ingredients: 2 tablespoons olive oil | 2 pounds Brussels sprouts | 2 garlic cloves, minced
1 teaspoon thyme, chopped | a pinch of salt and black pepper | 1 cup mozzarella, shredded
¼ cup Parmesan, grated | 1 tablespoon parsley, chopped

Directions: Put some water in a pot, bring to a boil over medium-high heat, add sprouts, cook them for 10 minutes, transfer them to a bowl filled with ice water, cool them down and drain them well. In a bowl, combine the Brussels sprouts with salt, pepper, oil, garlic and thyme, toss and smash them a bit. Spread smashed Brussels sprouts on a lined baking sheet, sprinkle mozzarella and parmesan on top, introduce in the oven and bake them at 425°F for 20 minutes. Sprinkle parsley on top, divide between plates and serve

Bacon-Wrapped Sausage Skewers

Preparation Time: 10 minutes | **Cooking Time:** 8 minutes | **Servings:** 4 | **Calories**: 331

Ingredients: 5 Italian chicken sausages | 10 slices bacon

Directions: Preheat your deep fryer to 370°F/190°C. Cut the sausage into four pieces. Slice the bacon in half. Wrap the bacon over the sausage. Skewer the sausage. Fry for 4-5 minutes until browned.

Celery and Chili Peppers Stir Fry

Preparation Time: 10 minutes | **Cooking Time:** 5 minutes | **Servings:** 6 | **Calories**: 162

Ingredients: 2 tablespoons olive oil | 3 chili peppers, dried and crushed | 4 cups celery, julienned
2 tablespoons coconut aminos

Directions: Heat up a pan with the oil at medium-high heat, add chili peppers, stir and cook them for 2 minutes. Add the celery and the coconut aminos, stir, cook for 3 minutes more, divide between plates and serve as a side dish.

Acorn Squash Puree

Preparation Time: 10 minutes | **Cooking Time:** 20 minutes | **Servings:** 4 | **Calories**: 182

Ingredients: ½ cup water | 2 acorn squash, deseeded and halved | salt and black pepper, to taste
2 tablespoons ghee, melted | ½ teaspoon nutmeg, grated

Directions: Put the squash halves and the water in a pot, bring to a simmer, cook for 20 minutes, drain, scrape squash flesh, transfer to a bowl, add salt, pepper, ghee and nutmeg, mash well, divide between plates and serve as a side dish.

Squash Wedges

Preparation Time: 10 minutes | **Cooking Time:** 10 minutes | **Servings:** 4 | **Calories**: 202

Ingredients: 1 pound butternut squash, cut into medium wedges | olive oil for frying
a pinch of salt and black pepper | ¼ teaspoon baking soda

Directions: Heat a pan with olive oil at medium-high heat, put squash wedges, season with salt, pepper and the baking soda, cook until they are gold on all sides, drain grease, divide between plates then serve.

Turnips Mash

Preparation Time: 10 minutes | **Cooking Time:** 20 minutes | **Servings:** 4 | **Calories**: 201

Ingredients: 4 turnips, peeled and chopped | ½ cup veggie stock | salt and black pepper, to taste
1 yellow onion, chopped | ¼ cup coconut cream

Directions: In a pot, combine the turnips with stock and onion, stir, bring to a simmer, cook for 20 minutes and blend using an immersion blender. Add salt, pepper and cream blend again, divide between plates and serve as a side dish.

Celery and Mozzarella Side Salad

Preparation Time: 10 minutes | **Cooking Time:** 0 minutes | **Servings:** 4 | **Calories**: 100

Ingredients: 8 ounces mozzarella, shredded | 2 cups cherry tomatoes, halved | 3 celery stalks, chopped
juice of 1 lemon | 3 tablespoons olive oil | a pinch of salt and black pepper | ½ teaspoon oregano, dried

Directions: In a bowl, place and combine the tomatoes with the celery, oregano, mozzarella, lemon juice, salt, pepper and the oil, toss, divide between plates then serve.

Turmeric Peppers Platter

Preparation Time: 10 minutes | **Cooking Time:** 20 minutes | **Servings:** 4 | **Calories**: 120

Ingredients: 2 green bell peppers, cut into wedges | 2 red bell peppers, cut into wedges
2 yellow bell peppers, cut into wedges | 2 tablespoons avocado oil | 2 garlic cloves, minced
1 bunch basil, chopped | a pinch of salt and black pepper | 2 tablespoons balsamic vinegar

Directions: Warm a pan with the oil on medium heat, add the garlic and the vinegar and cook for 2 minutes. Add the peppers and the other ingredients, toss, cook over medium heat for 18 minutes, arrange them on a platter and serve as an appetizer.

Mushroom Cakes

Preparation Time: 10 minutes | **Cooking Time:** 12 minutes | **Servings:** 6 | **Calories**: 222

Ingredients: 1 cup shallots, chopped | 3 garlic cloves, minced | 1 pound mushrooms, minced
2 tablespoons almond flour | ¼ cup coconut cream | 1 tablespoon flaxseed with 2 tablespoons water
¼ cup parsley, chopped | 2 tablespoons olive oil

Directions: In a bowl, combine the shallots with the garlic, the mushrooms, and the other ingredients except for the oil, stir well and shape medium cakes out of this mix. Heat a pan with the oil over medium heat, add the mushroom cakes, cook for 6 minutes on each side, arrange them on a platter and serve.

Cabbage Sauté

Preparation Time: 5 minutes | **Cooking Time:** 10 minutes | **Servings:** 2 | **Calories**: 148

Ingredients: 3 ounces kale | 2 ounces green cabbage | 2 ounces red cabbage | 1 tablespoon lemon juice
2 tablespoons olive oil | ¼ teaspoon black pepper | salt, to taste

Directions: Tear the kale leaves from stems, and cut the cabbage into thin pieces. Take a skillet and heat the oil over a low to medium heat. Put everything into a skillet. Pour some lemon juice and season the mixture with some salt and pepper. Stir everything together. Leave the skillet over medium heat and cook the mixture for 5-10 minutes or until you notice it became tender and golden at the edges.

Creamy Cabbage

Preparation Time: 5 minutes | **Cooking Time:** 10 minutes | **Servings:** 2 | **Calories**: 149

Ingredients: 6 ounces cabbage | 1 garlic clove | 1 tablespoon butter (or coconut oil)
1 ounce vegetable broth (or water) | 1-½ ounces heavy cream (or coconut cream) | salt, to taste

Directions: Cut the cabbage into thin slices and crush the garlic. Take a large skillet and melt the butter over medium-high heat. Add in cabbage and garlic and cook for 3-4 minutes until you notice cabbage got tender. Pour the broth and cream to the skillet and stir everything together. Wait until everything simmers and then cook it for 3-4 more minutes. You will know you are done when the cream is thick, and the cabbage is softer. Serve the meal while it's hot.

Walnuts Broccoli Salad

Preparation Time: 10 minutes | **Cooking Time:** 20 minutes | **Servings:** 6 | **Calories**: 197

Ingredients: 6 cups broccoli florets | 14 oz. tomato paste | 1 tablesp. olive oil | 1 yellow onion, chopped
1 teaspoon thyme, dried | salt and black pepper, to taste | ½ cup walnuts, chopped

Directions: Heat up a pan with the oil at medium-high heat, add the onion, stir and cook for 5 minutes. Add broccoli, tomato paste, thyme, salt and pepper, toss, cook for 10 minutes, divide between plates, sprinkle walnuts on top and serve as a side dish.

Creamy Coleslaw

Preparation Time: 10 minutes | **Cooking Time:** 2 minutes | **Servings:** 2 | **Calories**: 222

Ingredients: 3 oz. green cabbage | 1 oz. red cabbage | 2 oz. cucumber | 1 tablespoon scallions
4 tablespoons mayonnaise | ½ tablespoon lemon juice | 1 tablespoon dill | 1 tablespoon parsley
6 black olives | salt, to taste

Directions: Cut the red and green cabbage, olives, scallions, and cucumber into bite-sized pieces and add them to a bowl. Add some salt. Put the lemon juice and mayo in another bowl. Mince the parsley and dill and combine them in. Mix the wet and dry ingredients so you can prepare coleslaw. You can wait for the mixture to marinate a little bit and leave it aside for an hour or simply serve it right away

Chili Cauliflower Mix

Preparation Time: 10 minutes | **Cooking Time:** 35 minutes | **Servings:** 4 | **Calories:** 271

Ingredients: 2 tablespoons sweet chili sauce | 3 tablespoons olive oil | 3 garlic cloves, minced
juice of 1 lime | 1 cauliflower head, florets separated | 1 teaspoon cilantro, chopped
a pinch of salt and black pepper

Directions: In a bowl, the chili sauce with the oil, garlic, lime juice, salt, pepper, cilantro and the cauliflower, toss well, spread on a lined baking sheet, introduce in the oven and cook at 425 degrees F for 35 minutes. Divide the cauliflower between plates and serve as a side dish.

Mozzarella Broccoli Mix

Preparation Time: 10 minutes | **Cooking Time:** 15 minutes | **Servings:** 4 | **Calories**: 261

Ingredients: 2 tablespoons olive oil | 1 broccoli head, florets separated | 2 garlic cloves, minced
½ cup mozzarella, shredded | ¼ cup Parmesan, grated | ½ cup coconut cream | 1 tbsp. parsley, chopped

Directions: Heat up a pan with the oil over medium-high heat add broccoli, salt, pepper and garlic, stir and cook for 6 minutes. Add parmesan, mozzarella and cream, toss, introduce the pan in the oven and cook at 375 degrees F for 10 minutes. Add parsley, toss, divide between plates and serve as a side dish.

Parsley Bacon Brussels Sprouts

Preparation Time: 10 minutes | **Cooking Time:** 20 minutes | **Servings:** 6 | **Calories**: 261

Ingredients: 1 pound Brussels sprouts, halved | a pinch of salt & black pepper | 7 bacon slices, chopped
1 yellow onion, chopped | 2 tablespoons stevia | 2 tablespoons olive oil | 1 tablespoon parsley, chopped
2 teaspoons sweet paprika

Directions: Heat up a pan with the oil over medium-high heat, add the onion, stir and sauté for 4-5 minutes. Add the bacon, stir and cook for 3 minutes more. Add the sprouts, salt, pepper, stevia, paprika and parsley, toss, cook for 10 minutes more, divide between plates and serve as a side dish.

Mozzarella and Artichoke Mix

Preparation Time: 10 minutes | **Cooking Time:** 10 minutes | **Servings:** 4 | **Calories**: 277

Ingredients: 14 oz canned artichoke hearts, drained | pinch of salt & black pepper | 2 cups baby spinach
2 tablespoons parsley, chopped | 1 cup mozzarella, shredded | 1 and ¾ cups coconut milk | juice 1 lemon
½ cup chicken stock | 2 garlic cloves, minced | 3 tablespoons ghee, melted | a pinch of red pepper flakes

Directions: Heat up a pan with the ghee over medium-high heat, add the garlic, stir and cook for 2 minutes. Add lemon juice, coconut milk, stock, artichokes, salt and pepper, stir and cook for 5 minutes. Add spinach, pepper flakes and mozzarella, toss, cook for 3 minutes more, divide between plates, sprinkle parsley on top and serve as a side dish.

Roast Beef and Mozzarella Plate

Preparation Time: 5 minutes | **Cooking Time:** 0 minutes | **Servings:** 2 | **Calories**: 267

Ingredients: 4 slices of roast beef | ½ ounce chopped lettuce | 1 avocado, pitted | ½ cup mayonnaise
2 oz mozzarella cheese, cubed | Seasoning: ¼ tsp salt | 1/8 tsp ground black pepper | 2 tbsp avocado oil

Directions: Scoop out flesh from the avocado and divide it evenly between two plates. Add slices of roast beef, lettuce, and cheese and then sprinkle with salt and black pepper. Serve with avocado oil and mayonnaise.

Baked Zucchini Gratin

Preparation Time: 10 minutes | **Cooking Time:** 25 minutes | **Servings:** 2 | **Calories**: 355

Ingredients: 1 large zucchini, cut into ¼-inch-thick slices | 1 ounce brie cheese, rind trimmed off | salt
1 tbsp butter | freshly ground black pepper | ⅓ cup shredded Gruyère cheese | ¼ cup crushed pork rinds

Directions: Salt the zucchini slices and put them in a colander in the sink for 45 minutes; the zucchini will shed much of their water. Preheat the oven to 400°F. When the zucchini been "weeping" for about 30 minutes, in a small saucepan over medium-low heat, heat the Brie and butter, stirring occasionally, until the cheese has melted and the mixture is fully combined, about 2 minutes. Arrange the zucchini in an 8-inch baking dish so the zucchini slices are overlapping a bit. Season with pepper. Pour the Brie mixture over the zucchini, and top with the shredded Gruyère cheese. Sprinkle the crushed pork rinds over the top. Bake for about 25 minutes, until the dish is bubbling and the top is nicely browned, and serve.

Parmesan and Pork rind Green Beans

Preparation Time: 5 minutes | **Cooking Time:** 15 minutes | **Servings:** 2 | **Calories**: 175

Ingredients: ½ pound fresh green beans | 2 tablespoons crushed pork rinds | 2 tablespoons olive oil
1 tablespoon grated Parmesan cheese | pink Himalayan salt | freshly ground black pepper

Directions: Preheat the oven to 400°F. In a medium bowl, combine the green beans, pork rinds, olive oil, and Parmesan cheese. Season with pink Himalayan salt and pepper, and toss until the beans are thoroughly coated. Spread the bean mixture on a baking sheet in a single layer, and roast for about 15 minutes. At the halfway point, give the pan a little shake to move the beans around, or just give them a stir. Divide the beans between two plates and serve.

Roasted Radishes with Brown Butter Sauce.

Preparation Time: 10 minutes | **Cooking Time:** 15 minutes | **Servings:** 2 | **Calories**: 181

Ingredients: 2 cups halved radishes | 1 tablespoon olive oil | pink Himalayan salt
freshly ground black pepper | 2 tablespoons butter | 1 tablespoon chopped fresh flat-leaf Italian parsley

Directions: Preheat the oven to 450°F. In a medium bowl, toss the radishes in the olive oil and season with pink Himalayan salt and pepper. Spread the radishes on a baking sheet in a single layer. Roast for 15 minutes, stirring halfway through. Meanwhile, when the radishes have been roasting for about 10 minutes, in a small, light-colored saucepan over medium heat, melt the butter completely, stirring frequently, and season with pink Himalayan salt. When the butter begins to bubble and foam, continue stirring. When the bubbling diminishes a bit, the butter should be a nice nutty brown. The browning process should take about 3 minutes total. Transfer the browned butter to a heat-safe container (I use a mug). Remove the radishes from the oven, and divide them between two plates. Spoon the brown butter over the radishes, top with the chopped parsley, and serve.

Rosemary Veggie Mix

Preparation Time: 10 minutes | **Cooking Time:** 20 minutes | **Servings:** 4 | **Calories**: 199

Ingredients: 1-pound Brussels sprouts, halved | 2 tablespoons olive oil | 1 teaspoon rosemary, chopped 1 tablespoon balsamic vinegar | 1 teaspoon thyme, chopped | ½ cup cranberries, dried

Directions: Spread the sprouts on a lined baking sheet, add rosemary, vinegar, oil and thyme, toss, introduce in the oven and cook at 400 degrees F for 20 minutes. Divide between plates, sprinkle cranberries on top and serve as a side dish.

Celeriac Stuffed Avocado

Preparation Time: 5 minutes | **Cooking Time:** 0 minutes | **Servings:** 2 | **Calories**: 285

Ingredients: ¼ tsp salt | ½ lemon, juiced, zested | 1 avocado | 1 celery root, finely chopped 2 tbsp mayonnaise

Directions: Prepare avocado and for this, cut avocado in half and then remove its pit. Put remaining ingredients in a bowl, combine thoroughly until combined and evenly stuff this mixture into avocado halves.

Roasted Brussels Sprouts

Preparation Time: 10 minutes | **Cooking Time:** 25 minutes | **Servings:** 4 | **Calories:** 200

Ingredients: 1 pound Brussels sprouts, halved | 2 tablespoons olive oil | a pinch of salt and black pepper

Directions: Spread the sprouts on a lined baking sheet, add the oil, salt and pepper, toss, introduce in the oven and bake at 425 degrees F for 25 minutes. Divide between plates and serve as a side dish.

Awesome Roasted Acorn Squash

Preparation Time: 40 to 45 minutes | **Cooking Time:** 0 minutes | **Servings:** 4 | **Calories**: 253

Ingredients: ¼ teaspoon black pepper | ¼ cup Parmesan cheese, grated | 8 fresh thyme sprigs 2-½ tablespoons olive oil | 1 large acorn squash, cut in half lengthwise

Directions: First of all, please certify you've all the ingredients on the market. Preheat the oven to 400° F. /200° C. Now remove the seed from squash & cut into ¾ slices. Add squash slices, parmesan cheese, olive oil, thyme, pepper, and salt in a bowl and toss to coat. One thing remains to be done. Then spread squash onto a baking tray & roast in preheated oven for about 25 to 30 minutes or until golden brown.

Chia Seed Crackers

Preparation Time: 5 minutes | **Cooking Time:** 35 minutes | **Servings:** 8 | **Calories:** 120

Ingredients: 1/2 cup ground chia seeds | 1-1/2 cups water | 1/4 teaspoon paprika | 1/4 teaspoon salt 1/4 teaspoon black pepper | 1/4 teaspoon dried oregano | 3 oz. shredded cheddar cheese 2 tablespoons almond meal | 1/4 teaspoon garlic powder | 4 tablespoons olive oil

Directions: Preheat oven to 375°F and in the meantime take a large bowl and mix oregano, garlic powder, almond meal, paprika, chia seeds, salt and pepper. Mix together until all the ingredients are well combined. Take the olive oil and pour into the mixture. Whisk until fully blended. Pour water into the mixture and keep mixing until you see the smoothness. Add the shredded cheddar cheese, mix it well with the mixture using a spatula and then prepare the dough kneading with your hands. Spread the dough on a parchment paper in the baking sheet, cover with another parchment paper from the top and make it 0.125 inch thin with the help of a roller. Place in the preheated oven and bake for 30 minutes. Cut into the shapes you like after removing from the oven and place in the oven again to bake for 5 minutes more or until the time you are satisfied. Remove from the oven once properly baked and transfer to the wire rack to cool before you serve the delicious chia seed crackers.

Keto Bread

Preparation Time: 5 minutes | **Cooking Time:** 25 minutes | **Servings:** 12 slices | **Calories:** 165

Ingredients: 5 tablespoons butter, at room temperature, divided | 6 large eggs, lightly beaten
1 ½ cups almond flour | 3 teaspoons baking powder | 1 scoop MCT oil powder (optional)
pinch of pink Himalayan salt

Directions: Preheat the oven to 390°F. Coat a 9-by-5-inch of loaf pan with a tablespoon of butter. In a large bowl, utilize a hand mixer to mix the eggs, almond flour, remaining 4 tablespoons of butter, baking powder, MCT oil powder (if using), and pink Himalayan salt until thoroughly blended. Pour into the prepared pan. Bake it for approximately 25 minutes. Slice and serve.

Chicken-Pecan Salad Cucumber Bites

Preparation Time: 15 minutes | **Cooking Time:** 0 minutes | **Servings:** 2 | **Calories:** 323

Ingredients: 1 cup diced cooked chicken breast | 2 tablespoons mayonnaise | ¼ cup chopped pecans
¼ cup diced celery | pink Himalayan salt | black pepper | 1 cucumber, peeled and cut into ¼-inch slices

Directions: In a bowl, mix together the chicken, mayonnaise, pecans, and celery. Season with pink Himalayan salt and pepper. Lay the cucumber slices out on a plate, and add a pinch of pink Himalayan salt to each. Put a spoonful of the chicken-salad mixture on top of each cucumber slice and serve.

Chicken Liver Pate

Preparation Time: 10 minutes | **Cooking Time:** 10 minutes | **Servings:** 7 | **Calories:** 173

Ingredients: 1 pound chicken liver | 1 teaspoon salt | 4 tablespoons butter | ½ teaspoon dried cilantro
1 teaspoon ground black pepper | 5 oz. chive stems | 1 cup water

Directions: Chop the chicken liver roughly and place it in the air fryer basket tray. Dice the chives. Pour the water in the air fryer basket tray and add the diced chives. Preheat the air fryer to 360°F and cook the chicken liver for 10 minutes. Once cooked, strain the chicken liver mixture to discard the liquid. Transfer the chicken liver into a blender. Add the butter, ground black pepper, and dried cilantro. Blend the mixture till you get the pate texture. Transfer the liver pate to a bowl and serve it immediately.

Zucchini Fritters with Cheddar

Preparation Time: 10 minutes | **Cooking Time:** 8 minutes | **Servings:** 7 | **Calories:** 133

Ingredients: 4 oz. mozzarella | 3 oz. cheddar cheese | 1 zucchini, grated | 2 tablespoon dried dill
1 tablespoon coconut flour | 1 tablespoon almond flour | ¼ teaspoon salt | 1 teaspoon butter

Directions: Shred the Cheddar and Mozzarella. Combine the grated zucchini with the shredded cheese. Add dried dill and coconut flour. Add almond flour and salt. Stir carefully with a fork. Mix well to combine and leave to marinade for 3 minutes. Preheat the air fryer to 400°F. Melt the butter in the air fryer tray. Make the fritters from the zucchini mixture and put them in the melted butter. Cook the fritters for 5 minutes. Turn the zucchini fritters over and cook for 3 min more.

Cauliflower Casserole

Preparation Time: 5 minutes | **Cooking Time:** 20 minutes | **Servings:** 4 | **Calories:** 240

Ingredients: 2 cups cauliflower florets, separated | 4 eggs, whisked | 1 teaspoon sweet paprika
2 tablespoons butter, melted | a pinch of salt and black pepper

Directions: Heat up your air fryer at 320 degrees F, grease with the butter, add cauliflower florets on the bottom, then add eggs whisked with paprika, salt and pepper, toss and cook for 20 minutes. Divide between plates and serve for breakfast.

Parsley Shrimp Tails

Preparation Time: 10 minutes | **Cooking Time:** 14 minutes | **Servings:** 6 | **Calories**: 155

Ingredients: 1 pound shrimp tails | 1 tablespoon olive oil | 1 teaspoon dried dill
½ teaspoon dried parsley | 2 tablespoons coconut flour | ½ cup heavy cream | 1 teaspoon chili flakes

Directions: Peel the shrimp tails and sprinkle them with the dried dill and dried parsley. Mix the shrimp tails carefully in a mixing bowl. Combine the coconut flour, heavy cream, and chili flakes in a separate bowl and whisk until smooth. Preheat the air fryer to 330°F. Place the shrimp tails in the cream mix and stir. Grease the air fryer rack and put the shrimp tails inside. Cook the shrimp tails for 7 minutes. Turn the shrimp. Cook the shrimp tails for 7 minutes more.

Calamari Almond Rings

Preparation Time: 12 minutes | **Cooking Time:** 8 minutes | **Servings:** 4 | **Calories:** 190

Ingredients: 1 cup almond flour | 9 oz. calamari | 1 egg | ½ teaspoon lemon zest | 1 teaspoon fresh lemon juice | ½ teaspoon turmeric | ¼ teaspoon salt | ¼ teaspoon ground black pepper

Directions: Wash and peel the calamari. Slice the calamari into thick rings. Crack the egg in a bowl and whisk it. Add lemon zest, turmeric, salt, and ground black pepper to the bowl and mix. Sprinkle the calamari rings with fresh lemon juice. Place the calamari rings in the whisked egg and stir. Leave the calamari rings in the egg mixture for 4 minutes. Coat the calamari rings in the almond flour mixture well. Preheat the air fryer to 360°F. Transfer the calamari rings to the air fryer rack, and cook for 8 minutes.

Turkey Stuffed Peppers

Preparation Time: 13 minutes | **Cooking Time:** 30 minutes | **Servings:** 4 | **Calories:** 267

Ingredients: 2 large and sweet peppers, halved and seeded | 1 teaspoon garlic salt | 12 oz ground turkey
3/4 cup ricotta cheese | 1 cup mozzarella

Directions: At 400 degrees F, preheat the oven. Place the pepper halves in a baking dish and drizzle ¼ teaspoons garlic salt on the top. Divide the ground turkey into each pepper half. Drizzle remaining garlic salt on top. Bake the turkey stuffed peppers for 25 minutes in the preheated oven. Top the stuffed peppers with ricotta cheese and mozzarella cheese. Bake the peppers again for 5 mins to melt the cheese & serve.

Keto Beef Bombs

Preparation Time: 15 minutes | **Cooking Time:** 14 minutes | **Servings:** 7 | **Calories:** 155

Ingredients: 6 oz. ground chicken | 6 oz. ground beef | 6 oz. ground pork | 2 oz chive stems
3 garlic cloves, minced | 1 tbsp dried parsley | ½ tsp salt | ½ tsp chili flakes | 1 egg | 1 tbsp butter

Directions: Put the ground chicken, ground beef, and ground pork in a mixing bowl. Add the diced chives, minced garlic, dried parsley, salt, and chili flakes. Crack the egg into the bowl with the ground meat. Stir the meat mixture using your hands. Melt butter and add it to the ground meat mixture. Stir. Leave the ground meat mixture for 5 minutes to rest. Preheat the air fryer to 370°F. Make small meatballs from the meat mixture and put them in the air fryer. Cook the meatballs for 14 min. Cool before serving.

Paprika Mozzarella Balls

Preparation Time: 10 minutes | **Cooking Time:** 10 minutes | **Servings:** 6 | **Calories:** 262

Ingredients: 5 oz. bacon, sliced | 10 oz. mozzarella | ¼ tsp ground black pepper | ¼ tsp paprika

Directions: Sprinkle the sliced bacon with ground black pepper and paprika. Wrap the mozzarella balls in the bacon. Secure the mozzarella balls with toothpicks. Preheat the air fryer to 360°F. Put the mozzarella balls in the air fryer rack and cook for 10 minutes.

Toasted Macadamia & Nuts Mix

Preparation Time: 5 minutes | **Cooking Time:** 9 minutes | **Servings:** 4 | **Calories:** 230

Ingredients: ¼ cup hazelnuts | ¼ cup walnuts | ½ cup pecans | ½ cup macadamia nuts
1 tablespoon olive oil | 1 teaspoon salt

Directions: Preheat the air fryer to 320°F. Place the hazelnuts, walnuts, pecans, and macadamia nuts in the air fryer. Cook for 8 minutes stirring halfway through. Drizzle the nuts with olive oil and salt and shake them well. Cook the nuts for 1 minute. Transfer the cooked nuts ramekins.

Flax Mozzarella Wraps

Preparation Time: 10 minutes | **Cooking Time:** 2 minutes | **Servings:** 2 | **Calories**: 143

Ingredients: 1 cucumber | 1 egg | 3 oz. flax seeds | 3 oz. mozzarella, grated | 1 tablespoon water
½ tablespoon butter | ¼ teaspoon baking soda | ¼ teaspoon salt

Directions: Crack the egg into a bowl and whisk it. Sprinkle the whisked egg with the flax seeds, grated mozzarella, water, baking soda, and salt. Whisk the mixture. Preheat the air fryer to 360°F. Toss the butter in the air fryer basket and melt it. Separate the egg liquid into 2 servings. Pour the first part of the serving in the air fryer basket. Cook it for 1 minute on one side. Turnover and cook for another minute. Repeat the same steps with the remaining egg mixture. Cut the cucumber into cubes. Separate the cubed cucumber into 2 parts. Place the cucumber cubes in the center of each egg pancake. Wrap the eggs.

Keto Almond Buns

Preparation Time: 15 minutes | **Cooking Time:** 13 minutes | **Servings:** 10 | **Calories**: 72

Ingredients: 1 cup almond flour | 5 tablespoons sesame seeds | 1 tablespoon pumpkin seeds, crushed
1 teaspoon stevia extract | ½ tablespoon baking powder | 1 teaspoon apple cider vinegar | 4 eggs
¼ teaspoon salt | ½ cup water, hot

Directions: Place the almond flour, sesame seeds, crushed pumpkin seeds, baking powder, and salt in a large mixing bowl. Then crack the eggs in a separate bowl. Whisk them and add stevia extract and apple cider vinegar. Stir the egg mixture gently. Pour the hot water into the almond flour mixture. Stir and add the whisked egg mixture. Knead the dough until well combined. Preheat the air fryer to 350°F. Cover the air fryer basket with some parchment paper. Make 10 small buns from the dough and put them in the air fryer. Cook the sesame cloud buns for 13 minutes. Check if the buns are cooked. If they require a little more time – cook for 1 minute more. Allow to cool before serving.

Unique Scrambled Tofu

Preparation Time: 5 to 10 minutes | **Cooking Time:** 0 minutes | **Servings:** 1 | **Calories**: 256

Ingredients: pepper to taste | 1-½ tablespoon grapeseed oil | 1 tablespoon vegetable broth
¼ teaspoon garlic powder | 1 teaspoon nutritional yeast | 14 ounces soft tofu | ¾ teaspoon salt
1 teaspoon onion powder | ¼ teaspoon turmeric powder

Directions: First off all go ahead and assemble all the ingredients at one place. In a small bowl, thoroughly combine nutritional yeast, spices, salt, and pepper. Set aside. Now crumble the tofu depending on how "chunky" you want the scramble to be. Set aside. Please heat oil in a pan on moderate. Now we can plow ahead to succeeding the most significant step. Add tofu & stir until heated through. Add vegetable broth and the spice mix. Now stir until the tofu is evenly coated with the spices. Only one thing remains to be done now. Take off the warmth once most of the liquid is absorbed. Finally, serve hot or warm. Finally, we've completed the recipe. Enjoy.

Roasted Brussels Sprouts with Bacon

Preparation Time: 5 minutes | **Cooking Time:** 25 minutes | **Servings:** 2 | **Calories**: 248

Ingredients: ½ pound Brussels sprouts, cleaned, trimmed, and halved | 1 tablespoon olive oil pink Himalayan salt | freshly ground black pepper | 1 teaspoon red pepper flakes | 6 bacon slices
1 tablespoon grated parmesan cheese

Directions: Preheat the oven to 400°F. In a bowl, mix the Brussels sprouts with the olive oil, season with pink Himalayan salt and pepper, then sprinkle the red pepper flakes. Cut the bacon strips into 1-inch pieces. (I use kitchen shears.) Place the Brussels sprouts and bacon on a baking sheet in a single layer. Roast for about 25 minutes. About halfway through the baking time, give the pan a little shake to move the sprouts around, or give them a stir. You want your Brussels sprouts crispy and browned on the outside. Remove the Brussels sprouts from the oven. Divide them between two plates, top each serving with Parmesan cheese, and serve.

Avocado in Bacon Wraps

Preparation Time: 15 minutes | **Cooking Time:** 11 minutes | **Servings:** 8 | **Calories**: 216

Ingredients: 2 avocado, pitted | 1 tablespoon coconut flakes | ½ teaspoon salt | 1 teaspoon paprika
1 teaspoon turmeric | ½ teaspoon ground black pepper | 1 teaspoon olive oil | 5 oz. bacon, sliced
1 egg | 1 teaspoon dried rosemary

Directions: Peel the avocados and cut them into medium strips. Crack the egg in a bowl and whisk it. Sprinkle the whisked egg with the coconut flakes, salt, paprika, turmeric, ground black pepper, and dried rosemary. Put the avocado strips in the egg mixture. Then wrap the avocado in the sliced bacon. Preheat the air fryer to 360°F. Place the wrapped avocado sticks in the air fryer rack. Cook for 6 minutes on one side. Turn the avocado over. Cook for 5 minutes more and serve.

Chicken Broccoli Casserole

Preparation Time: 15 minutes | **Cooking Time:** 20 minutes | **Servings**: 6 | **Calories**: 213

Ingredients: 2 cups cooked chicken, shredded | 1 medium broccoli, cut into florets | 1/2 cup chicken stock | 6 oz cream cheese, softened | 1/2 cup cheddar cheese, shredded | salt and black pepper, to taste

Directions: At 390 degrees F, preheat the oven. Add cooked and shredded chicken to the casserole dish and spread it evenly. Pour ½ cup chicken stock to a saucepan and place it over medium heat. Stir in cream cheese and salt and black pepper, mixing well until smooth. Pour this sauce over the shredded chicken. Spread the broccoli florets on top and press them a little. Drizzle cheese on top and bake for 20 minutes in the preheated oven. Serve warm.

Spinach Balls with Chicken

Preparation Time: 15 minutes | **Cooking Time:** 11 minutes | **Servings**: 7 | **Calories**: 159

Ingredients: 4 large eggs | 1 cup spinach | 1 tablespoon minced garlic | 8 oz. ground chicken
2 tablespoons almond flour | 1 teaspoon olive oil | 1 teaspoon smoked paprika | 1 teaspoon coconut flour
½ teaspoon salt

Directions: Crack the eggs and transfer them to a blender. Add the spinach, salt, minced garlic, almond flour, smoked paprika, and coconut flour. Blend until well combined. Transfer the mixture into a bowl. Add the ground chicken and stir. Make your hands wet and make medium balls from the spinach mixture. Preheat the air fryer to 370°F. Grease the air fryer basket with olive oil. Put the spinach balls in the air fryer and cook for 11 minutes. Serve the snack immediately or keep it in a plastic container in the fridge.

Almond Coconut Egg Wraps

Preparation Time: 5 minutes | **Cooking Time:** 5 minutes | **Servings:** 4 | **Calories**: 111

Ingredients: 5 organic eggs | 1 tbsp coconut flour | 25 tsp sea salt | 2 tbsp almond meal

Directions: Combine the fixings in a blender and work them until creamy. Heat a skillet using the med-high temperature setting. Pour two tablespoons of batter into the skillet and cook – covered about three min. Turn it over to cook for another 3 minutes. Serve the wraps piping hot.

Herbed Crab Cakes

Preparation Time: 15 minutes | **Cooking Time:** 10 minutes | **Servings:** 6 | **Calories**: 107

Ingredients: 12 oz crabmeat | ¼ tcaspoon salt | 1 teaspoon chili powder | 1 tablespoon butter | 1egg
1 teaspoon ground white pepper | 1 tablespoon almond flour | 1 tablespoon chives

Directions: Chop the crabmeat into small pieces and place in a bowl. Sprinkle the crabmeat with salt, chili powder, ground white pepper, and chives. Stir the mixture gently with a spoon. Then crack the egg into the crabmeat. Add almond flour and stir carefully until you have a smooth texture. Preheat the air fryer to 400°F. Take 2 spoons and place a small amount of the crabmeat mixture in one of them. Cover it with the second spoon and make the crab cake. Toss the butter in the air fryer and melt it. Transfer the crab cakes to the air fryer and cook them for 10 minutes turning halfway through. Cool before serving.

Jalapeno Bacon Bites

Preparation Time: 15 minutes | **Cooking Time:** 11 minutes | **Servings:** 5 | **Calories**: 198

Ingredients: 6 oz. bacon, sliced | 1 cup jalapeno pepper | ½ teaspoon salt | ½ teaspoon paprika
1 teaspoon olive oil

Directions: Wash the jalapeno peppers carefully. Combine the salt, paprika, and olive oil together. Stir gently. Brush the jalapeno peppers with the olive oil mixture generously. Wrap each jalapeno pepper in the bacon slices. Secure the jalapeno bites with toothpicks. Preheat the air fryer to 360°F. Put the jalapeno bites in the air fryer rack. Cook for 11 minutes or until the bacon is crisp. Transfer the cooked jalapeno pepper bites to a plate and cover them with paper towels to remove excess grease before serving.

Buffalo Chicken Dip

Preparation Time: 10 minutes | **Cooking Time:** 20 minutes | **Servings:** 2 | **Calories**: 859

Ingredients: 1 large cooked boneless chicken breast, shredded | 8 oz cream cheese | butter or oil
½ cup shredded cheddar cheese | ½ cup chunky blue cheese dressing | ¼ cup buffalo wing sauce

Directions: Preheat the oven to 375°F. Grease a small baking pan. In a bowl, combine together the chicken, cream cheese, Cheddar cheese, blue cheese dressing, and wing sauce. Move the mixture into the prepared baking pan. Bake for 20 minutes. Pour into a dip dish and serve hot.

Chicken Nuggets

Preparation Time: 15 minutes | **Cooking Time:** 10 minutes | **Servings:** 7 | **Calories**: 212

Ingredients: 1 pound chicken fillet | ½ teaspoon salt | ½ teaspoon ground black pepper | 2 eggs
½ teaspoon chili pepper | ½ cup coconut flour

Directions: Cut the chicken fillet into nugget size pieces. Crack the eggs into a bowl and whisk them. Combine the coconut flour, chili pepper, salt, and ground black pepper in a large mixing bowl. Mix well to combine. Dip the nuggets in the whisked egg. Coat the chicken nuggets in the almond flour mixture. Preheat the air fryer to 360°F. Transfer the coated chicken nuggets to the air fryer rack and cook for 10 minutes. Serve hot.

Moroccan Lamb Balls

Preparation Time: 15 minutes | **Cooking Time:** 14 minutes | **Servings:** 6 | **Calories**: 137

Ingredients: 1 teaspoon cumin seeds | 1 teaspoon coriander seeds | 1 garlic clove, sliced | 1 egg
12 oz. ground lamb | 2 tablespoons fresh lemon juice | 1 teaspoon dried mint | 2 tablespoons heavy cream

Directions: Combine the ground lamb and sliced garlic in a bowl. Sprinkle the meat mixture with the coriander seeds and cumin seeds. Coat the ground lamb with the fresh lemon juice and dried mint. Stir the ground lamb mixture with a fork. Crack the egg into the mixture. Stir well. Preheat the air fryer 360° F. Make the meatballs from the lamb mixture and place them in the air fryer. Cook for 8 mins. Drizzle the lamb balls with the heavy cream and cook for 6 mins. Place a cocktail stick in every lamb ball and serve.

Ginger Chicken Wings

Preparation Time: 15 minutes | **Cooking Time:** 14 minutes | **Servings:** 4 | **Calories:** 234

Ingredients: 1 pound chicken wings | 1 teaspoon garlic powder | ¼ teaspoon ground black pepper
¼ teaspoon cayenne pepper | ½ teaspoon ground ginger | 1 tablespoon mustard | ½ teaspoon salt
1 tablespoon tomato puree

Directions: Place the chicken wings in a mixing bowl. Coat the wings with salt, garlic powder, ground black pepper, cayenne pepper, ground ginger, and mustard. Mix well. Add the tomato puree and mix into the chicken wings. Marinade for 10 minutes. Preheat the air fryer to 370°F. Place the chicken wings in the air fryer basket tray and cook for 14 minutes.

Pesto Cauliflower Steaks

Preparation Time: 15 minutes | **Cooking Time:** 20 minutes | **Servings:** 2 | **Calories**: 448

Ingredients: 2 tablespoons olive oil, plus more for brushing | ½ head cauliflower | ¼ cup almonds
freshly ground black pepper | 2 cups fresh basil leaves | ½ cup grated Parmesan cheese
½ cup shredded mozzarella cheese | pink Himalayan salt

Directions: Preheat the oven to 425°F. Brush a baking sheet with olive oil or line with a silicone baking mat. To prep the cauliflower steaks, remove and discard the leaves and cut the cauliflower into 1-inch-thick slices. You can roast the extra floret crumbles that fall off with the steaks. Place the cauliflower steaks on the prepared baking sheet, and brush them with the olive oil. You want the surface just lightly coated so it gets caramelized. Season with pink Himalayan salt and pepper. Roast the cauliflower steaks for 20 minutes. Meanwhile, put the basil, Parmesan cheese, almonds, and 2 tablespoons of olive oil in a food processor (or blender), and season with pink Himalayan salt and pepper. Mix until combined. Spread some pesto on top of each cauliflower steak, and top with the mozzarella cheese. Return to the oven and bake until the cheese melts, about 2 mins. Place the cauliflower steaks on two plates, serve hot.

Crunchy Pork Rind Zucchini Sticks

Preparation Time: 15 minutes | **Cooking Time:** 25 minutes | **Servings:** 2 | **Calories:** 238

Ingredients: 2 medium zucchinis, halved lengthwise and seeded | ¼ cup crushed pork rinds
¼ cup grated Parmesan cheese | 2 garlic cloves, minced | 2 tablespoons melted butter
pink Himalayan salt | freshly ground black pepper | olive oil, for drizzling

Directions: Preheat the oven to 400°F. Line a baking sheet with aluminum foil or a silicone baking mat. Place the zucchini halves cut-side up on the prepared baking sheet. In a medium bowl, combine the pork rinds, Parmesan cheese, garlic, and melted butter, and season with pink Himalayan salt and pepper. Mix until well combined. Spoon the pork-rind mixture onto each zucchini stick, and drizzle each with a little olive oil. Bake for about 20 minutes, or until the topping is golden brown. Turn on the broiler to finish browning the zucchini sticks, 3 to 5 minutes, and serve.

Lamb Chives Burgers

Preparation Time: 15 minutes | **Cooking Time:** 9 minutes | **Servings:** 6 | **Calories:** 178

Ingredients: 1 pound ground lamb | 3 oz. chive stems | 1 teaspoon minced garlic | 1 teaspoon salt ½ teaspoon chili pepper | 1 teaspoon ground black pepper | 1 large egg | 2 tablespoons coconut flour 1 teaspoon olive oil

Directions: Combine the ground lamb with the diced chives. Stir carefully and sprinkle the mixture with minced garlic and salt. Add chili pepper, ground black pepper, and coconut flour. Crack the egg into the mixture and mix with your hands. Place the mixture in the fridge for 10 minutes. Meanwhile, preheat the air fryer to 400°F. Make 6 large balls from the ground lamb mixture and flatten them to make the shape of a burger patty. Place the burgers in the air fryer rack and drizzle them with olive oil. Cook for 6 minutes. Turn them using a spatula. Cook the lamb burgers for 3 minutes. Serve hot.

Cheddar-stuffed Mushrooms

Preparation Time: 10 minutes | **Cooking Time:** 5 minutes | **Servings:** 7 | **Calories**: 121

Ingredients: 9 oz. mushroom tops | 6 oz. cheddar cheese, shredded | 1 teaspoon dried dill 1 teaspoon dried parsley | ½ teaspoon salt | 1 tablespoon butter

Directions: Remove the flesh from the mushroom tops and chop finely. Combine the ground mushroom flesh with the dried dill and dried parsley. Add salt and soft butter and mix. Combine the mixture with the shredded cheese. Stir. Fill the mushroom tops with the cheese mixture. Preheat the air fryer to 400°F. Put the mushrooms in the air fryer rack and cook them for 5 minutes. Transfer to a serving plate.

Parmesan Turnip Slices

Preparation Time: 12 minutes | **Cooking Time:** 10 minutes | **Servings:** 8 | **Calories**: 66

Ingredients: 1 teaspoon garlic powder | 1 pound turnip | 1 teaspoon salt | 3 oz. Parmesan, shredded 1 tablespoon olive oil

Directions: Peel the turnip and slice it. Sprinkle the sliced turnip with salt and garlic powder. Drizzle the turnip slices with olive oil. Preheat the air fryer to 360°F. Put the turnip slices in the air fryer basket and cook them for 10 minutes. Serve.

Salty Cucumber Chips

Preparation Time: 10 minutes | **Cooking Time:** 11 minutes | **Servings:** 12 | **Calories:** 8

Ingredients: 1 pound cucumber | 1 teaspoon salt | 1 tbsp smoked paprika | ½ tsp garlic powder

Directions: Wash the cucumbers carefully and slice them into chips. Sprinkle the chips with salt, smoked paprika, and garlic powder. Preheat the air fryer to 370°F. Place the cucumber slices in the air fryer rack. Cook the cucumber chips for 11 minutes. Transfer the cucumber chips to a paper towel and allow to cool. Serve the cucumber chips immediately or keep them in a paper bag.

Eggplant Chips

Preparation Time: 15 minutes | **Cooking Time:** 13 minutes | **Servings:** 10 | **Calories**: 46

Ingredients: 1 teaspoon onion powder | 1 teaspoon salt | 3 eggplants | 1 teaspoon paprika ½ teaspoon ground black pepper | 1 tablespoon olive oil

Directions: Wash the eggplants and slice them into chips. Sprinkle the eggplant slices with salt and let it absorb the eggplant juice and bitterness. Dry the eggplant slices and sprinkle them with onion powder, paprika, and ground black pepper. Stir the eggplant slices using your fingertips. Then preheat the air fryer to 400°F. Place the eggplant slices in the air fryer rack and cook them for 13 minutes. The temperature of cooking depends on the thickness of the eggplant slices.

Spicy Kale Chips

Preparation Time: 10 minutes | **Cooking Time:** 8 minutes | **Servings:** 14 | **Calories:** 22

Ingredients: 1 pound kale | 1 teaspoon salt | 1 teaspoon chili pepper | 2 teaspoon olive oil

Directions: Wash the kale and dry well. Tear the kale roughly. Preheat the air fryer to 370°F. Sprinkle the kale with salt, chili pepper, and olive oil. Mix well. Place the kale on the air fryer rack and cook for 5 minutes. Shake the kale and cook it for 3 minutes more. Chill the chips and keep them in a dry place.

Creamy Broccoli Crisps

Preparation Time: 15 minutes | **Cooking Time:** 13 minutes | **Servings:** 6 | **Calories**: 80

Ingredients: 3 tablespoons heavy cream | 1 tablespoon almond flour | ½ teaspoon salt
½ teaspoon turmeric | 1 teaspoon ground black pepper | 1 pound broccoli

Directions: Wash the broccoli and separate it into small florets. Then combine the almond flour, salt, turmeric, and ground black pepper in a shallow spice bowl. Shake to combine well. Sprinkle the florets with the spice mixture. Stir carefully. Drizzle the broccoli florets with the heavy cream and mix well. Sprinkle the broccoli florets with the remaining spices one more time. Preheat the air fryer to 360°F. Put the Prepared broccoli florets in the air fryer rack. Cook the broccoli florets for 10 minutes. Shake the broccoli carefully. Cook the broccoli crisps for 3 minutes more. Let the cooked broccoli crisps cool before serving.

Cheese Chips and Guacamole

Preparation Time: 10 minutes | **Cooking Time:** 20 minutes | **Servings:** 2 | **Calories:** 323

Ingredients: For the cheese chips: 1 cup shredded cheese | For the Guacamole: 1 avocado, mashed
juice of ½ lime | 1 teaspoon diced jalapeño | 2 tablespoons chopped fresh cilantro leaves
pink Himalayan salt

Directions: Preheat the oven to 350°F. Line a baking sheet with parchment paper or a silicone baking mat. Add ¼-cup mounds of shredded cheese to the pan, leaving plenty of space between them, and bake until the edges are brown and the middles have fully melted, about 7 minutes. Set the pan on a cooling rack, and let the cheese chips cool for 5 minutes. The chips will be floppy when they first come out of the oven but will crisp as they cool.

Tomato, Avocado, and Cucumber Salad

Preparation Time: 10 minutes | **Cooking Time:** 30 minutes | **Servings:** 2 | **Calories:** 248

Ingredients: ½ cup grape tomatoes, halved | ¼ cup crumbled feta cheese | 1 avocado, finely chopped
4 small Persian cucumbers or 1 English cucumber, peeled and finely chopped | pink Himalayan salt
freshly ground black pepper | 2 tablespoons vinaigrette salad dressing

Directions: In a large bowl, combine the tomatoes, cucumbers, avocado, and feta cheese. Add the vinaigrette, and season with pink Himalayan salt and pepper. Toss to thoroughly combine. Divide the salad between two plates and serve.

Roasted Almond Nuts

Preparation Time: 5 minutes | **Cooking Time:** 10 minutes | **Servings:** 6 | **Calories**: 285

Ingredients: 1 teaspoon of ground cumin | 1 teaspoon of salt | 1 cup of walnuts
1 teaspoon of paprika powder | 1 tablespoon of coconut oil

Directions: Put all the ingredients into a medium sized pan and cook on medium-high heat for 10 minutes, stirring all the while. Set aside to cool for a few minutes before serving as a snack. Note: You can store the nuts in an airtight container at room temperature.

Beef Slices

Preparation Time: 10 minutes | **Cooking Time:** 20 minutes | **Servings:** 6 | **Calories:** 176

Ingredients: 8 oz. ground pork | 7 oz. ground beef | 6 oz chive stems | 1 egg | 1 tablespoon almond flour
1 tablespoon chives | 1 teaspoon salt | 1 teaspoon cayenne pepper | 1 tablespoon dried oregano
1 teaspoon butter | 1 teaspoon olive oil

Directions: Crack the egg into a large bowl. Add the ground beef and ground pork. Add the almond flour, chives, salt, cayenne pepper, dried oregano, and butter. Dice the chives. Put the diced chives in the ground meat mixture. Use your hands to combine the mixture. Preheat the air fryer to 350°F. Make the meatloaf form from the ground meat mixture. Grease the air fryer basket with the olive oil and place the meatloaf inside. Cook the meatloaf for 20 mins. Allow the meatloaf to rest for a few mins. Slice and serve.

Salami, Pepperoncini, and Cream Cheese Pinwheels.

Preparation Time: 20 minutes | **Cooking Time:** 0 minutes | **Servings:** 2 | **Calories**: 448

Ingredients: 8 ounces cream cheese, at room temperature | ¼ pound salami, thinly sliced
2 tablespoons sliced pepperoncini

Directions: Lay out a sheet of plastic wrap on a large cutting board or counter. Place the cream cheese in the center of the plastic wrap, and then add another layer of plastic wrap on top. Using a rolling pin, roll the cream cheese until it is even and about ¼ inch thick. Try to make the shape somewhat resemble a rectangle. Pull off the top layer of plastic wrap. Place the salami slices so they overlap to completely cover the cream-cheese layer. Place a new piece of plastic wrap on top of the salami layer so that you can flip over your cream cheese–salami rectangle. Flip the layer so the cream cheese side is up. Remove the plastic wrap and add the sliced pepperoncini in a layer on top. Roll the layered ingredients into a tight log, pressing the meat and cream cheese together. (You want it as tight as possible.) Then wrap the roll with plastic wrap and refrigerate for at least 6 hours so it will set. Use a sharp knife to cut the log into slices and serve.

Almond Flour Crackers

Preparation Time: 10 minutes | **Cooking Time:** 20 minutes | **Servings:** 14 | **Calories:** 51

Ingredients: a quarter teaspoon of cumin | 3 tablespoons of water | 1 cup of almond flour
a pinch of chili powder | a quarter teaspoon of sea salt | a quarter teaspoon of paprika
1 tablespoon of flax flour | a quarter teaspoon of garlic powder | a quarter teaspoon of onion powder

Directions: Preheat your oven to 370°F. Throw all the ingredients into a large mixing bowl, in no particular order. Stir the ingredients until well combined. The dough will firm up as you stir so don't worry about it being a bit moist in the beginning. The dough should be firm enough after about a minute continuous stirring. Grease your palms before handling the dough so that it doesn't stick, then shape them into small balls and set them aside to rest for 10 minutes. Line a baking dish with parchment paper. Place the dough balls into the baking dish and shape them into rectangles. Cover the dough with another piece of parchment then press with the palm of your hand to flatten the dough so that it sticks to the parchment. Use a rolling pin to flatten the dough to your decide thickness further. Remove the top parchment and use a slightly wet knife to cut the dough into clean rectangles. If you shaped them perfectly before, you shouldn't have any cut out dough. Make sure you leave enough space between each of the crackers to make sure they all have crisp borders. Place into the oven and bake for 20 minutes, checking it at five minute intervals so that it doesn't burn. Remove from the oven and leave to cool in the baking dish for 5-10 minutes, then transfer to a cooling rack being careful not to break them. The longer they sit and cool, the harder they get. You can store yours in airtight containers or glass jars for up to 10 days.

Keto Mug Bread

Preparation Time: 2 minutes | **Cooking Time:** 2 minutes | **Servings:** 1 | **Calories:** 416

Ingredients: 1/3 cup almond flour | ½ tsp baking powder | ¼ tsp salt |1 whole egg
1 tbsp. melted butter

Directions: Mix all ingredients in a microwave-safe mug. Microwave for 90 sec. Cool for 2 minutes

Keto Pizza Crust

Preparation Time: 10 minutes | **Cooking Time:** 6 minutes | **Servings:** 8 | **Calories:** 165

Ingredients: 1 cup almond flour | 2 cups shredded mozzarella | 2 tbsp. cream cheese | pinch of salt

Directions: Combine both cheeses in a bowl and melt in the microwave. Stir then gradually knead in the salt and almond flour. Roll out to flatten in between sheets of parchment. Bake at 350°F for 6 minutes. Put choice of toppings on and bake for another 5-10 minutes.

Keto Blender Buns

Preparation Time: 5 minutes | **Cooking Time:** 25 minutes | **Servings:** 6 | **Calories:** 200

Ingredients: 4 whole eggs | ¼ cup melted butter | ½ tsp salt | ½ cup almond flour | 1 tsp Italian spices

Directions: Preheat oven to 425°F. Pulse all ingredients in a blender. Divide batter into a 6-hole muffin tin. Bake for 25 minutes.

Avocado Flatbread

Preparation Time: 25 minutes | **Cooking Time:** 5 minutes | **Servings:** 6 | **Calories**: 80

Ingredients: 130 grams mashed avocado | ¾ cup chickpea flour | 1 tsp cumin powder | ½ tsp salt

Directions: Combine all ingredients in a bowl. Stir until mixture comes together into a dough. Knead the dough briefly on a lightly floured surface. Leave the dough to rest for 15 minutes. Divide the dough into four portions. Take each portion of dough and flatten with a rolling pin. Toast flatbread in a lightly oiled skillet for about 2 minutes per side.

Keto Cheese Bread

Preparation Time: 9 minutes | **Cooking Time:** 25 minutes | **Servings:** 6 | **Calories**: 203

Ingredients: 1 teaspoon baking powder | ¼ teaspoon salt | 1/3 cup milk | 1 cup almond flour
2 large whole eggs | ½ cup grated parmesan | 1/3 cup cream cheese, softened

Directions: Preheat oven to 350°F. Whisk together almond flour, baking powder, and salt in a bowl. In a separate, bowl beat eggs and add cream cheese. Gradually stir in the milk. Stir the wet mixture into the dry ingredients. Fold in the grated Parmesan. Coat a 6-hole muffin tin with non-stick spray. Divide the batter into the pan and bake for 25 minutes.

Curry-Spiked Vegetable Latkes

Preparation Time: 15 minutes | **Cooking Time:** 6 minutes | **Servings:** 6 | **Calories**: 123

Ingredients: 100 grams carrots, spiralized | 100 grams zucchini, spiralized | 100 grams cauliflower, minced | 50 grams white onion, minced | 5 grams parsley, chopped | ¼ cup almond flour | 1 tbsp. flax seeds, soaked in 2 tbsp. water | 2 tsp curry powder | ½ tsp salt | 2 tbsp. olive oil plus more for frying

Directions: Mix shredded vegetables, onions, parsley, almond flour, egg, salt, and curry powder in a bowl. Heat olive oil in a non-stick skillet. Spoon the vegetable mixture into the hot oil, shaping each latke with an egg ring. Fry the latkes for 3 minutes per side over medium heat. Drain on paper towels.

Bulgogi-Spiced Tofu Wraps

Preparation Time: 2 hours | **Cooking Time:** 5 minutes | **Servings:** 6 | **Calories:** 198

Ingredients: 400 g firm tofu | 200 grams iceberg lettuce for wrapping
For the Marinade: 50 g chopped leeks | 2 tbsp. soy sauce | 1 tsp erythritol | 2 tbsp. sesame oil
For the Slaw: 50 g white radish, julienne | 50 g cucumber, julienne | 50 g carrots, julienne
20 g scallions, julienne | For the Dip:1 tbsp. ml light soy sauce | 2 tbsp. ml sesame oil | 1 tsp erythritol
1 tbsp. gochujang

Directions: Combine all ingredients for the tofu marinade in a bowl. Whisk until fully combined. Cut tofu into 1-inch thick slices and allow to marinate for not less than 2 hours. While marinating prepare the slaw. Whisk all ingredients for the dressing. Toss in all chopped vegetables. Cover and refrigerate. Grill the tofu and cut into approximately 1"x3" strips. Toss chopped tofu with the prepared slaw. Serve with lettuce leaves for wrapping. Allow to cool before slicing.

Avocado Stuffed with Tomato and Mushrooms

Preparation Time: 10 minutes | **Cooking Time:** 10 minutes | **Servings:** 4 | **Calories**: 245

Ingredients: 4 avocados, pitted and halved | 2 tablespoons olive oil | 1 onion, chopped
2 cups button mushrooms, chopped | 1 teaspoon garlic, crushed | salt and black pepper, to taste
1 teaspoon deli mustard | 1 tomato, chopped

Directions: Scoop out about 2 teaspoons of avocado flesh from each half; reserve the scooped avocado flash. Heat the oil in a sauté pan that is preheated over a moderately high flame. Now, cook the mushrooms, onion, and garlic until the mushrooms are tender and the onion is translucent. Add the reserved avocado flash to the mushroom mixture and mix to combine. Now, add the salt, black pepper, mustard, and tomato. Divide the mushroom mixture among the avocado halves and serve immediately.

Tofu-Kale Dip with Crudités

Preparation Time: 15 minutes | **Cooking Time:** 25 minutes | **Servings:** 2 | **Calories**: 75

Ingredients: 2 cups kale | 1 cup tofu, pressed, drained and crumbled | 2 teaspoons nutritional yeast
2 garlic cloves, minced | 2 teaspoons olive oil | 1 teaspoon sea salt | | 1/2 cup soy milk | 1 tsp. dried basil
1/4 teaspoon ground black pepper | 1/2 teaspoon paprika | 1/2 teaspoon dried dill weed

Directions: Start by preheating your oven to 400 degrees F. Lightly oil a casserole dish with a nonstick cooking spray. Now, parboil the kale leaves until it is just wilted. Puree the remaining ingredients in your food processor or blender. Stir in the kale; stir until the mixture is homogeneous. Bake approximately 13 minutes. Now, serve with a crudités platter. Bon appétit!

Never Fear Thin Bagels Pieces

Preparation Time: 10 minutes | **Cooking Time:** 40 minutes | **Servings:** 8 | **Calories**: 129

Ingredients: 3 tablespoon of ground flaxseed | ½ a cup of tahini | ½ a cup of psyllium husk powder | 1 cup of water | 1 teaspoon of baking powder | just a pinch of salt | sesame seeds for garnish

Directions: Preheat your oven to 375 degrees Fahrenheit. Take a mixing bowl and add Psyllium Husk, baking powder, ground flax seeds, salt and keep whisking until combined. Add water to the dry mix and keep mixing until the water has been absorbed fully. Add tahini and keep mixing until the dough forms. Knead well. Form patties from the dough that have a diameter of 4 inches and a thickness of ¼ inch. Lay them carefully on your baking tray. Cut up a small hole in the middle. Add sesame seeds on top. Bake for 40 minutes until a golden brown texture is seen. Cut them in half and toast if you like. Top them up with your favorite Keto-Vegan compliant spread. Enjoy!

Keto Vegan Bagels

Preparation Time: 20 minutes | **Cooking Time:** 40 minutes | **Servings:** 6 | **Calories:** 308

Ingredients: a pinch salt | half a cup of ground golden flaxseed | 2 tablespoons of coconut oil (melted) 1 teaspoon of baking powder | a quarter cup of psyllium husk powder | half a cup of almond butter (unsweetened and unsalted)

Toppings: 1/4 teaspoon of salt | 1 teaspoon of sesame seeds | 1 teaspoon of dried onion flakes 6 tablespoons of vegan cream cheese | 1 teaspoon of dried garlic flakes | 1 teaspoon of poppy seeds

Directions: For the bagels: Preheat your oven to 375°F. Use a tablespoon of coconut oil to grease the sections of a doughnut pan. Put the baking powder, psyllium husk powder, salt and ground flax seed into a bowl, stir until well combined. Put the almond butter into a large bowl, add a cup of warm water and whisk until smooth. Add dry ingredients and stir until well combined until a moldable dough is formed. Cut the dough into six portions and set aside. For the toppings: put the sesame seeds, poppy seeds, sea salt, onion flakes and garlic flakes into a small bowl and stir to combine then set aside. To bake: roll the dough into long logs by just rolling them back and forth, then press them into the greased molds. Coat the top of bagels with the rest of the coconut oil using a marinating brush. Sprinkle an even amount of the toppings over the bagels. Bake for 40 minutes or until the bagels are a dark golden color. Leave in the mold to cool in the tray before moving to a wire rack to cool completely. Serve with some vegan cream cheese and enjoy.

Note: If the bagels do not cool well enough before being removed from the mold, they'll break, so let it cool in the mold for 10 minutes at least.

Keto Vegan Protein Bites

Preparation Time: 10 minutes | **Cooking Time:** 10 minutes | **Servings:** 16 | **Calories:** 249

Ingredients : For cookie dough base : two tablespoons of coconut oil | a quarter cup of almond flour a quarter cup of dairy free chocolate chips | half a cup of softened coconut butter or any nut seed butter two tablespoons of shredded coconut (unsweetened) | half a teaspoon of sea salt | one tsp cinnamon 1 teaspoon of vanilla extract or 2 teaspoons of vanilla bean powder | 4 tbsp of raw honey or maple syrup a quarter cup of vegan protein powder

For pumpkin spice flavor: cookie dough base | one teaspoon of maple syrup | a pinch of ground mace four tablespoons of plain pumpkin puree (unsweetened) | a quarter teaspoon of ground ginger half a teaspoon of ground cinnamon | one tablespoon of almond flour | three drops of liquid stevia two tablespoons of shredded coconut (unsweetened) | a quarter teaspoon of ground cloves chocolate mint flavor | a quarter cup of shredded coconut (unsweetened) | chocolate cherry flavor one teaspoon of peppermint extract | two tablespoons of coconut oil | three tablespoons of cocoa powder one tablespoon of cocoa powder | one teaspoon of chopped pepper mint leaves one teaspoon of maple syrup | two tablespoons of coconut oil | two tablespoons unsulfured dried cherries

Directions: In a medium bowl, add but butter or coconut, honey or maple syrup, vanilla and coconut oil. Stir until fully combined. Put in the dry ingredients and stir until well combined using the back of a spoon as the dough is very sticky. Put in the chocolate chips or any other flavoring. Cut the dough into bite sized balls and role between the flat of your palms. Line a baking dish or tray with pieces of parchment paper. Transfer the rolled dough balls into a pre-lined baking sheet. Refrigerate for an hour to get a firm chewy consistency. Serve and enjoy. Note: The bites can last for as long as a week if kept in an airtight container and refrigerated in a fixed temperature.

Vegan Baked Jelly Doughnuts

Preparation Time: 1.5 hours | **Cooking Time:** 10 minutes | **Servings:** 12 | **Calories:** 251

Ingredients: 1 tbsp. yeast | 2 tbsp. warm water | 180 ml soymilk | 1 tbsp. erythritol maple syrup
1 gram baking soda | ¼ tsp salt | 1 tbsp. flaxseed meal | 3 tbsp. water | 2 tbsp. olive oil
500 grams almond flour | 150 grams desiccated coconut | sugar-free fruit jelly (for filling)

Directions: Sprinkle yeast over warm water and allow to bloom for about five minutes. Stir flaxseed meal in water and bloom for 5 minutes. In a large bowl, mix together yeast mixture, flaxseed mixture, soymilk, erythritol, and olive oil. Whisk almond flour and baking soda in a separate bowl. Gradually beat flour into the wet ingredients. Knead the resulting dough for about 5 minutes or until smooth and elastic. Place the dough in a lightly oiled bowl and cover. Leave to rise for about an hour in a warm place. Turn the dough onto a floured surface. Roll out into ½" thickness and cut into circles. Transfer to a sheet pan, cover, and leave again to rise for another hour. Bake for 8-10 minutes at 420°F. Place on a rack to cool. Fill each doughnut with your choice of jelly using a pastry injector. Coat with desiccated coconut.

Keto Hummus Quesadillas

Preparation Time: 20 minutes | **Cooking Time:** 20 minutes | **Servings:** 6 | **Calories:** 158

Ingredients: For the Hummus: 200 grams cauliflower | ¼ cup olive oil | 1 tbsp. lemon juice
1 tbsp. curry powder | 1 clove garlic, minced | ½ tsp salt | ¼ tsp chili powder
For the Flatbread: ½ cup almond flour | 2 tbsp. psyllium husk | ¼ tsp baking soda | pinch of salt
1 tbsp. olive oil | 1 cup lukewarm water

Directions: Prepare the Flatbread: whisk together the almond flour, psyllium husk, baking soda, and salt in a bowl. Add in the water and olive oil. Knead until everything comes together into a smooth dough. Leave to rest for about 15 minutes. Divide the dough into 6 equal-sized portions. Roll each portion into a ball, then flatten with a rolling pin in between sheets of parchment paper. Refrigerate until ready to use. To cook, heat in a non-stick pan for 2-3 minutes per side. Prepare the hummus: Boil cauliflower for 5 minutes, or until tender. Drain. Put cauliflower in a food processor together with the rest of the ingredients for the hummus in a food processor. Blend until smooth. Assemble the tortillas: Take a piece of flatbread. Spread a generous amount of prepared hummus to one side. Fold the tortilla in half. Toast the filled tortillas for 1-2 minutes each side in a non-stick skillet. Slice up and serve.

Keto Hamburger Buns

Preparation Time: 5 minutes | **Cooking Time:** 15 minutes | **Servings:** 5 | **Calories:** 294

Ingredients: 1-1/4 cups almond flour | 1-1/2 cups mozzarella cheese, part skim grated | 1 large egg
2 oz. cream cheese | 2 tablespoons oat fiber | 500 protein powder | 1 tablespoon baking powder
1 metal plate or a pan which you care less about

Directions: Using a microwave safe bowl, put the cream cheese and mozzarella cheese. Microwave the cheese for I minutes. Remove the bowl, stir and microwave again for 40 seconds to another minute. Scrape out the cheese and place it together with the egg into a food processor. Stop when it's smooth. Add your dry ingredients, processing it till dough is formed. (It is normally very sticky) Let the dough cool. Preheat your oven to 400°F, placing the rack in the middle. Line your baking sheet with parchment paper and place the cheap metal plate or pan at the bottom of the oven. Once the oven is ready, separate the dough into 5 equal portions. Apply oil on your hands (not too much) and roll the portions into balls. Place them on the parchment paper, flattening them a bit while creating a domed shape. Put 5 or 6 ice cubes on the metal pan and place the buns inside the oven. The steam from the cubes will make the buns rise. Bake them for about fifteen minutes. They should be done once they brown on the outside. If not, give them more minutes in the oven.

Low-Carb Coconut Hamburger Buns

Preparation Time: 10 minutes | **Cooking Time:** 20 minutes | **Servings:** 4 | **Calories**: 218

Ingredients: 1/2 cup coconut flour | 1-1/2 cups mozzarella cheese, shredded | 2 large eggs
2 tablespoons cream cheese, softened | 2 tablespoons flax meal | 1 tablespoon baking powder
1 tablespoon sesame seeds | 1/2 teaspoon salt

Directions: Preheat your oven to 380°F. Using a mixing bowl, whisk your flax meal, coconut flour, salt and baking soda. In another bowl, put your cream cheese and mozzarella cheese. Microwave your cheese for 45 seconds to a minute. Stir it and microwave once more until it becomes melted. Beat your eggs, adding into the first bowl which has the dry ingredients. Add the cheese too to the bowl. You can use your hand mixer to make the dough. Separate the dough into four equal portions. Use these portions to make the buns and sprinkle sesame seeds. Press the seeds to prevent them from falling out. Line the baking sheet with parchment paper and place your buns. Bake for 20 minutes or until they brown on the outside. Leave them to cool.

Paleo Keto Buns

Preparation Time: 10 minutes | **Cooking Time:** 45 minutes | **Servings:** 10 | **Calories**: 208

Ingredients: 1-1/2 cup almond meal | 1/2 cup coconut flour | 1/2 cup flax meal | 480 ml boiling water
2/3 cup psyllium husks | 6 egg whites, large | 2 eggs, large | 5 tablespoons sesame seeds
2 teaspoons garlic powder | 2 teaspoons cream of tarta | apple cider vinegar | 2 teaspoon onion powder |
1 teaspoon baking soda | 1 teaspoon sea salt/ pink Himalayan | 2 tablespoons erythritol

Directions: Preheat your oven to 350°F. Mix all your dry ingredients in a mixing bowl. Add your egg whites and eggs. Use a hand mixer to process it till your dough becomes thick. Add the boiling water and process until it combines. Line your baking sheet with parchment paper. Use a spoon to make the buns and create a dome shape. Sprinkle the sesame seeds on the buns. Press the seeds into the buns to prevent them from falling out. Bake for 45 minutes.

Seeded Buns

Preparation Time: 10 minutes | **Cooking Time:** 35 minutes | **Servings:** 6 | **Calories**: 73

Ingredients: 1 cup almond flour | 2 tsp. baking powder | 3 egg whites | 1.25 cup hot water
2 tbsp. sesame seeds | 5 tbsp. psyllium husk powder | 1 tsp. salt | 2 tsp. apple cider vinegar
medium saucepan | standard sized flat sheet

Directions: Warm the water in a saucepan until it starts to bubble. Transfer to a glass dish. In the meantime, prepare a flat sheet with a layer of baking lining and set to the side. Blend the water with the almond flour, baking powder, psyllium husk, salt, and apple cider vinegar until it becomes a thick consistency. Section into 6 equal portions and form mounds. Apply pressure to flatten the mounds to approximately 1 inch thick. Arrange on the prepped flat sheet and glaze with the melted butter. Dust with the sesame seeds and heat for approximately 35 minutes. Serve immediately and enjoy!

Sweet Potato Toast

Preparation Time: 3 minutes | **Cooking Time:** 20 minutes | **Servings:** 4 | **Calories**: 132

Ingredients: 1 ripe avocado | 1 large sweet potato | pepper and salt | ½ cup roughly-chopped pistachios
3 tbsp. olive oil | crushed red pepper flakes

Directions: Warm up the oven to 400°F. Prepare a baking sheet with aluminum foil. Slice the potato into 1/4-inch rounds. Arrange on the baking sheet and toss it with the oil, salt, and pepper. Bake for 20 minutes and garnish with the avocado and pistachios. Add a few pepper flakes.

Keto Burger Buns

Preparation Time: 10 minutes | **Cooking Time:** 12 minutes | **Servings:** 6 | **Calories**: 216

Ingredients: 1 cup almond flour | ¼ cup psyllium husk powder | 1 tsp baking powder
1 cup mozzarella cheese | ¼ cup cream cheese | 1 egg | tbsp. sesame seeds

Directions: Preheat oven to 400°F. Melt the two cheeses together in the microwave. Blend the melted cheese together then stir in the egg. Whisk together the almond flour, psyllium husk, and baking powder in a separate bowl. Mix the dry ingredients into the cheese mixture until a dough is formed. Divide the dough into 6 and roll each portion into a ball. Top each ball with sesame seeds. Arrange on a baking sheet lined with parchment and bake for 12 minutes. Leave to cool for 10-15 minutes before slicing into halves.

Coco-Cilantro Flatbread

Preparation Time: 10 minutes | **Cooking Time:** 15 minutes | **Servings:** 6 | **Calories**: 46

Ingredients: ½ cup coconut flour | 2 tablespoons flax meal | ¼ teaspoon baking soda
1 tablespoon coconut oil | 2 tablespoons chopped cilantro | ¼ teaspoon salt | 1 cup lukewarm water

Directions: In a medium bowl, whisk together the coconut flour, flax, baking soda, and salt. Add in the water, coconut oil, and chopped cilantro. Knead until everything comes together into a smooth dough. Leave to rest for about 15 minutes. Divide the dough into 6 equal-sized portions. Roll each portion into a ball, then flatten with a rolling pin in between sheets of parchment paper. Refrigerate until ready to use. To cook, heat in a non-stick pan for 2-3 minutes per side.

Low-Carb Dinner Rolls

Preparation Time: 10 minutes | **Cooking Time:** 10 minutes | **Servings:** 6 | **Calories**: 219

Ingredients: 1 cup almond flour | 1/4 cup flaxseed, ground | 1 cup mozzarella, shredded | 1 egg
1 oz. cream cheese | 1/2 teaspoon baking soda

Directions: Preheat your oven to 400°F. Using a microwave-safe mixing bowl, microwave cream cheese and the mozzarella for a minute. Stir them till they become smooth. Add eggs in the bowl while stirring to mix well. In another clean bowl, put your almond flour, baking soda and flaxseed and mix the dry ingredients. Pour your egg and cheese mix into the bowl with dry ingredients. Use your hand mixer or hands to make dough by kneading. Slightly wet your hands with coconut oil or olive oil and roll your dough to six balls. Top them with sesame seeds and place them on the parchment paper. Bake them for 10 minutes. A golden brown look will indicate that they are done. Leave them to cool.

Low-Carb Clover Rolls

Preparation Time: 10 minutes | **Cooking Time:** 20 minutes | **Servings:** 8 | **Calories**: 283

Ingredients: 1/3 cup coconut flour | 1-1/2 cups mozzarella cheese, shredded | 2 large eggs
1-1/2 teaspoons baking powder | 1/4 cup Parmesan cheese, grated | 2 ounces cream cheese

Directions: Preheat your oven to 350°F. Put your almond flour and baking powder in a clean bowl and mix. Using another bowl, put your Mozzarella and cream cheese and microwave for a minute. Stir it well after it melts. Add eggs to the cheese and stir. Add the egg-cheese mix to the bowl with dry ingredients and mix thoroughly. Wet your hands and knead dough into a sticky ball. Put the dough ball on the parchment paper and slice into fourths. Slice each fourth or quarter into 6 smaller portions. Roll each small portion into balls. Roll the balls into the parmesan cheese light for them to coat it. Grease your muffin pan and place 3 dough balls in each cup of the pan. Bake it for 20 minutes at 350°F.

Keto Bread Rolls

Preparation Time: 10 minutes | **Cooking Time:** 20 minutes | **Servings:** 8 | **Calories:** 216

Ingredients: 1-1/3 cups almond flour | 1-1/2 cups shredded mozzarella cheese, part skim | 3 eggs
2 oz. cream cheese, full fat | 1-1/2 tablesp. baking powder, aluminum free | 2 tablespoons coconut flour

Directions: Preheat your oven to 350°F. In a clean bowl, put almond flour, coconut flour and baking powder. Mix well and set it aside. Using a microwave-safe bowl, put the cream cheese and mozzarella in it and microwave for 30 seconds. Remove the bowl, stir and microwave again for 30 seconds. This should go on until the cheese has entirely melted. Using a food processor add the cheese, the eggs and flour mix. Process at high speed for uniformity of the dough. (It is normally sticky.) Knead the dough into a dough ball and separate it into 8 equal pieces. Slightly wet your hands with oil for this step. Roll each piece with your palms to form a ball and place each ball on the baking sheet. (should be 2 inches apart) In a bowl, add the remaining egg and whisk. Brush the egg wash on the rolls. Bake for 20 minutes or until they are golden brown.

Moutabelle with Keto Flatbread

Preparation Time: 20 minutes | **Cooking Time:** 20 minutes | **Servings:** 6 | **Calories:** 171

Ingredients: For the Moutabelle : 500 grams eggplant | 75 grams white onion | 10 grams flat parsley
2 tbsp. tahini paste | 2 tbsp. lemon juice | ¼ cup olive oil | salt and pepper, to taste
For the Flatbread: ½ cup almond flour | 2 tbsp. psyllium husk | ¼ tsp baking soda | pinch of salt
1 tbsp. olive oil | 1 cup lukewarm water

Directions: Prepare the Flatbread: Whisk together the almond flour, psyllium husk, baking soda, and salt in a bowl. Add in the water and olive oil. Knead until everything comes together into a smooth dough. Leave to rest for about 15 minutes. Divide the dough into 6 equal-sized portions. Roll each portion into a ball, then flatten with a rolling pin in between sheets of parchment paper. Refrigerate until ready to use. To cook, heat in a non-stick pan for 2-3 minutes per side. Prepare the Moutabelle: split each eggplant in half lengthwise. Brush with olive oil and season with salt. Grill over high heat until fully cooked. Set aside until cool enough to handle. Peel the grilled eggplants, and transfer the flesh to a blender or food processor. Add in remaining ingredients and process until smooth. You may add a little warm water if it is too thick to process.

Avocado Taco Boats

Preparation Time: 5 minutes | **Cooking Time:** 20 minutes | **Servings:** 4 | **Calories:** 430

Ingredients: 4 grape tomatoes | 2 large avocados | 1 lbs. ground beef | 4 tablespoons taco seasoning
3/4 cup shredded sharp cheddar cheese | 4 slices pickled jalapeño | 1/4 cup salsa | 2/3 cup water
3 shredded romaine leaves | 1/4 cup sour cream

Directions: Take a skillet of large size, grease it with oil and heat it over medium high heat. Cook the ground beef in it for 10-15 minutes or until it gives brownish look. Once the beef gets brown, drain the grease from the skillet and add the water and the taco seasoning. Reduce the heat once the taco seasoning gets mixed well and simmer for 8-10 minutes. Take both avocados and prepare their halves using a sharp knife. Take each avocado shell and fill it with ¼ of the shredded romaine leaves. Fill each shell with ¼ of the cooked ground beef. Do the topping with sour cream, cheese, jalapeno, salsa and tomato before you serve the delicious avocado taco boats.

Brussels Sprouts with Bacon

Preparation Time: 15 minutes | **Cooking Time:** 40 minutes | **Servings:** 6 | **Calories**: 113

Ingredients: bacon (16 oz.) | Brussels sprouts (16 oz.) | black pepper

Directions: Warm the oven to reach 400° Fahrenheit. Slice the bacon into small lengthwise pieces. Put the sprouts and bacon with pepper. Bake within 35 to 40 minutes. Serve.

Veggie Wraps with Glorious Tahini Sauce

Preparation Time: 10 minutes | **Cooking Time:** 0 minutes | **Servings:** 8 | Calories: 120

Ingredients: ¼ cup of sliced carrots | 2 tablespoon of sauerkraut | 2 tablespoon of tahini sauce

Directions: De-vein your leaves and wash them well. Add carrots, sauerkraut and wrap them up well. Pour the sauce directly/use as a dip. Enjoy!

Vegan Cheese Fondue

Preparation Time: 5 minutes | **Cooking Time:** 20 minutes | **Servings:** 4 | **Calories:** 126

Ingredients: 70 grams raw cashews | 1 tbsp. nutritional yeast | 1 tsp garlic powder | 2 tsp cider vinegar
2 tbsp. gelatin | 1 tbsp. turmeric powder | 1 tsp salt | 2 cups water | 200 grams zucchini, cut into sticks

Directions: Boil cashews over high heat in a saucepan for 14 minutes. Blend garlic powder, cashews, gelatin, vinegar, turmeric powder, water, yeast, and salt until smooth. Add the puree to a saucepot and boil for about 4-5 minutes, while constantly stirring. Stir until the mixture is smooth. Put it to a fondue pot and enjoy alongside zucchini sticks.

Avocado Kale Keto Bowl

Preparation Time: 10 minutes | **Cooking Time:** 0 minutes | **Servings:** 2 | **Calories:** 230

Ingredients: ½ avocado, sliced | 1 cup kale leaves | 1 banana, sliced | ½ cup raspberries
1 cup almond milk | 1 kiwi, sliced | 2 drops stevia | ½ cup ice | 1 tsp chia seeds

Directions: Place avocado, kale, stevia, banana, almond milk, and ice in a blender. Process until smooth and cream. Transfer to a bowl. Serve and decorate the bowl by placing chia seeds, kiwi, and raspberries.

Baked Zucchini Chips

Preparation Time: 20 minutes | **Cooking Time:** 2 hours 45 minutes | **Servings:** 10 | **Calories:** 23.5

Ingredients: 2 medium zucchinis, sliced with a mandolin | 1 tbsp. olive oil | 1/2 tsp salt

Directions: Preheat your oven to 200 degrees F. Prepare your baking sheets by lining with parchment paper. Add all ingredients to a large mixing bowl and toss to coat the zucchini with oil and salt thoroughly. Arrange the zucchini slices in a single layer on the baking sheet. They can touch but they should not overlap. Bake for 2 and a half hours or until the zucchini chips are golden and crispy. Turn off the oven and allow them to cool with the oven door cropped slightly open. This will allow the zucchini chips to crisp up even more as they cool.

Vegetable Latkes Spiked with Curry

Preparation Time: 15 minutes | **Cooking Time:** 6 minutes | **Servings:** 6 | **Calories:** 123

Ingredients: 100 grams carrots, spiralized | 100 grams zucchini, spiralized | ¼ cup almond flour
100 grams cauliflower, minced | 50 grams minced white onion | 5 grams parsley, chopped
1 tbsp. flax seeds, soaked in 2 tbsp. water | 2 tsp curry powder | ½ tsp salt | 2 tbsp. olive oil for frying

Directions: In a bowl, mix almond flour, egg, parsley, onions, curry powder, and salt. In a non-stick skillet over medium heat, heat olive oil. Using a spoon, add vegetable mixture to the hot oil, while you shape every latke like an egg ring. Over medium heat, fry each side for about 3 minutes. Use paper towels to drain

Pepperoni Pizza Cups

Preparation Time: 10 minutes | **Cooking Time:** 8 minutes | **Servings:** 24 | **Calories**: 70

Ingredients: 24 mini mozzarella balls | 24 small basil leaves | 24 pepperoni slices in sandwich style
1 small jar pizza sauce | sliced black olives, optional

Directions: Preheat oven to 400°F, in the meantime take each pepperonis slice and make half inch cuts at the edges, giving it a shape of circular cross. Make sure that the center remains uncut. Take the muffin pan, grease it with oil and adjust all the prepared pepperonis into it. Place in the preheated oven and bake for 5 minutes or until the edges get crispy and the color is still red. Remove from the oven and set aside to cool for 5 minutes, then transfer to the paper towel, so that the excess oil gets absorbed. Clean the pan with a paper towel and place the cups again into the pan. Put basil leaf in the center of each pepperoni, then add ½ tsp pizza sauce, mozzarella ball and olive slice in the end. Bake in the oven for another 3 minutes or until the time when cheese starts melting. Remove from the oven and set aside to cool for 5 minutes before transferring to the serving plate.

Fathead Sausage Rolls

Preparation Time: 15 minutes | **Cooking Time:** 30 minutes | **Servings:** 6 | **Calories:** 470

Ingredients: 1 egg | pre-shredded grated mozzarella cheese (170 g) | 6 sausages | almond flour (85 g) |
2 tablespoons cream cheese full fat | 1 teaspoon onion flakes | pinch salt, to taste | onion flakes, to garnish

Directions: Preheat oven to 350°F and in the meantime remove the casing of all sausages and discard them. Transfer the sausages to the lined baking pan. Place in the preheated oven and bake for around 10 minutes. Take a medium size bowl, add almond flour and cheese to it. Mix them together completely. Add the cream cheese to the mixture, whisk until fully blended. Microwave the mixture for 60 seconds and remove, then stir a bit and microwave again for 30 seconds, remove and stir. Crack the egg into the mixture, add the onion flakes and salt. Keep mixing and pressing with a spoon to prepare a soft dough. Spread the dough over a parchment paper, place another parchment paper at the top, press with your hands and give it a shape of rectangle using a roller. Make sure that you roll evenly on all sides to prepare a good fat head pastry. Cut a piece of the prepared fat head pastry and wrap it around a sausage. Repeat it with all the remaining sausages. Cut the wrapped sausage rolls in your desired sizes, transfer them to the baking sheet and sprinkle the sesame seeds over the top if you prefer. Heat the oven to 425°F, and bake for 15 minutes or until you get a golden brown look. Remove from the oven once baked, and serve with your favorite keto sauce.

Mozzarella Sticks

Preparation Time: 8 minutes | **Cooking Time:** 2 minutes | **Servings:** 2 | **Calories**: 430

Ingredients: 1 large whole egg | 3 sticks mozzarella cheese in half (overnight frozen) | 1/2 teaspoon salt
2 tablespoons grated Parmesan cheese | 1/2 cup almond flour | 1/4 cup coconut oil
2-1/2 teaspoons Italian seasoning blend | 1 tablespoon chopped parsley

Directions: Heat the coconut oil in a cast iron skillet of medium size over low medium heat. Crack the egg in a small bowl in the meantime and beat it well. Take another bowl of medium size and add parmesan cheese, almond flour and seasonings to it. Whisk together the ingredients until a smooth mixture is prepared. Take the overnight frozen mozzarella stick and dip in the beaten egg, then coat it well with the dry mixture. Do the same with all the remaining cheese sticks. Place all the coated sticks in the preheated skillet and cook them for 2 minutes or until they start giving a golden-brown look from all sides. Remove from the skillet once cooked properly and place over paper towel so that any extra oil gets absorbed. Sprinkle parsley over the sticks if you desire and serve with keto marinara sauce.

Stuffed Portobello Mushrooms

Preparation Time: 10 minutes | **Cooking Time:** 10 minutes | **Servings:** 4 | **Calories:** 135.2

Ingredients: 2 Portobello mushrooms | 1 cup spinach, chopped, steamed | 1 tablespoon coconut cream
2 oz artichoke hearts, drained, chopped | 1 tablespoon cream cheese | 1 teaspoon minced garlic
1 tablespoon fresh cilantro, chopped | 3 oz cheddar cheese, grated | ½ teaspoon ground black pepper
2 tablespoons olive oil | ½ teaspoon salt

Directions: Sprinkle mushrooms with olive oil and place in the tray. Transfer the tray in the preheated to 360F oven and broil them for 5 minutes. Meanwhile, blend artichoke hearts, coconut cream, cream cheese, minced garlic, and chopped cilantro. Add grated cheese in the mixture and sprinkle with ground black pepper and salt. Fill the broiled mushrooms with the cheese mixture and cook them for 5 minutes more. Serve the mushrooms only hot.

Spiced Tofu and Broccoli Scramble

Preparation Time: 5 minutes | **Cooking Time:** 3 minutes | **Servings:** 3 | **Calories:** 231

Ingredients: 400 grams firm tofu, drained and pressed | 1 tbsp. tamari | 1 tbsp. garlic powder
2 tsp paprika powder | 2 tsp turmeric powder | 150 grams broccoli, rough-chopped | 2 tbsp. olive oil

Directions: Crumble the tofu in a bowl with the garlic powder, paprika, turmeric, and nutritional yeast. Heat olive oil in a pan. Sautee broccoli for a minute. Stir in spiced tofu. Cook for 1-2 minutes. Season with tamari. Serve hot.

LUNCH AND DINNER

Low Carb Broccoli Leek Soup

Preparation Time: 15 minutes | **Cooking Time:** 15 minutes | **Servings:** 2 | **Calories:** 231

Ingredients: ½ leek | 100 g cream cheese | 150 g broccoli | ½ cup heavy cream | 1 cup of water
¼ tablespoon black pepper | ½ vegetable bouillon cube | ¼ cup basil | 1 teaspoon garlic | salt

Directions: Put water into a pan and put broccoli chopped, leek chopped, and salt. Boil on high. Simmer on low. Put the remaining items, simmer for 1 minute. Remove. Blend the soup mixture into a blender. Serve.

Lucky Mediterranean Style Pasta

Preparation Time: 10 to 15 minutes | **Cooking Time:** 5 minutes | **Servings:** 4 | **Calories:** 231

Ingredients: 1 cup spinach | salt and black pepper, to taste | 2-½ tablespoons olive oil
2 tablespoons butter | 5 cloves garlic (minced) | ¼ cup feta cheese (crumbled) | 2 tablespoons capers
¼ cup sun-dried tomatoes | ¼ cup Parmesan cheese(shredded) | 2 zucchinis (spiralized)
2 tablespoons Italian flat-leaf parsley (chopped) | 10 kalamata olives (halved)

Directions: First of all, please confirm you've all the ingredients on the market. Now please heat oil and butter in a large pan& sauté the garlic, spinach, zucchini, in its seasoned with salt & pepper until the spinach wilts & zucchini becomes tender. Now drain any extra liquid. One thing remains to be done. Now quickly add the rest of the ingredients except the cheese and stir cook properly for about 2 to 5 minutes. Finally, remove from the flame & toss in the cheese.

Quick Creamed Coconut Curry Spinach

Preparation Time: 30 to 35 minutes | **Cooking Time:** 5 minutes | **Servings:** 6 | **Calories:** 191

Ingredients: 1 small can whole fat coconut milk | cashews, for garnish | 1-½ teaspoon lemon zest
2-½ teaspoons yellow curry paste | 1 pound frozen spinach, thawed and drained of moisture

Directions: First of all, please certify you've all the ingredients out there. Please heat a medium-sized available. Please heat a medium-sized pan to medium-high heat, then add the curry paste & cook appropriately for about 30 to 40 seconds. Then add a small amount of the coconut milk & stir to combine and then cook until the paste is aromatic. This step is essential. Add the spinach, and then season. Now quickly add the rest of the ingredients, apart from the cashews, & allow the sauce to reduce slightly. One thing remains to be done. Keep the sauce creamy, but reduce it to coat the spinach thoroughly. Finally, serve with chopped cashews.

Kale Mushroom Soup

Preparation Time: 16 minutes | **Cooking Time:** 60 minutes | Servings: 4 | **Calories:** 276

Ingredients: 1 lb. sausage cooked, casings removed and sliced | 29 oz. chicken bone broth | pepper
6-½ oz. fresh kale, cut into bite-sized pieces | 6-½ oz. sliced mushrooms | 2 garlic cloves, minced | salt

Directions: Pour chicken broth and an equal amount of water to a cooking pot. Place the pot on medium heat and cook to a boil. Stir in mushrooms, garlic, sausage, and kale. Adjust seasoning with black pepper and salt. Cover and cook the broccoli soup on low heat for 1 hour. Serve warm.

Bun less Burger - Keto Style

Preparation Time: 15 minutes | **Cooking Time:** 25 minutes | **Servings:** 6 | **Calories:** 479

Ingredients: ground beef 1 lb. | Worcestershire sauce 1 tbsp. | steak seasoning 1 tbsp. | olive oil 2 tbsp. onions 4 oz.

Directions: Mix the beef, olive oil, Worcestershire sauce, and seasonings. Grill the burger. Prepare the onions by adding one tablespoon of oil in a skillet to med-low heat. Sauté. Serve.

Creamy Parmesan Shrimp

Preparation Time: 10 minutes | **Cooking Time:** 20 minutes | **Servings:** 4 | **Calories**: 524

Ingredients: 1-1/2 lbs shrimp | 1/2 cup chicken stock | 1/4 tsp red pepper flakes | salt & pepper
1 cup parmesan cheese, grated | 1 cup fresh basil leaves | 1-1/2 cups heavy cream | 1/4 tsp paprika
3 oz roasted red peppers, sliced | 1/2 onion, minced | 1 tbsp garlic, minced | 3 tbsp butter

Directions: Melt 2 tbsp butter in a pan over medium heat. Season shrimp with pepper and salt and sear in a pan for 1-2 minutes. Transfer shrimp on a plate. Add remaining butter in a pan. Add red chili flakes, paprika, roasted peppers, garlic, onion, pepper, and salt and cook for 5 minutes. Add stock and stir well and cook until liquid reduced by half. Turn heat to low and add cream and stir for 1-2 minutes. Add basil and parmesan cheese and stir for 1-2 minutes. Return shrimp to the pan, cook for 1-2 minutes and serve.

Pesto Flavored Steak

Preparation Time: 15 minutes | **Cooking Time:** 17 minutes | **Servings:** 4 | **Calories**: 226

Ingredients: ¼ c. fresh oregano, chopped | 1-½ tbsp. garlic, minced | 1 tbsp. fresh lemon peel, grated
½ tsp. red pepper flakes, crushed | salt and freshly ground black pepper, to taste | 1 cup pesto
1 lb.(1 inch thick) grass-fed boneless beef top sirloin steak | ¼ cup feta cheese, crumbled

Directions: Preheat the gas grill to medium heat. Lightly, grease the grill grate. In a bowl, add the oregano, garlic, lemon peel, red pepper flakes, salt and black pepper and mix well. Rub the garlic mixture onto the steak evenly. Place the steak onto the grill and cook, covered for about 12-17 minutes, flipping occasionally. Remove from the grill and place the steak onto a cutting board for about 5 minutes. With a sharp knife, cut the steak into desired sized slices. Divide the steak slices and pesto onto serving plates and serve with the topping of the feta cheese.

Flawless Grilled Steak

Preparation Time: 21 minutes | **Cooking Time:** 10 minutes | **Servings:** 5 | **Calories**: 271

Ingredients: ½ tsp. dried thyme, crushed | ½ tsp. dried oregano, crushed | 1 tsp. red chili powder
½ tsp. ground cumin | ¼ tsp. garlic powder | salt and freshly ground black pepper, to taste
1-½ lb. grass-fed flank steak, trimmed | ¼ c. Monterrey Jack cheese, crumbled

Directions: In a large bowl, add the dried herbs and spices and mix well. Add the steaks and rub with mixture generously. Set aside for about 15-20 minutes. Preheat the grill to medium heat. Grease the grill grate. Place the steak onto the grill over medium coals and cook for about 17-21 minutes, flipping once halfway through. Remove the steak from grill and place onto a cutting board for about 10 minutes before slicing. With a sharp knife, cut the steak into desired sized slices. Top with the cheese and serve.

Turkey Meatballs

Preparation Time: 15 minutes | **Cooking Time:** 20 minutes | **Servings:** 2 | **Calories**: 281

Ingredients: 1 pound of ground turkey | 1 tablespoon of fish sauce | 1 diced onion | 1/2 almond flour
2 tablespoon of soy sauce | 1/8 cup of ground beef | 1/2 teaspoon of garlic powder | 1/2 teaspoon of salt
1/2 teaspoon of ground ginger | 1/2 teaspoon of thyme | 1/2 teaspoon of curry | 5 tablespoons of olive oil

Directions: Combine ground turkey, fish sauce, one diced onion, soy sauce, ground beef, seasonings, oil, and flour in a large mixing bowl. Mix it thoroughly. Form meatballs depending on preferred size. Heat skillet and pour in 3 tablespoons of oil [you may need more depending on the size of meat balls]. Cook meatballs until evenly browned on each side. Serve hot.

Coffee BBQ Pork Belly

Preparation Time: 15 minutes | **Cooking Time:** 60 minutes | **Servings:** 4 | **Calories**: 644

Ingredients: beef stock 1.5 cups | pork belly 2 lb. | olive oil 4 tbsp | low-carb barbecue dry rub instant espresso powder 2 tbsp.

Directions: Set the oven at 350° Fahrenheit. Heat-up the beef stock in a small saucepan. Mix in the dry barbecue rub and espresso powder. Put the pork belly, skin side up in a shallow dish and drizzle half of the oil over the top. Put the hot stock around the pork belly. Bake within 45 minutes. Sear each slice within three minutes per side. Serve.

Garlic & Thyme Lamb Chops

Preparation Time: 15 minutes | **Cooking Time:** 10 minutes | **Servings:** 6 | **Calories**: 252

Ingredients: lamb chops 6 | whole garlic cloves 4 | thyme sprigs 2 | ground thyme 1 tsp.
olive oil 3 tbsp.

Directions: Warm-up a skillet. Put the olive oil. Rub the chops with the spices. Put the chops in the skillet with the garlic and sprigs of thyme. Sauté within 3 to 4 minutes and serve.

Jamaican Jerk Pork Roast

Preparation Time: 15 minutes | **Cooking Time:** 4 hours | **Servings:** 12 | **Calories**: 282

Ingredients: olive oil 1 tbsp. | pork shoulder 4 lb. | beef broth .5 cup | Jamaican jerk spice blend .25 cup

Directions: Rub the roast well the oil and the jerk spice blend. Sear the roast on all sides.
Put the beef broth. Simmer within four hours on low. Shred and serve.

Keto Meatballs

Preparation Time: 15 minutes | **Cooking Time:** 20 minutes | **Servings:** 10 | **Calories:** 153

Ingredients: egg 1 | grated Parmesan .5 cup | shredded mozzarella .5 cup | ground beef 1 lb.
garlic 1 tbsp.

Directions: Warm-up the oven to reach 400°F. Combine all of the fixings. Shape into meatballs. Bake within 18-20 minutes. Cool and serve.

Cheesy Roasted Chicken

Preparation Time: 15 minutes | **Cooking Time:** 10 minutes | **Servings:** 6 | **Calories:** 387

Ingredients: 3 cups of chopped roasted chicken | 2 cups of shredded cheddar cheese
2 cups white of shredded cheddar cheese | 3 cups of shredded parmesan cheese

Directions: Oven: 350°F. Be sure to rub butter or to spray with non-stick cooking spray. In a bowl, put in all the cheese and mix well. Microwave the cheese till it melts. Put in the chicken and toss thoroughly. Put two tablespoons of the cheese chicken combo in a pile on the baking sheet. Be sure to leave space between piles. Bake for 4-6 minutes. The moment they turn golden brown at the edges, take them off. Serve hot.

Mixed Vegetable Patties - Instant Pot

Preparation Time: 15 minutes | **Cooking Time:** 10 minutes | **Servings:** 4 | **Calories:** 220

Ingredients: cauliflower florets 1 cup | vegetables 1 bag | water 1.5 cups | flax meal 1 cup
olive oil 2 tbsp.

Directions: Steam the veggies to the steamer basket within 4 to 5 minutes. Mash in the flax meal.
Shape into 4 patties. Cook the patties within 3 minutes per side. Serve.

Roasted Leg of Lamb

Preparation Time: 15 minutes | **Cooking Time:** 1 hour 30 minutes | **Servings:** 6 | **Calories**: 223

Ingredients: reduced-sodium beef broth .5 cup | 2 lb. lamb legs| 6 garlic cloves | 1 tbsp. rosemary leaves 1 tbsp. black pepper

Directions: Warm-up oven temperature to 400 Fahrenheit. Put the lamb in the pan and put the broth and seasonings. Roast 30 minutes and lower the heat to 350º F. Cook within one hour. Cool and serve.

Garlic Pork Loin

Preparation Time: 15 minutes | **Cooking Time:** 1 hour | **Servings:** 6 | **Calories:** 235

Ingredients: 1-½ lb. pork loin roast | 4 cloves garlic, sliced into slivers | salt and pepper, to taste

Directions: Preheat your oven to 425 degrees F. Make several slits all over the pork roast. Insert garlic slivers. Sprinkle with salt and pepper. Roast in the oven for 1 hour.

Beef with Bell Peppers

Preparation Time: 15 minutes | **Cooking Time:** 10 minutes | **Servings:** 6 | **Calories**: 274

Ingredients: 1 tbsp olive oil | 1 pound grass-fed flank steak | 1 red bell pepper | 1 green bell pepper 1 tbsp ginger | 3 tbsp low-sodium soy sauce | 1-½tbsp balsamic vinegar | 2 tsp Sriracha

Directions: Sear the steak slices within 2 minutes. Cook bell peppers within 2–3 minutes. Transfer the beef mixture. Boil the remaining fixing within 1 min. Add the beef mixture & cook within 1–2 min. Serve.

Cheesy Bacon Ranch Chicken

Preparation Time: 40 minutes | **Cooking Time:** 35 minutes | **Servings:** 8 | **Calories:** 387

Ingredients: 8 boneless and skinned chicken breasts | 1 cup of olive oil | 8 thick slices bacon | 3 cups of shredded mozzarella | 1-1/4 tablespoon of ranch seasoning | 1 small chopped onion | chopped chives | kosher salt or pink salt | black pepper

Directions: Preheat skillet and heat little oil, and cook bacon evenly on both sides. Save four tablespoons of drippings and put the others away. Add in salt and pepper in a bowl and rub it over chicken to season. Put 1/2 oil on the flame to cook the chicken from each side for 5 to 7 minutes. When ready, reduce the heat and put in the ranch seasoning, then add mozzarella. Cover and cook on a low flame for 3-5 minutes. Put in bacon fat and chopped chives, then bacon and cover it. Take off and serve warm.

Turkey Breast with Tomato-Olive Salsa

Preparation Time: 20 minutes | **Cooking Time:** 10 minutes | **Servings:** 4 | **Calories**: 387

Ingredients: For turkey: 4 boneless turkey, skinned | 3 tablespoons olive oil | salt | pepper
For salsa: 6 chopped tomatoes | 1/2 diced onions | 5 ounces of pitted and chopped olives 2 crushed garlic cloves | 2 tablespoons of chopped basil | 1 large diced jalapeno | pepper | salt

Directions: In a bowl, put salt, pepper, and three spoons of oil, mix and coat the turkey with this mixture. Place it on a preheated grill and grill for ten minutes. In another bowl, mix garlic, olives, tomatoes, pepper, and drop the rest of the oil. Sprinkle salt and toss. Serve with turkey is warm.

Braised Lamb Shanks

Preparation Time: 15 minutes | **Cooking Time:** 2 hours 35 minutes | **Servings:** 6 | **Calories**: 109.3

Ingredients: 4 grass-fed lamb shanks | 2 tbsp butter | salt | ground black pepper | 6 garlic cloves
6 rosemary sprigs | 1 cup chicken broth

Directions: Warm-up oven to 450°F. Coat the shanks with butter and put salt plus pepper. Roast within 20 minutes. Remove then reduce to 325°F. Place the garlic cloves and rosemary over and around the lamb. Roast within 2 hours. Put the broth into a roasting pan. Increase to 400°F. Roast within 15 minutes more. Serve.

Chicken Pot Pie

Preparation Time: 15 minutes | **Cooking Time:** 25 minutes | **Servings:** 4 | **Calories:** 341

Ingredients: For the filling: 1/2 medium onion, chopped | 2 celery stalks, chopped |
1/2 cup fresh or frozen peas | 2 tablespoons butter | 1 garlic clove, minced | 1-1/2 pounds chicken thighs
1 cup chicken broth | 1/2 cup heavy (whipping) cream | ½ cup shredded low-moisture mozzarella cheese
1 teaspoon dried thyme | 1/2 teaspoon pink Himalayan sea salt | 1/2 teasp. freshly ground black pepper
For the crust: 1 cup almond flour | 2 tablespoons butter, at room temperature | 2 tablespoons sour cream
1 large egg, white | 1 tablespoon ground flaxseed | 1 teaspoon xanthan gum | 1 teaspoon baking powder
1/2 teaspoon garlic powder | 1/4 teaspoon pink Himalayan sea salt | 1/4 teaspoon dried thyme

Directions: Filling: In a saucepan, combine the onion, celery, peas, butter, and garlic over medium heat. Cook for about 5 minutes, until the onion starts to turn translucent. In a large skillet, cook the chicken thighs for 3 to 5 minutes, until there is no more visible pink. Add the cooked chicken and all juices to the pan with the vegetables. Add the broth, cream, mozzarella, thyme, salt, and pepper to the pan. Simmer it until sauce thickens, stirring occasionally. Preheat the oven to 400°F. In a bowl or container, combine the almond flour, butter, sour cream, egg white, flaxseed, xanthan gum, baking powder, garlic powder, salt, and thyme. Form this into a dough. Place the dough between 2 sheets of parchment paper and roll out into a 10-inch round that is 1/4 inch thick. Fill an 8-inch pie pan or 4 (6-ounce) ramekins with the chicken filling. Top the pie pan with the crust, flipping it onto the filling and peeling away the parchment paper. If using ramekins, cut circles of the dough and fit them onto the ramekins. Pinch to seal the edges, and trim off any excess. Baking time: 10-12 minutes. Let cool for 5 minutes, then serve.

Mongolian Beef

Preparation Time: 15 minutes | **Cooking Time:** 10 minutes | **Servings:** 4 | **Calories**: 266

Ingredients: 1 lb. grass-fed flank steak, cut into thin slices against the grain | 2 tsp. arrowroot starch
salt, to taste | ¼ cup avocado oil | 1 piece fresh ginger, grated (1-inch) | 4 garlic cloves, minced
½ tsp. red pepper flakes, crushed | ¼ cup water | 1/3 cup low-sodium soy sauce
1 tsp. red boat fish sauce | 3 scallions, sliced | 1 tsp. sesame seeds

Directions: In a bowl, add the steak slices, arrowroot starch and salt and toss to coat well. In a larger skillet, heat oil over medium-high heat and cook the steak slices for about 1½ minutes per side. With a slotted spoon, transfer the steak slices onto a plate. Drain the oil from the skillet but leaving about 1 tbsp. inside. In the same skillet, add the ginger, garlic and red pepper flakes and sauté for about 1 minute. Add the water, soy sauce and fish sauce and stir to combine well. Stir in the cooked steak slices and simmer for about 3 minutes. Stir in the scallions and simmer for about 2 minutes. Remove from the heat and serve hot with the garnishing of sesame seeds.

Beef & Veggie Casserole

Preparation Time: 20 minutes | **Cooking Time:** 55 minutes | **Servings:** 4 | **Calories**: 472

Ingredients: 3 tbsp butter | 1 pound grass-fed ground beef | 1 yellow onion | 2 garlic cloves
1 cup pumpkin | 1 cup broccoli | 2 cups cheddar cheese | 1 tbsp Dijon mustard | 6 organic eggs
½cup heavy whipping cream | salt | ground black pepper

Directions: Cook the beef within 8–10 minutes. Transfer. Cook the onion and garlic within 10 minutes. Add the pumpkin and cook within 5–6 minutes. Add the broccoli and cook within 3–4 minutes. Transfer to the cooked beef, combine. Warm-up oven to 350ºF. Put 2/3 of cheese and mustard in the beef mixture, combine. In another mixing bowl, add cream, eggs, salt, and black pepper, and beat. In a baking dish, place the beef mixture and top with egg mixture, plus the remaining cheese. Bake within 25 minutes. Serve.

Broccoli and Chicken Casserole

Preparation Time: 15 minutes | **Cooking Time:** 35 minutes | **Servings:** 6 | **Calories**: 431

Ingredients: 2 tablespoons butter | 1/4 cup cooked bacon, crumbled | 2-1/2 cups cheddar cheese, shredded and divided | 4 ounces cream cheese, softened | 1/4 cup heavy whipping cream
1/2 pack ranch seasoning mix | 2/3 cup homemade chicken broth | 1-1/2 cups small broccoli florets
2 cups cooked grass-fed chicken breast, shredded

Directions: Preheat your oven to 350ºF. Arrange a rack in the upper portion of the oven. For the chicken mixture: In a large wok, melt the butter over low heat. Add the bacon, 1/2 cup of cheddar cheese, cream cheese, heavy whipping cream, ranch seasoning, and broth, and with a wire whisk, beat until well combined. Cook for about 5 minutes, stirring frequently. Meanwhile, in a microwave-safe dish, place the broccoli and microwave until desired tenderness is achieved. In the wok, add the chicken and broccoli and mix until well combined. Remove from the heat and transfer the mixture into a casserole dish. Top the chicken mixture with the remaining cheddar cheese. Bake for about 25 minutes. Now, set the oven to broiler. Broil the chicken mixture for about 2–3 minutes or until cheese is bubbly. Serve hot.

Veggies & Walnut Loaf

Preparation Time: 15 minutes | **Cooking Time:** 1 hour 10 minutes | **Servings:** 3 | **Calories**: 242

Ingredients: 1 tablespoon olive oil | 2 yellow onions | 2 garlic cloves | 1 teaspoon dried rosemary
1 cup walnuts | 2 carrots |1 celery stalk | 1 green bell pepper | 1 cup button mushrooms | 5 organic eggs
1-¼cups almond flour | salt | ground black pepper

Directions: Warm-up oven to 350ºF. Sauté the onion within 4–5 minutes. Add the garlic and rosemary and sauté within 1 minute. Add the walnuts and vegetables within 3–4 minutes. Put aside. Beat the eggs, flour, sea salt, and black pepper. Mix the egg mixture with vegetable mixture. Bake within 50–60 minutes. Serve.

Rib Roast

Preparation Time: 15 minutes | **Cooking Time:** 3 hours | **Servings:** 6 | **Calories**: 329

Ingredients: 1 rib roast | 12 cloves garlic, chopped | 2 teaspoons lemon zest | salt, to taste
6 tablespoons fresh rosemary, chopped | 5 sprigs thyme

Directions: Preheat your oven to 325 degrees F. Season all sides of rib roast with salt. Place the rib roast in a baking pan. Sprinkle with garlic, lemon zest and rosemary. Add herb sprigs on top. Roast for 3 hours. Let rest for a few minutes and then slice and serve.

Shrimp & Bell Pepper Stir-Fry

Preparation Time: 20 minutes | **Cooking Time:** 10 minutes | **Servings:** 3 | **Calories:** 221

Ingredients: ½ cup low-sodium soy sauce | 2 tablespoons balsamic vinegar | 2 tablespoons erythritol
1 tablespoon arrowroot starch | 1 tablespoon ginger | ½ teaspoon red pepper flakes | 2 scallion greens
3 tablespoons olive oil | ½ red bell pepper | ½ yellow bell pepper | ½ green bell pepper | 1 onion
1 red chili | 1-½ pounds shrimp

Directions: Mix soy sauce, vinegar, erythritol, arrowroot starch, ginger, and red pepper flakes. Set aside. Stir-fry the bell peppers, onion, and red chili within 1–2 minutes. In the center of the wok, place the shrimp and cook within 1–2 minutes. Stir the shrimp with bell pepper mixture and cook within 2 minutes. Stir in the sauce and cook within 2–3 minutes. Stir in the scallion greens and remove. Serve hot.

Salad Skewers

Preparation Time: 10 minutes | **Cooking Time:** 0 minutes | **Servings:** 1 | **Calories:** 315

Ingredients: two wooden skewers, soaked in water for 30 minutes before use | eight large black olives
one yellow pepper, cut into eight squares | ½ red onion, chopped in half and separated into eight pieces
3.5 oz (10 cm) cucumber, cut into 4 slices & halved ounce of feta, cut into eight cubes | 8 cherry tomatoes
For the dressing: 1 tablespoon extra-virgin olive oil | 1 teaspoon balsamic vinegar | juice of ½ lemon
few leaves basil, finely chopped (or ½ tsp dried mixed herbs to replace basil and oregano)
a right amount of salt and freshly ground black pepper | few leaves oregano, finely chopped
½ clove garlic, peeled and crushed

Directions: Thread each skewer in the order with salad ingredients: olive, tomato, yellow pepper, red onion, cucumber, feta, basil, olive, yellow pepper, red ointment, cucumber, feta. Put all the ingredients of the dressing in a small bowl and blend well together. Pour over the spoils.

Chicken Quesadilla

Preparation Time: 15 minutes | **Cooking Time:** 25 minutes | **Servings:** 4 | **Calories:** 299

Ingredients: 1 tbsp. extra-virgin olive oil | 1 bell pepper, sliced | 1/2 yellow onion, sliced
1/2 tsp. chili powder | kosher salt | freshly ground black pepper | 3 cups shredded Monterey Jack
3 cups shredded cheddar | 4 cups shredded chicken | 1 avocado, thinly sliced | 1 green onion, thinly sliced
sour cream, for serving

Directions: Let the oven preheat to 400°F. Prepare two baking sheets with a baking mat or parchment paper. Heat oil. Put pepper and onion and season with chili powder, salt, and pepper. Cook until soft, 5 minutes. Transfer to a plate. In a medium bowl, stir together cheeses. Put 1 1/2 cups of cheese mixture onto both prepared baking sheets centers. Spread the cheese evenly in a circle shape, like a flour tortilla. Bake the quesadilla for about 20 minutes. Put onion-pepper mixture, shredded chicken, and avocado slices to one half of each. Let cool slightly. Then use the parchment paper and a little spatula to gently lift. Fold the cheese tortillas empty side over the filling side. Place the quesadilla baking sheet in the oven to heat, 3 to 5 minutes more. Decorate with green onion and sour cream and serve.

Avocado Mayonnaise

Preparation Time: 10 minutes | **Cooking Time:** 1 minute | **Servings:** 4 | **Calories:** 90

Ingredients: 1 avocado | 3 tbsp. olive oil | ½ jalapeño, chopped | 3 garlic cloves, chopped | salt, to taste
½ lemon, juiced | 6/10 parsley sprigs, chopped

Directions: Combine all ingredients in a blender and pulse on high until smooth. Keep refrigerated.

Beef Stir Fry

Preparation Time: 15 minutes | **Cooking Time:** 10 minutes | **Servings:** 4 | **Calories**: 247

Ingredients: 1 tablespoon soy sauce | 1 tablespoon ginger, minced | 1 teaspoon cornstarch
1 teaspoon dry sherry | 12 oz. beef, sliced into strips | 1 teaspoon toasted sesame oil
2 tablespoons oyster sauce | 1 lb. baby Bok choy, sliced | 3 tablespoons chicken broth

Directions: Mix soy sauce, ginger, cornstarch and dry sherry in a bowl. Toss the beef in the mixture. Pour oil into a pan over medium heat. Cook the beef for 5 minutes, stirring. Add oyster sauce, Bok choy and chicken broth to the pan. Cook for 1 minute.

Sweet & Sour Pork

Preparation Time: 15 minutes | **Cooking Time:** 15 minutes | **Servings:** 6 | **Calories**: 414

Ingredients: 1 lb. pork chops | salt and pepper to taste | ½ cup sesame seeds
2 tablespoons peanut oil | 2 tablespoons soy sauce | 3 tablespoons apricot jam | chopped scallions

Directions: Season pork chops with salt and pepper. Press sesame seeds on both sides of pork. Pour oil into a pan over medium heat. Cook pork for 3 to 5 minutes per side. Transfer to a plate. In a bowl, mix soy sauce and apricot jam. Simmer for 3 minutes. Pour sauce over the pork and garnish with scallions before serving.

Grilled Pork with Salsa

Preparation Time: 30 minutes | **Cooking Time:** 15 minutes | **Servings:** 8 | **Calories**: 219

Ingredients: salsa | 1 onion, chopped | 1 tomato, chopped | 1 peach, chopped | 1 apricot, chopped
1 tablespoon olive oil | 1 tablespoon lime juice | 2 tablespoons fresh cilantro, chopped | salt, to taste
pepper, to taste | pork | 1 lb. pork tenderloin, sliced | 1 tablespoon olive oil | ½ teaspoon ground cumin
¾ teaspoon chili powder

Directions: Combine salsa ingredients in a bowl. Cover and refrigerate. Brush pork tenderloin with oil. Season with salt, pepper, cumin and chili powder. Grill pork for 5 to 7 minutes per side. Slice pork and serve with salsa.

Lamb Chops and Herb Butter

Preparation Time: 15 minutes | **Cooking Time:** 4 minutes | **Servings:** 4 | **Calories:** 722.3

Ingredients: eight lamb chops | one tbsp. olive oil | butter | pepper | salt
For the herb butter: five ounces butter | one clove garlic | half tbsp. garlic powder | four tbsps. parsley
one tsp. lemon juice | one-third tsp. salt

Directions: Season the lamb chops with pepper and salt. Warm-up olive oil and butter in an iron skillet. Add the lamb chops. Fry within four minutes. Mix all the listed items for the herb butter in a bowl. Cool. Serve with herb butter.

Crispy Cuban Pork Roast

Preparation Time: 15 minutes | **Cooking Time:** 4 minutes | **Servings:** 6 | **Calories:** 910.3

Ingredients: five pounds pork shoulder | four tsp salt | two tsp. cumin | one tsp. black pepper
2 tbsps. oregano | 1 red onion | 4 cloves garlic | orange juice | lemons juiced | one-fourth cup of olive oil

Directions: Rub the pork shoulder with salt in a bowl. Mix all the remaining items of the marinade in a blender. Marinate the meat within eight hours. Cook within forty minutes. Warm-up your oven at 200 degrees. Roast the pork within thirty minutes. Remove the meat juice. Simmer within twenty minutes. Shred the meat. Pour the meat juice. Serve.

Low Carb Crack Slaw Egg Roll in a Bowl Recipe

Preparation Time: 15 minutes | **Cooking Time:** 20 minutes | **Servings:** 2 | **Calories**: 116

Ingredients: 1 lb. ground beef | 4 cups shredded coleslaw mix | 1 tbsp. avocado oil | 1 tsp. sea salt
¼ tsp. black pepper | 4 cloves garlic | 3 tbsp. ginger | ¼ cup coconut amines | 2 tsp. toasted sesame oil
¼ cup green onions

Directions: Warm-up avocado oil in a large pan, put in the garlic, and cook. Add the ground beef and cook within 10 mins, put salt and black pepper. Lower the heat and add the coleslaw mix and the coconut amines. Stir to cook for 5 minutes. Remove and put in the green onions and the toasted sesame oil. Serve.

Keto Sloppy Joes

Preparation Time: 15 minutes | **Cooking Time:** 1 hour 10 minutes | **Servings:** 2 | **Calories**: 215

Ingredients: 1-¼ cup almond flour | 5 tbsp. ground psyllium husk powder | 1 tsp. sea salt | 3 white eggs
2 tsp. baking powder | 2 tsp. cider vinegar | 1-¼ cups boiling water | 1-½ lb. ground beef | 1 yellow onion
4 garlic cloves | 14 oz. crushed tomatoes | 1 tbsp. chili powder | 1 tbsp. Dijon powder | 2 tsp. salt
1 tbsp. red wine vinegar | 4 tbsp. tomato paste | ¼ tsp ground black pepper | ½ cup mayonnaise
6 oz. cheese | 2 tbsp. olive oil

Directions: Warm-up the oven to 350 degrees and then mix all the dry fixing. Add some vinegar, egg whites, and boiled water. Whisk for 30 seconds. Form the dough into 5 or 8 pieces of bread. Cook within 55 minutes. Cook the onion and garlic. Add the ground beef and cook. Put the other fixing and cook. Simmer for 10 minutes in low. Serve.

Chicken for Tacos

Preparation Time: 10 minutes | **Cooking Time:** 24 minutes | **Servings:** 2 | **Calories:** 947

Ingredients: 2 pounds of chicken drumsticks, skin-on | 1/3 cup balsamic vinegar | 1/4 cup honey
4 cloves of garlic, minced | salt and black pepper, to taste

Directions: Take a small bowl and combine together vinegar, salt, pepper, honey, and garlic. Pour this sauce into the instant pot. Place chicken drumsticks on top of the sauce and push it down, so the chicken submerges in the sauce. Cook on high pressure for 20 minutes. Once the cooking time completes, let the steam release, using the quick release method. Now, turn on the sauté button so that the sauce boils and get reduced. Now, place the drumsticks on parchment paper. Preheat the oven to 350 degrees F. Place the chicken inside the oven to broil for 4 minutes. Then remove the chicken from the oven and transfer to the platter. Pour the instant pot sauce over the top. Serve and enjoy over tacos if liked.

Indian Buttered Chicken

Preparation Time: 15 minutes | **Cooking Time:** 30 minutes | **Servings:** 4 | **Calories:** 456

Ingredients: 3 tablespoons unsalted butter | 1 medium yellow onion, chopped | 2 garlic cloves, minced
1 teaspoon fresh ginger, minced | 1-1/2 pounds grass-fed chicken breasts, cut into 3/4-inch chunks
2 tomatoes, chopped finely | 1 tablespoon garam masala | 1 teaspoon red chili powder | 1 cup heavy cream
1 teaspoon ground cumin | salt & ground black pepper, to taste | 2 tablespoons fresh cilantro, chopped

Directions: In a wok, melt butter and sauté the onions for about 5–6 minutes. Now, add in ginger and garlic and sauté for about 1 minute. Add the tomatoes and cook for about 2–3 minutes, crushing with the back of the spoon. Stir in the chicken spices, salt, and black pepper, and cook for about 6–8 minutes or until the desired doneness of the chicken. Put in the cream and cook for about 8–10 more minutes, stirring occasionally. Garnish with fresh cilantro and serve hot.

Bacon-Wrapped Meatloaf

Preparation Time: 15 minutes | **Cooking Time:** 1 hour | **Servings:** 4 | **Calories:** 1020.3

Ingredients: For the Meatloaf: two tbsps. butter | one onion | two pounds beef | one large egg
half cup whipping cream | two ounces cheese | one tbsp. oregano | one tsp. salt | half tsp. black pepper
seven ounces bacon | For the gravy: 1-1/2 cup whipping cream | half tbsp. tamari soy sauce

Directions: Warm-up your oven at 200 degrees Celsius. Dissolve the butter in a pan. Add the onion. Cook within four minutes. Keep aside. Combine onion, ground meat, and the remaining fixing except for the bacon in a large bowl. Make a firm loaf. Use bacon strips for wrapping the loaf. Bake the meatloaf for forty-five minutes. Put the juices from the baking dish and cream, then boil. Simmer within ten minutes. Add thc soy sauce. Slice and serve with gravy.

Cheesy Ham Quiche

Preparation Time: 10 minutes | **Cooking Time:** 30 minutes | **Servings:** 6 | **Calories:** 362

Ingredients: 8 eggs | 1 cup zucchini | .50 c. shredded heavy cream | 1 cup ham, diced | 1 tbsp mustard
salt | dash

Directions: For this recipe, you can start off by prepping your stove to 375°F and getting out a pie plate for your quiche. Next, it is time to prep the zucchini. First, you will want to go ahead and shred it into small pieces. Once this is complete, take a paper towel and gently squeeze out the excess moisture. This will help avoid a soggy quiche. When the step from above is complete, you will want to place the zucchini into your pie plate along with the cooked ham pieces and your cheese. Once these items are in place, you will want to whisk the seasonings, cream, and eggs together before pouring it over the top. Now that your quiche is set, you are going to pop the dish into your stove for about forty minutes. By the end of this time, the egg should be cooked through, and you will be able to insert a knife into the center and have it come out clean. If the quiche is cooked to your liking, take the dish from the oven and allow it to chill slightly before slicing and serving.

Chicken Parmigiana

Preparation Time: 15 minutes | **Cooking Time:** 25 minutes | **Servings:** 5 | **Calories:** 398

Ingredients: 5 grass-fed skinless, boneless chicken breasts | 1/4 cup Parmesan cheese, grated
1 large organic egg, beaten | 1/2 cup superfine blanched almond flour | 1/2 teaspoon dried parsley
1/2 teaspoon paprika | 1/2 teaspoon garlic powder | salt and ground black pepper, as required
1/4 cup olive oil | 1 cup sugar-free tomato sauce | 5 ounces mozzarella cheese, thinly sliced
2 tablespoons fresh parsley, chopped

Directions: Preheat your oven to 375°F. Arrange one chicken breast between 2 pieces of parchment paper. With a meat mallet, pound the chicken breast into a 1/2-inch thickness. Repeat with the remaining chicken breasts. Add the beaten egg into a shallow dish. Place the almond flour, Parmesan, parsley, spices, salt, and black pepper in another shallow dish, and mix well. Dip chicken breasts into the whipped egg and then coat with the flour mixture. Heat the oil in a deep wok over medium-high heat and fry the chicken breasts for about 3 minutes per side. The chicken breasts must be transferred onto a paper towel-lined plate to drain. At the bottom of a casserole, place about 1/2 cup of tomato sauce and spread evenly. Arrange the chicken breasts over marinara sauce in a single layer. Put sauce on top plus the mozzarella cheese slices. Bake for about 20 minutes or until done completely. Remove from the oven and serve hot with the garnishing of parsley.

Buttered Cod

Preparation Time: 5 minutes | **Cooking Time:** 5 minutes | **Servings:** 4 | **Calories:** 295

Ingredients: 1-½ lb. cod fillets, sliced | 6 tablespoons butter, sliced | ¼ teaspoon garlic powder
¾ teaspoon ground paprika | salt and pepper to taste | lemon slices | chopped parsley

Directions: Mix the garlic powder, paprika, salt and pepper in a bowl. Season cod pieces with seasoning mixture. Add 2 tablespoons butter in a pan over medium heat. Let half of the butter melt. Add the cod and cook for 2 minutes per side. Top with the remaining slices of butter. Cook for 3 to 4 minutes. Garnish with parsley and lemon slices before serving.

Salmon with Red Curry Sauce

Preparation Time: 10 minutes | **Cooking Time:** 22 minutes | **Servings:** 4 | **Calories:** 553

Ingredients: 4 salmon fillets | 2 tablespoons olive oil | salt and pepper, to taste | 14 oz. coconut cream
1-½ tablespoons red curry paste | 1 tablespoon fresh ginger, chopped | 1-½ tablespoons fish sauce

Directions: Preheat your oven to 350 degrees F. Cover baking sheet with foil. Brush both sides of salmon fillets with olive oil and season with salt and pepper. Place the salmon fillets on the baking sheet. Bake salmon in the oven for 20 minutes. In a pan over medium heat, mix the curry paste, ginger, coconut cream and fish sauce. Sprinkle with salt and pepper. Simmer for 2 minutes. Pour the sauce over the salmon before serving.

Salmon with Pepita and Lime

Preparation Time: 15 minutes | **Cooking Time:** 15 minutes | **Servings:** 4 | **Calories:** 185

Ingredients: 2 tbsp. pepitas, ground | ¼ tsp. chili powder | 1 lb. salmon fillet, cut 4 p.| 2 tbsp. lime juice

Directions: In a large saucepan, place a trivet and pour a cup of water into the pan. Bring it to a boil. Place salmon in a heatproof dish that fits inside a saucepan. Drizzle lime juice on the fillet. Season with salt, pepper, and chili powder. Garnish with ground pepitas. Seal dish with foil. Place the dish on the trivet inside the saucepan. Cover and steam for 15 minutes. Serve and enjoy.

Steamed Chili-Rubbed Tilapia

Preparation Time: 15 minutes | **Cooking Time:** 15 minutes | **Servings:** 4 | **Calories:** 211

Ingredients: 1 lb. tilapia fillet, skin removed | 2 tbsp. chili powder | 3 cloves garlic, peeled and minced
2 tbsp. extra virgin olive oil | 2 tbsp soy sauce

Directions: In a large saucepan, place a trivet and pour a cup or two of water into the pan. Bring it to a boil. Place tilapia in a heatproof dish that fits inside a saucepan. Drizzle soy sauce and oil on the filet. Season with chili powder and garlic. Seal dish with foil. Place the dish on the trivet inside the saucepan. Cover and steam for 15 minutes. Serve and enjoy.

Sesame-Crusted Tuna with Green Beans

Preparation Time: 15 minutes | **Cooking Time:** 5 minutes | **Servings:** 4 | **Calories:** 420

Ingredients: ¼ cup white sesame seeds | ¼ cup black sesame seeds | 4 ahi tuna steaks
salt and pepper | 1 tablespoon olive oil | 1 tablespoon coconut oil | 2 cups green beans

Directions: In a shallow dish, mix the two kinds of sesame seeds. Season the tuna with pepper and salt. Dredge the tuna in a mixture of sesame seeds. Heat up to high heat the olive oil in a skillet, then add the tuna. Cook for 1 to 2 minutes until it turns seared, then sear on the other side. Remove the tuna from the skillet, and let the tuna rest while using the coconut oil to heat the skillet. Fry the green beans in the oil for 5 minutes then use sliced tuna to eat.

Salmon Teriyaki

Preparation Time: 15 minutes | **Cooking Time:** 25 minutes | **Servings:** 6 | **Calories:** 312

Ingredients: 3 tbsp. sesame oil | 2 teaspoons fish sauce | 3 tbsp. coconut amino | 2 tsp ginger, grated
4 cloves garlic, crushed | 2 tablespoons xylitol | 1 tablespoon green lime juice | 2 tsp green lime zest
cayenne pepper, to taste | 6 salmon fillets | 1 teaspoon arrowroot starch | ¼ cup water | sesame seeds

Directions: Preheat your oven to 400 degrees F. Combine the sesame oil, fish sauce, coconut amino, ginger, garlic, xylitol, green lime juice, zest and cayenne pepper in a mixing bowl. Create 6 packets using foil. Add half of the marinade in the packets. Add the salmon inside. Place in the baking sheet and cook for about 20 to 25 minutes. Add the remaining sauce in a pan over medium heat. Dissolve arrowroot in water, and add to the sauce. Simmer until the sauce has thickened. Place the salmon on a serving platter and pour the sauce on top. Sprinkle sesame seeds on top before serving.

Grilled Salmon and Zucchini with Mango Sauce

Preparation Time: 5 minutes | **Cooking Time:** 10 minutes | **Servings:** 4 | **Calories:** 350

Ingredients: 4 boneless salmon fillets | 1 tablespoon olive oil | 1 large zucchini, sliced in coins
2 tablespoons fresh lemon juice | ½ cup chopped mango | ¼ cup fresh chopped cilantro
1 teaspoon lemon zest | ½ cup canned coconut milk | salt and pepper

Directions: Preheat a grill pan to heat, and sprinkle with cooking spray liberally. Brush with olive oil to the salmon and season with salt and pepper. Apply lemon juice to the zucchini, and season with salt and pepper. Put the zucchini and salmon fillets on the grill pan. Cook for 5 minutes then turn all over and cook for another 5 minutes. Combine the remaining ingredients in a blender and combine to create a sauce. Serve the side-drizzled salmon filets with mango sauce and zucchini.

Thyme-Sesame Crusted Halibut

Preparation Time: 20 minutes | **Cooking Time:** 15 minutes | **Servings:** 2 | **Calories**: 246

Ingredients: 8 oz. halibut, cut into 2 portions | 1 tbsp. lemon juice, freshly squeezed
1 tsp. dried thyme leaves | 1 tbsp. sesame seeds, toasted

Directions: In a large saucepan, place a trivet and pour a cup or two of water into the pan. Bring it to a boil. Place halibut in a heatproof dish that fits inside a saucepan. Season with lemon juice, salt, and pepper. Sprinkle with dried thyme leaves and sesame seeds. Seal dish with foil. Place the dish on the trivet inside the saucepan. Cover and steam for 15 minutes. Serve and enjoy.

Steamed Mustard Salmon

Preparation Time: 15 minutes | **Cooking Time:** 15 minutes | **Servings:** 4 | **Calories**: 402

Ingredients: 2 tbsp Dijon mustard | 2 cloves of garlic, minced | 4 salmon fillets, skin removed
1 tbsp dill weed | 1 whole lemon

Directions: Slice lemon in half. Slice one lemon in circles and juice the other half in a small bowl. Whisk in mustard, garlic, and dill weed in a bowl of lemon—season with pepper and salt. In a large saucepan, place a trivet and pour a cup or two of water into the pan. Bring to a boil. Place lemon slices in a heatproof dish that fits inside a saucepan—Season salmon with pepper and salt. Slather mustard mixture on top of salmon. Seal dish with foil. Place the dish on the trivet inside the saucepan. Cover and steam for 15 minutes. Serve and enjoy.

Steamed Cod with Ginger

Preparation Time: 15 minutes | **Cooking Time:** 15 minutes | **Servings:** 4 | **Calories**: 514

Ingredients: 4 cod fillets, skin removed | 3 tbsp. lemon juice, freshly squeezed
2 tbsp. coconut aminos | 2 tbsp. grated ginger | 6 scallions, chopped

Directions: In a large saucepan, place a trivet and pour a cup or two of water into the pan. Bring to a boil. In a small bowl, whisk well lemon juice, coconut aminos, coconut oil, and grated ginger. Place scallions in a heatproof dish that fits inside a saucepan. Season scallion's moon with pepper and salt. Drizzle with ginger mixture. Sprinkle scallions on top. Seal dish with foil. Place the dish on the trivet inside the saucepan. Cover and steam for 15 minutes. Serve and enjoy.

Halibut en Papillote

Preparation Time: 10 minutes | **Cooking Time:** 15 minutes | **Servings:** 4 | **Calories**: 410

Ingredients: 4 halibut fillets | ½ tbsp. grated ginger | 1 cup chopped tomatoes | 1 lemon
1 shallot, thinly sliced

Directions: Slice lemon in half. Slice one lemon in circles. In a small bowl, squeeze the other half of the lemon. Mix in grated ginger and season with pepper and salt. In a large saucepan, place a trivet and pour a cup or two of water into the pan. Bring to aboil. Get 4 large foil and place one fillet in the middle of each foil. Season with fillet salt and pepper. Drizzle with olive oil. Add the grated ginger, tomatoes, and shallots equally. Fold the foil to generate a pouch and crimp the edges. Place the foil containing the fish on the trivet. Cover saucepan and steam for 15 minutes. Serve and enjoy in pouches.

Chili-Garlic Salmon

Preparation Time: 10 minutes | **Cooking Time:** 15 minutes | **Servings:** 4 | **Calories**: 409

Ingredients: 5 tbsp. sweet chili sauce | ¼ cup coconut aminos | 3 tbsp. green onions, chopped
3 cloves garlic, peeled and minced | 4 salmon fillets

Directions: In a large saucepan, place a trivet and pour a cup or two of water into the pan. Bring to a boil. In a small bowl, whisk well sweet chili sauce, garlic, and coconut aminos. Place salmon in a heatproof dish that fits inside a saucepan. Season salmon with pepper. Drizzle with sweet chili sauce mixture. Sprinkle green onions on top of the filet. Seal dish with foil. Place the dish on the trivet inside the saucepan. Cover and steam for 15 minutes. Serve and enjoy.

Chili-Lime Shrimps

Preparation Time: 5 minutes | **Cooking Time:** 10 minutes | **Servings:** 4 | **Calories**: 306

Ingredients: 1-½ lb. raw shrimp, peeled and deveined | 1 tbsp. chili flakes | 5 tbsp sweet chili sauce
2 tbsp. lime juice, freshly squeezed | 1 tsp cayenne pepper

Directions: In a small bowl, whisk well chili flakes, sweet chili sauce, cayenne pepper, and water. On medium-high fire, heat a non-stick saucepan for 2 minutes. Add oil to a pan and swirl to coat bottom and sides. Heat oil for a minute. Stir fry shrimp, around 5 minutes. Season lightly with salt and pepper. Stir in sweet chili mixture and toss well shrimp to coat. Turn off fire, drizzle lime juice and toss well to coat. Serve and enjoy.

Flounder with Dill and Capers

Preparation Time: 10 minutes | **Cooking Time:** 15 minutes | **Servings:** 4 | **Calories**: 447

Ingredients: 4 flounder fillets | 1 tbsp. chopped fresh dill | 2 tbsp. capers, chopped | 4 lemon wedges

Directions: In a large saucepan, place a trivet and pour a cup or two of water into the pan. Bring to a boil. Place flounder in a heatproof dish that fits inside a saucepan. Season snapper with pepper and salt. Drizzle with olive oil on all sides. Sprinkle dill and capers on top of the filet. Seal dish with foil. Place the dish on the trivet inside the saucepan. Cover and steam for 15 mins. Serve and enjoy with lemon wedges.

Spicy Keto Chicken Wings

Preparation Time: 20 minutes | **Cooking Time:** 30 minutes | **Servings:** 4 | **Calories**: 465

Ingredients: chicken wings | 2 lbs. Cajun spice | 1 tbsp smoked paprika |2 tbsp turmeric | .50 tbsp salt
2 tbsp baking powder | pepper | dash

Directions: When you first begin the Ketogenic Diet, you may find that you won't be eating the traditional foods that may have made up a majority of your diet in the past. While this is a good thing for your health, you may feel you are missing out! The good news is that there are delicious alternatives that aren't lacking in flavor! To start this recipe, you'll want to prep the stove to 400°F. As this heat up, you will want to take some time to dry your chicken wings with a paper towel. This will help remove any excess moisture and get you some nice, crispy wings! When you are all set, take out a mixing bowl and place all of the seasonings along with the baking powder. If you feel like it, you can adjust the seasoning levels however you would like. Once these are set, go ahead and throw the chicken wings in and coat evenly. If you have one, you'll want to place the wings on a wire rack that is placed over your baking tray. If not, you can just lay them across the baking sheet. Now that your chicken wings are set, you are going to pop them into the stove for thirty minutes. By the end of this time, the tops of the wings should be crispy. If they are, take them out from the oven and flip them so that you can bake the other side. You will want to cook these for an additional thirty minutes. Finally, take the tray from the oven and allow to cool slightly before serving up your spiced keto wings. For additional flavor, serve with any of your favorite, keto-friendly dipping sauce.

Easy Meatballs

Preparation Time: 10 minutes | **Cooking Time:** 20 minutes | **Servings:** 4 | **Calories**: 454

Ingredients: 1 lb. ground beef | 1 egg, beaten | salt and pepper, to taste | 1 teaspoon garlic powder
1 teaspoon onion powder | 2 tablespoons. butter | ¼ cup mayonnaise | ¼ cup pickled jalapeños
1 cup cheddar cheese, grated

Directions: Combine the cheese, mayonnaise, pickled jalapenos, salt, pepper, garlic powder and onion powder in a large mixing bowl. Add the beef and egg and combine using clean hands. Form large meatballs. Makes about 12. Fry the meatballs in the butter over medium heat for about 4 minutes on each side or until golden brown. Servings warm with a keto-friendly side. The meatball mixture can also be used to make a meatloaf. Just preheat your oven to 400 degrees F, press the mixture into a loaf pan and bake for about 30 minutes or until the top is golden brown. Can be refrigerated for up to 5 days or frozen for up to 3 months.

Chicken Cordon Bleu with Cauliflower

Preparation Time: 10 minutes | **Cooking Time:** 45 minutes | **Servings:** 4 | **Calories**: 420

Ingredients: 4 boneless chicken breast halves (about 12 oz) | 4 slices deli ham | 4 slices Swiss cheese
1 large egg, whisked well | 2 ounces pork rinds -| ¼ cup almond flour | ¼ cup grated Parmesan cheese
½ teaspoon garlic powder | salt and pepper | 2 cups cauliflower florets

Directions: Preheat the oven to 350°F and add a foil on a baking sheet. Sandwich the breast half of the chicken between parchment parts and pound flat. Spread the bits out and cover with ham and cheese sliced over. Roll the chicken over the fillings and then dip into the beaten egg. In a food processor, mix the pork rinds, almond flour, parmesan, garlic powder, salt and pepper, and pulse into fine crumbs. Roll the rolls of chicken in the mixture of pork rind then put them on the baking sheet. Throw the cauliflower into the baking sheet with the melted butter and fold. Bake for 45 minutes until the chicken is fully cooked.

Curried Chicken with Instant Lemon

Preparation Time: 10 minutes | **Cooking Time:** 25 minutes | **Servings:** 6 | **Calories**: 321

Ingredients: 1 can coconut milk full fat | 1/4 cup lemon juice | 6 pcs. chicken breasts or thighs
1 tbsp. curry spice | 1 tsp turmeric

Directions: Set your instant pot on high heat. Add all ingredients and set on the manual setting. Secure the vent sealing and cover. Set the timer for about 4 hours. Serve hot!

Instant Pot Curried Lemon Coconut Chicken

Preparation Time: 10 minutes | **Cooking Time:** 25 minutes | **Servings:** 2 | **Calories:** 802

Ingredients: ½ cup coconut milk | ¼ cup of lemon juice | salt and black pepper, to taste
1.5 pounds chicken breasts or thighs | ½ teaspoon of lemon zest

Directions: Combine coconut milk, lemon zest, lemon juice, salt and black pepper in a bowl and mix well. Now pour this mixture into the bottom of the mini instant pot. Add the chicken thighs to the pot, stir ingredients well. Now, set the timer to 25 minutes at high pressures. Lock the lid and close the valve. After the cooking cycle complete, use the quick release and open the pot. Observe the chicken for doneness and then use the fork to shred the chicken inside the pot. Mix all the ingredients well. Serve with steamed rice and roasted vegetable of your choice. Enjoy.

Lemon Butter Pork Chops

Preparation Time: 5 minutes | **Cooking Time:** 25 minutes | **Servings:** 4 | **Calories**: 379

Ingredients: ½ teaspoon of sea salt | 1 teaspoon lemon-pepper seasoning | 1 teaspoon garlic powder
½ teaspoon dried thyme | 4 boneless pork chops | 5 tablespoons butter, divided | ¼ cup bone broth
2 tablespoons freshly squeezed lemon juice | 1 tablespoon minced garlic | ½ cup heavy (whipping) cream

Directions: In a small bowl, put and stir the lemon-pepper seasoning, salt, thyme, and garlic powder. Brush the spice mixture all around the pork chops. Get a skillet and heat it over medium-high heat then melt down 2 tablespoons of butter. Put the pork chops then cook for at least 5 minutes on each side until they are cooked through. Remove the chops from the pan. Reduce the heat to medium-low. Put the bone broth, garlic, lemon juice, and the remaining 3 tablespoons of butter. Put the pork chops and seethe for about 15 minutes, add the cream 1 tablespoon every few minutes, or up until the sauce turns thick. Remove from the heat and serve.

Fully Loaded Burger Bowls

Preparation Time: 15 minutes | **Cooking Time:** 30 minutes | **Servings:** 4 | **Calories:** 690

Ingredients: garlic powder (1 tsp) | extra lean beef (2lb) | butter (2 tablespoons)
Lawry's seasoned salt (2 ½ tsp) | ground black pepper (½ tsp) | sliced mushrooms (2 cups)
Worcestershire sauce (3 tsp) | shredded cheddar cheese (2 cups) | cooked bacon (10 slices)
BBQ sauce (for toppings) | diced chives(for toppings) | ranch (for toppings) | diced bacon (for toppings)

Directions: Mix up the beef, garlic powder, Worcestershire sauce, seasoned salt, and black pepper in a bowl. Line a baking sheet with a foil and neatly arrange four meat bowls on it. Use a clean can make the bowls. Get a small pan and shallow fry the mushrooms in butter. Add some pepper and salt for taste. Now divide into 4 parts. Now it's time to fill your meat bowls. Pour in a bit of cheese, diced bacon, mushrooms, and pour the rest of the cheese on top of all these. Leave to bake at 350°F loosely covered for about 30 minutes. Add your toppings: BBQ sauce, diced chives, ranch, and diced bacon.

Rosemary Roasted Pork with Cauliflower

Preparation Time: 10 minutes | **Cooking Time:** 20 minutes | **Servings:** 4 | **Calories:** 320

Ingredients: 1-½ pounds boneless pork tenderloin | 1 tablespoon coconut oil | 2 cups cauliflower florets
1 tablespoon fresh chopped rosemary | salt and pepper | 1 tablespoon olive oil

Directions: Rub the coconut oil into the pork, then season with the rosemary, salt, and pepper. Heat up the olive oil over medium to high heat in a large skillet. Add the pork on each side and cook until browned for 2 to 3 minutes. Sprinkle the cauliflower over the pork in the skillet. Reduce heat to low, then cover the skillet and cook until the pork is cooked through for 8 to 10 mins. Slice the pork with cauliflower and eat.

Keto Taco Skillet

Preparation Time: 10 minutes | **Cooking Time:** 5 minutes | **Servings:** 4 | **Calories:** 171

Ingredients: 1 cup textured vegetable protein | 1 packet taco seasoning mix | 2 tomatoes, diced
1 bell pepper, sliced into strips | 3 cups baby spinach | 2 tbsp. avocado oil

Directions: Stir together TVP and taco seasoning mix in a bowl. Pour in 2 cups of boiling water and leave for 10 minutes. Heat avocado oil in a skillet. Add seasoned TVP and stir for 2-3 minutes. Stir in baby spinach for another minute or until slightly wilted. Season to taste with salt and pepper as needed.

Chicken and Rice Congee

Preparation Time: 10 minutes | **Cooking Time:** 35 minutes | **Servings:** 1 | **Calories:** 493

Ingredients: 90 grams of rice, brown | 2 chicken drumsticks | ½ tablespoon ginger, sliced into strips
2 cups cold water | salt, to taste

Directions: First, rinse the rice under tap water by gently scrubbing the rice. Drain any milky water. Next step is to add ginger, rice, chicken drumsticks, and water to the instant pot. Do not add salt at this stage. Now close the lid of the pot and cook on high pressure for 30 minutes. Then, naturally release the steam. Open the lid carefully; check if the congee looks watery. Heat up the instant pot by pressing sauté button. Cook until desired thickness is obtained. Season it with salt and then use a fork to separate the meat from the bone. Remove the congee from the pot. Serve.

Whole Chicken

Preparation Time: 50 minutes | **Cooking Time:** 25 minutes | **Servings:** 6 | **Calories:** 236

Ingredients: 3 lb whole chicken | 1 whole yellow or red onion | 1 tbsp. coconut oil | 1 cup water

Directions: Pour a cup of water in your instant pot and lay the steam rack inside it. Heat coconut oil in a large skillet and add the chicken. Allow it to sear for about a minute on each side. Remove from heat. Arrange the chicken on the top of the steam rack of the instant pot. Secure the lid and set it to Chicken high pressure before adjusting the time. Assign 6 minutes for every pound of chicken. Add 2 minutes to the total cooking time. Allow steam to release for about 20 minutes. Serve while hot.

Chicken al Forno

Preparation Time: 18 minutes | **Cooking Time:** 30 minutes | **Servings:** 6 | **Calories:** 446

Ingredients: 2 lbs. chicken breast, cooked and diced | 1-1/2 cups vodka sauce jarred
1/2 cup parmesan cheese | 16 oz fresh mozzarella

Directions: At 400 degrees F, preheat the oven. Grease a casserole dish with cooking spray. Spread the cooked chicken in the casserole dish. Add vodka sauce, mozzarella, and parmesan cheese on top. Bake the saucy chicken casserole for 30 min. in the preheated oven. Serve warm.

Garlic Butter Chicken

Preparation Time: 40 minutes | **Cooking Time:** 25 minutes | **Servings:** 4 | **Calories:** 301

Ingredients: 4 pcs. chicken breast, chopped or whole | 10 cloves garlic, peeled and diced
1/4 cup turmeric ghee (or mix 1 tsp. turmeric with regular ghee) | salt, to taste

Directions: Place chicken breasts inside the instant pot. Add the turmeric ghee, garlic and salt. Set the instant pot on high pressure for about 35 minutes, following the instruction specifically on securing the valve and lid cover and in releasing pressure when cooking time is over. Shred chicken breasts while still in the pot and serve with additional ghee when needed.

Stuffed Chicken

Preparation Time: 10 minutes | **Cooking Time:** 25 minutes | **Servings:** 2 | **Calories:** 742

Ingredients: 4 chicken breasts, boneless, skinless butterfly cut | ½ cup frozen spinach | water
1/3 cup feta cheese, crumbled | 1/4 teaspoon of black pepper and salt | 2 tablespoon of coconut oil

Directions: Pound the chicken breast pieces into 1/4 inch thickness. Butterfly cut the chicken pieces and set aside for further use. Take a medium bowl and mix spinach, feta cheese, pepper, and salt. Divide this mixture evenly by spooning into the chicken breasts. Close the chicken breast and secure with a toothpick. Now, turn on the sauté mode of the instant pot and then add coconut oil to it. Sear the chicken breast in batches until golden brown. Then press the cancel button of the pot. Set aside the chicken and go for next steps. Now pour the water in the same pot and scrape the bottom to remove the seasoning. Now adjust the steamer rack in the pot and place chicken on top of the rack. Adjust the timer to 15 minutes at high pressure. Once the timer goes off, naturally release the steam. Serve the dish hot.

Shredded Chicken

Preparation Time: 30 minutes | **Cooking Time:** 25 minutes | **Servings:** 8 | **Calories:** 252

Ingredients: 4 lbs. chicken breasts | 1/2 tsp. black pepper | 1/2 cup chicken broth or water | 1 tsp. salt

Directions: Place ingredients in the instant pot. Cover the lid and secure the pressure valve to seal. Set the timer for 20 minutes cooking time at high temperature. Once the cooking time is complete, turn the valve venting to release pressure. When all pressure managed to escape, you can then open the lid. Place chicken on a platter or cutting board and shred to pieces using forks. Store chicken in an airtight container along with the liquid. This will keep the chicken constantly moist.

Roasted Lamb Rack

Preparation Time: 20 minutes | **Cooking Time:** 20 minutes | **Servings:** 4 | **Calories:** 736

Ingredients: 2 tablespoons fresh rosemary, chopped | 2 tablespoons garlic, minced | 1 teaspoon salt
¼ cup coconut flour | 1 tablespoon Dijon mustard | 4 tablespoons olive oil, divided
1 rack of lamb, trimmed (7 bone) | salt and freshly ground black pepper | ¼ teaspoon black pepper

Directions: Preheat the oven to 450°F. Add the rosemary, garlic, flour, mustard, ¼ teaspoon black pepper, 2 tablespoons of olive oil, and 1 teaspoon of salt in a large bowl. Mix well until well combined and set aside. On a flat work surface, season the lamb rack with salt and black pepper on both sides. In a skillet over high heat, heat the remaining olive oil until shimmering. Sear the lamb rack for 2 minutes per side. Remove from the heat and brush the rosemary mixture over the lamb rack. Wrap the lamb rack with aluminum foil and place it in a baking sheet. Cook in the heated oven for approximately 15 minutes until the internal temperature reads 145°F (63°C) on a meat thermometer. Take away from the oven and cool for 5 to 7 minutes before serving.

Pesto Chicken Casserole

Preparation Time: 10 minutes | **Cooking Time:** 30 minutes | **Servings:** 6 | **Calories**: 428

Ingredients: 1/2 cup heavy cream | 2 lb. cooked chicken breasts, cubed | 8 oz cream cheese softened
1/4 cup pesto | 8 oz mozzarella shredded

Directions: At 400 degrees F, preheat the oven. Grease a casserole dish with cooking spray. Mix pesto, cream cheese, and cream in a suitable mixing bowl. Toss in chicken and mix well to coat. Spread this chicken and cream mixture in the prepared baking dish. Drizzle shredded mozzarella on top then bake for 30 minutes. Serve warm.

Ranch Chicken Chili

Preparation Time: 10 minutes | **Cooking Time:** 15 minutes | **Servings:** 2 | **Calories**: 365

Ingredients: 8 ounces of white chili beans, not drained | 0.75 pounds of chicken breast, cubed
5 ounces of Rotel tomatoes and green chilies, not drained | ½ ounce of taco seasoning
½ ounce of ranch seasoning mix

Directions: Combine the white chili bean, Rotel, taco seasoning, and the ranch seasoning in a bowl. Add the chicken breasts to the bowl and mix well. Dump all the ingredients in an instant pot and then cook on high pressure for 15 minutes. Does a quick release steam, then serve.

Gooseberry Sauce

Preparation Time: 30 minutes | **Cooking Time:** 5 minutes | **Servings:** 4 | **Calories**: 35

Ingredients: 5 cups gooseberries, rinsed, topped and tailed | 5 garlic cloves, crushed
1 cup fresh dill, rinsed, stems removed | salt to taste

Directions: Combine gooseberries and dill in a blender and pulse until smooth. Add garlic and salt. Let stand for 30 minutes, covered.

Sesame Wings with Cauliflower

Preparation Time: 5 minutes | **Cooking Time:** 30 minutes | **Servings:** 4 | **Calories:** 400

Ingredients: 2-½ tablespoons soy sauce | 2 tablespoons sesame oil | 1-½ teaspoons balsamic vinegar
1 teaspoon minced garlic | 1 teaspoon grated ginger | salt | 1 pound chicken wing, the wings itself
2 cups cauliflower florets

Directions: In a freezer bag, mix the soy sauce, sesame oil, balsamic vinegar, garlic, ginger, and salt, then add the chicken wings. Coat flip, then chill for 2 to 3 hours. Preheat the oven to 400°F and line a foil-based baking sheet. Spread the wings along with the cauliflower onto the baking sheet. Bake for 35 minutes, then sprinkle on to serve with sesame seeds.

Beef and Broccoli Stir-Fry

Preparation Time: 20 minutes | **Cooking Time:** 15 minutes | **Servings:** 4 | **Calories:** 350

Ingredients: ¼ cup soy sauce | 1 tablespoon sesame oil | 1 teaspoon garlic chili paste
1 pound beef sirloin | 2 tablespoons almond flour | 2 tablespoons coconut oil
2 cups chopped broccoli florets | 1 tablespoon grated ginger | 3 cloves garlic, minced

Directions: In a small bowl, whisk the soy sauce, sesame oil, and chili paste together. In a plastic freezer bag, slice the beef and mix with the almond flour. Pour in the sauce and toss to coat for 20 minutes, then let rest. Heat up the oil over medium to high heat in a large skillet. In the pan, add the beef and sauce and cook until the beef is browned. Move the beef to the skillet sides, then add the broccoli, ginger, and garlic. Sauté until tender-crisp broccoli, then throw it all together and serve hot.

Chili-Garlic Edamame

Preparation Time: 5 minutes | **Cooking Time:** 10 minutes | **Servings:** 4 | **Calories:** 126

Ingredients: 300 grams edamame pods | 1 tbsp. olive oil | 3 cloves garlic, minced
½ tsp red chili flakes | pinch of salt

Directions: Steam edamame for 5 minutes. Heat olive oil in a pan. Sautee garlic and chili until aromatic. Add in steamed edamame and stir for a minute. Season with salt.

Parmesan-Crusted Halibut with Asparagus

Preparation Time: 10 minutes | **Cooking Time:** 15 minutes | **Servings:** 4 | **Calories**: 415

Ingredients: 2 tablespoons olive oil | ¼ cup butter, softened | salt and pepper | ¼ cup grated Parmesan
1 pound asparagus, trimmed | 2 tablespoons almond flour | 4 boneless halibut fillets | 1 tsp. garlic powder

Directions: Preheat the oven to 400°F and line a foil-based baking sheet. Throw the asparagus in olive oil and scatter over the baking sheet. In a blender, add the butter, Parmesan cheese, almond flour, garlic powder, salt and pepper, and mix until smooth. Place the fillets with the asparagus on the baking sheet, and spoon the Parmesan over the eggs. Bake for 10 to 12 mins, then broil until browned for 2 to 3 mins.

Hearty Beef and Bacon Casserole

Preparation Time: 25 minutes | **Cooking Time:** 30 minutes | **Servings:** 8 | **Calories**: 410

Ingredients: 8 slices uncooked bacon | 1 medium head cauliflower, chopped | 2 cloves garlic, minced
¼ cup canned coconut milk | 2 pounds ground beef (80% lean) | 8 ounces mushrooms, sliced
1 large yellow onion, chopped | salt and pepper

Directions: Preheat to 375°F on the oven. Cook the bacon in a skillet until it crispness, then drain and chop on paper towels. Bring to boil a pot of salted water, then add the cauliflower. Boil until tender for 6 to 8 minutes then drain and add the coconut milk to a food processor. Mix until smooth, then sprinkle with salt and pepper. Cook the beef until browned in a pan, then wash the fat away. Remove the mushrooms, onion, and garlic, then move to a baking platter. Place on top of the cauliflower mixture and bake for 30 minutes. Broil for 5 minutes on high heat, then sprinkle with bacon to serve.

Keto Vegan Chao Fan

Preparation Time: 10 minutes | **Cooking Time:** 5 minutes | **Servings:** 4 | **Calories:** 234

Ingredients: 1 cup textured vegetable protein, rehydrated | 300 g broccoli, riced in a food processor
2 tsp minced ginger | 1 shallot, minced | 4 cloves garlic, minced | ¼ cup chopped spring onions
2 tbsp. peanut oil | 2 tbsp. tamari

Directions: Heat peanut oil in a wok. Sautee garlic, ginger, and shallots until aromatic. Add hydrated TVP and stir for 2 minutes. Add broccoli and stir for another minute. Drizzle in tamari and stir until thoroughly mixed. Stir in chopped spring onions. Season with salt and pepper as needed.

Curried Cauliflower Mash

Preparation Time: 10 minutes | **Cooking Time:** 10 minutes | **Servings:** 4 | **Calories**: 110

Ingredients: 400 grams cauliflower | 1 liter vegetable stock | ½ cup coconut milk | 2 tbsp. curry powder
2 tbsp. tamari

Directions: Bring vegetable stock to a boil in a pot. Add cauliflower and simmer until fully tender and all the stock has evaporated. Stir in coconut milk, curry, and tamari. Puree with an immersion blender. Simmer for 1-2 minutes or until slightly thick. Season with salt as needed.

Homemade Vegan Sausages

Preparation Time: 10 minutes | **Cooking Time:** 15 minutes | **Servings:** 4 | **Calories:** 287

Ingredients: 1 cup vital wheat gluten | ¼ cup walnuts | ¼ cup minced onion | 1 tbsp. minced garlic
1 tsp cumin powder | 1 tsp smoked paprika | ½ tsp dried marjoram | ¼ tsp dried oregano | ¼ tsp salt
¼ tsp pepper | ¼ cup water | 2 tbsp. olive oil

Directions: Heat olive oil in a pan. Sautee onions and garlic until soft. Add onions and garlic together with the rest of the ingredients in a food processor. Pulse into a homogenous texture. Shape the mixture as desired. Wrap each sausage in cling film then with aluminum foil. Steam for 30 minutes. Sausages may be later heated up in a pan, in the oven, or on the grill.

Keto Tofu and Spinach Casserole

Preparation Time: 5 minutes | **Cooking Time:** 5 minutes | **Servings:** 4 | **Calories:** 222

Ingredients: 1 block firm tofu, drained, pressed, and cut into cubes | 1 bell pepper, diced
½ white onion, minced | 2 tbsp. olive oil | 100 grams fresh spinach | ½ cup diced tomatoes
1 tsp paprika | 1 tsp garlic powder | salt and pepper, to taste

Directions: Combine all ingredients in a pot. Simmer for 5 minutes

Low-Carb Jambalaya

Preparation Time: 10 minutes | **Cooking Time:** 10 minutes | **Servings:** 4 | **Calories**: 200

Ingredients: 200 grams seitan sausages, chopped | 400 grams cauliflower, riced | 1 cup vegetable broth
1 red bell pepper, diced | ¼ cup frozen peas | 3 cloves garlic, minced | ½ white onion, diced
3 tbsp. olive oil | 1 tbsp paprika | 1 tsp oregano | salt and pepper, to taste

Directions: Heat olive oil in a pot. Add seitan and sear until slightly brown. Add garlic, onions, and bell pepper. Sautee until aromatic. Add cauliflower, broth, oregano, paprika, salt, and pepper. Simmer for 5 minutes. Serve hot.

Eggplant Pomodoro

Preparation Time: 5 minutes | **Cooking Time:** 15 minutes | **Servings:** 4 | **Calories:** 101

Ingredients: 1 medium eggplant, diced | 1 cup diced tomatoes | ½ cup black olives, sliced
4 cloves garlic, minced | 2 tbsp. red wine vinegar | pinch of red pepper flakes | salt and pepper to taste
2 tbsp. olive oil | 4 cups shirataki pasta | fresh parsley for garnish

Directions: Heat olive oil in a pan. Sautee garlic and red pepper flakes until aromatic. Add eggplants, tomatoes, olives and red wine vinegar. Stir until eggplants are soft. Toss shirataki into the pan. Season with salt and pepper. Garnish with chopped fresh parsley for serving.

Vegetable Char Siu

Preparation Time: 5 minutes | **Cooking Time:** 15 minutes | **Servings:** 4 | **Calories:** 100

Ingredients: 100 grams raw jackfruit, deseeded and rinsed | 100 grams cucumbers, cut into thin strips
50 grams red bell pepper, cut into thin strips | 2 cloves garlic, minced | 1 shallot, minced
¼ cup Char Siu sauce | ¼ cup water | 2 tbsp. peanut oil

Directions: Heat peanut oil in a pan. Add jackfruit and stir until slightly brown. Add garlic and shallots and sauté until aromatic. Add water and Char Siu sauce. Simmer until jackfruit is tender. Shred jackfruit with forks. Toss in cucumbers and bell peppers.

Soy Chorizo

Preparation Time: 5 minutes | **Cooking Time:** 15 minutes | **Servings:** 6 | **Calories:** 249

Ingredients: 500 grams firm tofu, pressed and drained | ¼ cup soy sauce | ¼ cup red wine vinegar
¼ cup tomato paste | 1 tsp paprika | 1 tsp chili powder | 1 tsp garlic powder | ½ tsp onion powder
1 tsp cumin powder | ½ tsp black pepper | ½ tsp salt | ¼ cup olive oil

Directions: Crumble tofu in a bowl. Mix in all ingredients except for the olive oil. Heat olive oil in a non-stick pan. Add tofu mix and stir for 10-15 minutes. Serve in tacos, wraps, burritos, or rice bowls.

Vietnamese "Vermicelli" Salad

Preparation Time: 5 minutes | **Cooking Time:** 10 minutes | **Servings:** 4 | **Calories:** 249

Ingredients: 100 grams carrots, sliced into thin strips | 200 grams cucumbers, spiralized
2 tbsp. roasted peanuts, roughly chopped | ¼ cup fresh mint, chopped | ¼ cup fresh cilantro, chopped
1 tbsp. stevia | 2 tbsp. fresh lime juice | 1 tbsp. vegan fish sauce | 2 cloves garlic, minced
1 green chili, deseeded and minced | 2 tbsp. sesame oil

Directions: Whisk together sugar, lime juice, sesame oil, fish sauce, minced garlic, and chopped chili. Set aside. In a bowl, toss together cucumbers, carrots, cucumbers, peanuts, mint, cilantro, and prepared dressing. Serve chilled.

Kung Pao Tofu

Preparation Time: 5 minutes | **Cooking Time:** 10 minutes | **Servings:** 3 | **Calories:** 268

Ingredients: 250 grams firm tofu, cut into 1" cubes | ¼ cup vegetable oil, for frying
1 tsp minced ginger | 1 tsp minced garlic | 1 red bell pepper, cut into strips | 2 stalks green onions, sliced
1 tsp chili flakes | 2 tbsp. roasted peanuts | 1 tsp cornstarch | 1 tsp tomato paste | 1 tbsp. soy sauce
1 tbsp. hoisin sauce | 1 tsp erythritol | ½ cup water | 1 tsp sesame oil

Directions: Heat vegetable oil in a pan. Fry tofu until brown on all sides. Drain on paper towels. In a bowl, mix together water, cornstarch, tomato paste, hoisin sauce, soy sauce, and sugar. In a wok, heat 1 tablespoon of vegetable oil. Sautee ginger, garlic, green onions, chili flakes, and bell pepper until aromatic. Stir in the sauce mixture and simmer until thick. Toss in fried tofu and bring to a simmer. Take off the heat and drizzle in sesame oil.

Enoki Mushroom and Snow Pea Soba

Preparation Time: 5 minutes | **Cooking Time:** 5 minutes | **Servings:** 2 | **Calories**: 167

Ingredients: 75 grams snow peas | 100 grams shimeji mushrooms | 2 tsp minced ginger
¼ cup mirin | 3 tbsp. light soy sauce | 1 tsp erythritol | 1 tbsp. sesame oil | 1 tbsp. vegetable oil

Directions: Heat vegetable oil in a wok. Sautee ginger until aromatic. Add snow peas and stir fry for 1-2 minutes. Add shimeji mushrooms and stir for another minute. Add mirin, soy sauce, and erythritol. Turn off the heat and drizzle in sesame oil.

Grilled Cauliflower Steaks with Arugula Pesto

Preparation Time: 5 minutes | **Cooking Time:** 10 minutes | **Servings:** 3 | **Calories:** 283

Ingredients: 400 grams cauliflower, cut into 1" steaks | 2 tbsp. olive oil | ½tsp smoked paprika | ½ tsp garlic powder | ½ tsp onion powder | ¼ tsp salt | For the Pesto: 1 cup arugula leaves | ¼ cup pine nuts
2 tbsp. nutritional yeast | ¼ cup olive oil | 1 clove garlic, minced | salt and pepper, to taste

Directions: Combine all ingredients for the arugula pesto in a food processor. Pulse into a coarse paste. Marinate cauliflower steaks in olive oil, paprika, garlic powder, onion powder, and salt. Sear cauliflower steaks for 3 minutes per side on a hot grill. Serve hot with pesto on the side.

Vegan Potstickers

Preparation Time: 25 minutes | **Cooking Time:** 5 minutes | **Servings:** 8 | **Calories**: 118

Ingredients: 250 grams firm tofu, pressed and crumbled | ½ cup diced shiitake mushrooms
¼ cup finely chopped carrots | ¼ cup finely chopped spring onions | 1 tsp minced ginger
2 tbsp. soy sauce | 1 tbsp. sesame oil | 2 tbsp. peanut oil, plus more for pan-frying
1/2 tsp salt | ½ tsp pepper | 250 grams green cabbage

Directions: Heat peanut oil in a pan. Sautee minced ginger and spring onions until aromatic. Add tofu, mushrooms, and carrots. Sautee for 2-3 minutes. Take off the heat and season with soy sauce, sesame oil, salt, and pepper. Blanch cabbage leaves in boiling water to soften. Lay a piece cabbage leaf on your chopping board. Fill with about a tablespoon of the tofu mixture. Fold and secure with toothpicks. Repeat for remaining ingredients. Heat about 2 tbsp. of peanut oil in a pan. Arrange dumplings in and fry for 2 minutes over medium heat. Add about a quarter cup of water into the pan and cover. Steam over low heat until all water has evaporated.

Low-Carb Indian Pasta

Preparation Time: 5 minutes | **Cooking Time:** 5 minutes | **Servings:** 4 | **Calories:** 157

Ingredients: 400 grams shirataki pasta | 2 Roma tomatoes, diced | ¼ cup diced yellow onions
¼ cup green peas | 1 carrot, diced | ¼ cup sliced black olives | vinaigrette | 1/4 cup olive oil
2 cloves garlic, grated | ½ tsp red chili flakes | 1 tbsp. lemon juice | 1 tsp garam masala
2 tsp cumin powder | 1 tsp salt | ¼ tsp black pepper

Directions: Whisk together all ingredients for the vinaigrette in a large mixing bowl. Set aside. Bring a pot of water to a boil. Blanch shirataki for 1-2 minutes. Drain. Steam carrots and peas. Toss the shirataki, carrots, peas, olives, onions, and tomatoes with the vinaigrette.

Vegan Temaki Wraps

Preparation Time: 10 minutes | **Cooking Time:** 5 minutes | **Servings:** 4 | **Calories**: 125

Ingredients: 1 carrot, sliced into thin strips | 1 cucumber, sliced into thin strips | pinch of salt
2 red bell peppers, sliced into thin strips | 200 grams button mushrooms, sliced | 2 tbsp. sesame seeds
2 cups uncooked brown rice | 2 sheets nori, cut into squares | Dipping Sauce: 1 tsp gochujang
2 tbsp. sesame oil | 1 tbsp. lime juice | 2 tbsp. low-sodium soy sauce | 1 tsp erythritol

Directions: Whisk together all ingredients for the dressing in a bowl. Heat oil in a pan. Sautee mushrooms until brown, seasoning lightly with salt. When mushrooms are soft, toss in cucumber and peppers. Take off the heat and sprinkle in sesame seeds. Wrap in sheets of nori and serve with dipping sauce on the side.

Quorn Mince Keema

Preparation Time: 5 minutes | **Cooking Time:** 20 minutes | **Servings:** 4 | **Calories:** 125

Ingredients: 250 grams Quorn mince | 1/4 cup frozen peas | 2 tomatoes, diced | 4 cloves garlic, minced
1 tsp minced ginger | 1 shallot, minced | 2 pcs green chili, deseeded / chopped | 2 tbsp. tomato paste
2 tbsp. ghee | 1 tbsp. garam masala | ½ cup coconut milk | ½ cup water

Directions: Heat ghee in a pan. Add garlic, ginger, and green chili. Sautee until aromatic. Add shallots and tomatoes. Sautee until soft. Add tomato paste and garam masala. Roast briefly. Stir in Quorn mince. Add coconut milk and water. Cover and simmer for about 15 minutes. Add frozen peas and simmer for another 3 minutes. Season with salt and pepper as needed.

Salt and Pepper Scitan

Preparation Time: 5 minutes | **Cooking Time:** 5 minutes | **Servings:** 4 | **Calories**: 233

Ingredients: 400 grams seitan, cut into bit-sized pieces | 1 red bell pepper, diced | 1 green chili, sliced
2 cloves garlic, minced | 1 tsp minced ginger | ¼ cup sliced spring onions | 2 tbsp. vegetable oil
2 tsp sesame oil | vegetable oil for frying | ½ tsp Chinese five-spice powder | ½ tsp salt | ¼ tsp pepper

Directions: Put seitan pieces in a large mixing bowl. Season with salt, pepper, and five-spice. Heat about an inch deep of vegetable oil in a pan. Fry seitan over medium heat for about 5 minutes. Drain and set aside. Heat 1 tablespoon and 2 teaspoons sesame oil in a separate pan. Sauté bell peppers, green chili, garlic, ginger, and spring onions until aromatic. Toss in cooked seitan pieces. Season with salt as needed - Serve hot.

Mushrooms & Zucchini Starter

Preparation Time: 10 minutes | **Cooking Time:** 20 minutes | **Servings:** 4 | **Calories**: 78

Ingredients: 4 cups white mushrooms, rinsed, sliced | 3 cups zucchini, peeled, cut into sticks
1 onion, chopped | 1 tbsp. vegetable oil + 2 tbsp. | salt & pepper, to taste | 1 cup fresh parsley, chopped

Directions: Heat the vegetable oil in a saucepan and add mushrooms and zucchini. Cook, stirring, for 5 minutes over high heat. Add onion, salt, and pepper. Cook for 15 minutes. Top with parsley. Serve as a garnish or over keto toasts.

Vegan Bolognese

Preparation Time: 15 minutes | **Cooking Time:** 45 minutes | **Servings:** 6 | **Calories**: 124

Ingredients: 250 grams baby Bella mushrooms, minced | 250 grams riced cauliflower | ¼ cup olive oil
1 white onion, minced | 2 stalks celery, minced | ¼ cup minced carrots | 4/6 clove garlic, minced
1 tsp salt | ½ tsp black pepper | 1 cup dry red wine | 1/8 tsp nutmeg | 1 cup, plum tomatoes, crushed
300 grams zucchini, spiralized

Directions: Heat olive oil in a pot. Add onions and sauté until translucent. Add celery and garlic. Sauté until aromatic. Add mushrooms and cauliflower. Sauté briefly. Add oil remaining ingredients. Simmer for 40 minutes. Add in spiralized zucchini and toss for a minute.

Mushroom Goulash

Preparation Time: 15 minutes | **Cooking Time:** 20 minutes | **Servings:** 4 | **Calories**: 146

Ingredients: 5 cups white mushrooms, rinsed, boiled for 10 mins, chopped | 2 onions, chopped finely
2 garlic cloves, crushed | 3 tbsp. vegetable oil | 1 tbsp. ketchup | salt and pepper, to taste
1 tbsp. Keto friendly flour (almond/coconut)

Directions: Heat the vegetable oil in a saucepan and add mushrooms and onions. Cook, stirring, for 5-7 minutes. Add garlic and season with salt and pepper. Cook for 10 minutes. Add flour, ketchup, and some water covering ½ surface, and let stew for several minutes. Serve hot.

Brooklyn Salad

Preparation Time: 5 minutes | **Cooking Time:** 0 minutes | **Servings:** 2 | **Calories**: 131

Ingredients: 1 cup broccoli florets, blanched for 5 minutes in boiling water | 4 pickled cucumbers, sliced
3 cups white mushrooms, sliced or 1 200 g can mushrooms | 4 pickled ears corn, sliced
olive oil (1 tbsp. for frying + 2 tbsp. for the dressing)

Directions: If you are using fresh mushrooms, cook them in a pan with some olive oil until golden. Combine all ingredients in a salad bowl and dress with olive oil.

Cauliflower from the Oven

Preparation Time: 5 minutes | **Cooking Time:** 40 minutes | **Servings:** 2 | **Calories**: 221

Ingredients: 1 head cauliflower, leaves removed | 1 tbsp. olive oil | salt and paprika, to taste
For the dressing: 1-2 tbsp. mustard seeds | 2 tbsp. mustard oil | ½ lemon, juiced
small bunch of parsley, chopped

Directions: Place the whole cauliflower head onto a baking dish. Season with salt and paprika. Sprinkle with some olive oil. Bake for 40 minutes at 350°F. Or for 1 hour for softer option. Prepare the dressing by mixing together lemon juice, mustard seeds, and mustard oil. Add the chopped parsley and let stand until the cauliflower is done baking. Toss the cauliflower with the dressing and quarter the head. Serve.

Cauliflower Couscous

Preparation Time: 10 minutes | **Cooking Time:** 10 minutes | **Servings:** 3 | **Calories**: 145

Ingredients: ½ head cauliflower, pulsed in food processor | 3-4 kale leaves, de-stemmed, chopped
3 oz. sun dried tomatoes, drained | ¼ cup olives | 1 garlic clove, crushed | 3 tbsp. olive oil
1 tbsp. lemon juice | ½ tsp cumin, ground | 1 tsp oregano, dried | salt and pepper to taste
tofu, crumbled for topping (about 1 tbsp. per plate) | basil, chopped for topping (about 1 tbsp. per plate)

Directions: In a preheated pan with olive oil, add garlic and kale. Cook for 2 minutes, stirring. Add cauliflower and season with salt. Add the remaining ingredients and spices and cook for 2-3 minutes, stirring. Top with tofu and basil.

Fried Eggplant

Preparation Time: 5 minutes | **Cooking Time:** 25 minutes | **Servings:** 4 | **Calories**: 294

Ingredients: 2 eggplants, rinsed, cut in circles | 3/4 garlic cloves, crushed | salt and pepper, to taste
½ cup vegetable oil

Directions: Season eggplant circles with salt and pepper. In a preheated pan with 2 tbsp. oil, add eggplant circles in one layer. Fry for 1-2 minutes on each side until golden. Transfer to a plate and sprinkle with crushed garlic. Repeat with the remaining eggplants, adding more oil to a pan between batches.

Eggplant & Tomatoes Salad

Preparation Time: 25 minutes | **Cooking Time:** 10 minutes | **Servings:** 4 | **Calories**: 113

Ingredients: 2 eggplants, cut in circles | 2 red bell peppers, deseeded, cut in rings | pepper, to taste
3 tomatoes, cut in semi circles | 1 onion, cut in semi circles | 5/10 sprigs fresh parsley, chopped
olive oil (for frying the eggplants + salad dressing) | salt, to taste

Directions: Season eggplant circles with salt and let stand in a bowl while preparing the other ingredients. After all other vegetables are chopped, drain the eggplants and place in a preheated pan with oil. Fry on both sides until golden, 1-2 minutes per side. Combine the vegetables in a salad bowl, add chopped parsley, and dress with oil. Serve.

Eggplant Pate

Preparation Time: 15 minutes | **Cooking Time:** 1 hour | **Servings:** 4 | **Calories**: 165

Ingredients: 3-4 eggplants, peeled, cubed | 4 bell peppers, cubed | 3 tomatoes, cubed | 2 onions, cubed
2/3 garlic cloves, minced | a bunch of parsley, chopped | 3 tbsp. olive oil | salt and pepper, to taste

Directions: Season eggplants with salt and let stand in a bowl while preparing other vegetables. Combine all ingredients in a Crockpot. Season with salt and pepper. Add oil and stir. Select the "Stew" mode and cook for 1 hour, covered. After an hour, puree the cooked vegetables with a blender. Remove the excess liquid if there is any.

Pickled Eggplant

Preparation Time: 24 hours | **Cooking Time:** 25 minutes | **Servings:** 4 | **Calories**: 158

Ingredients: 2 eggplants, peeled, sliced | 1 large onion | 2/3 garlic cloves, crushed | 1 tsp salt
1 tsp Keto friendly sweetener | 2 tbsp. vegetable oil + more for baking | 1 tbsp. vinegar
3 sprigs parsley, chopped

Directions: Arrange the eggplants on a baking dish in one layer and oil them. Bake in the oven at 350°F for 25 minutes. In a bowl, combine onions, garlic, parsley, salt, sweetener, oil, and vinegar. Chop the baked eggplant and drop into the brine. Transfer to a jar, cover with lid, and refrigerate for 24 hours.

Eggplant Rolls

Preparation Time: overnight | **Cooking Time:** 35 minutes | **Servings:** 4 | **Calories:** 219

Ingredients: 3 eggplants, sliced lengthwise | 5 bell peppers | 3 tbsp. soy sauce | 2 tbsp. vegetable oil
2/3 garlic cloves, minced | 5 sprigs fresh parsley, minced | 5 sprigs fresh dill, minced | salt & pepper

Directions: Combine soy sauce with vegetable oil in a bowl. Lay out the eggplant slices on a baking tray and brush with the sauce. Place the whole peppers on a tray (take another tray if there isn't enough place left). Bake in the oven for 20 min at 350°F. Take the eggplants out and place on food wrap. Put the peppers back in the oven for 15 minutes more. Season the eggplant slices with salt, pepper, and garlic. Sprinkle with dill and parsley. Deseed the peppers and cut into strips. Place the pepper strips on eggplant and roll. Refrigerate the rolls overnight. Remove the wrap and cut up the rolls.

Korean Cucumber Salad

Preparation Time: 10 minutes | **Cooking Time:** 5 minutes | **Servings:** 4 | **Calories:** 112

Ingredients: 4 cucumbers, sliced | 1 onion, chopped in semi circles | 2/3 garlic cloves, crushed
2/3 sprigs spring onions, finely chopped | 3 tsp sesame seeds, toasted | 2 tsp red pepper flakes
3 tbsp. soy sauce | 3 tsp sesame oil | 2 tsp keto friendly sweetener you are using

Directions: Combine all ingredients. Stir well and serve.

Beets & Seeds Salad

Preparation Time: 15 minutes | **Cooking Time:** 1 minute | **Servings:** 2 | **Calories**: 251

Ingredients: 1 beet, boiled, grated | 1 tbsp. toasted sunflower seeds | 1 tbsp. toasted walnuts, chopped
3 prunes, chopped | 1 tbsp. flaxseeds
For the dressing: 1 tsp Tahini | 1 garlic clove, minced | 2 tbsp. olive oil | salt, to taste

Directions: Prepare the dressing by combining all dressing ingredients. Combine all salad ingredients in a bowl and mix well. Dress the salad and serve.

Stuffed Peppers

Preparation Time: 15 minutes | **Cooking Time:** 30 minutes | **Servings:** 2 | **Calories**: 199

Ingredients: 1 large bell pepper, halved, deseeded | 1 medium eggplant, rinsed, cubed | 2 sprigs basil
1 tomato, peeled, cubed | 1 onion, chopped | 1 carrot, grated | 1 garlic clove, crushed | 2 tbsp. olive oil
salt and pepper, to taste

Directions: Add half the onion to a preheated pan with olive oil. Season with salt and pepper. Add eggplant and fry until golden. In a stewpot sauté the remaining onion with carrots. Season with salt and pepper. Add tomatoes and garlic to the carrots. Cook for 10 minutes, covered, over medium heat. Fill the pepper halves with eggplant and onions. Place the stuffed peppers into the stewpot. Stew for 15 minutes until the pepper is soft.

Nori Salad Dressing

Preparation Time: 5 minutes | **Cooking Time:** 0 minutes | **Servings:** 6 | **Calories**: 18

Ingredients: 2 toasted nori sheets | 2 tbsp. sesame oil | ¾ cup rice wine vinegar | 1 tbsp. orange zest
½ tsp sea salt

Directions: Break the toasted nori into small pieces. Add all ingredients in a blender and pulse on high. Serve the nori dressing over roasted vegetables. Keep refrigerated.

Onion Fritters

Preparation Time: 5 minutes | **Cooking Time:** 20 minutes | **Servings:** 4 | **Calories**: 186

Ingredients: 3 large onions, peeled | 4 leeks | 6 tbsp. Keto friendly flour (almond/coconut)
¼ tsp fish seasoning | salt and pepper, to taste

Directions: Chop the onions and leeks and add to the food processor. Pulse until smooth. To the pureed onions add flour and seasonings. In a preheated pan with oil, spoon out the fritters and fry until golden on each side over high heat.

Walnut & Garlic Summer Squash

Preparation Time: 15 minutes | **Cooking Time:** 10 minutes | **Servings:** 4 | **Calories**: 239

Ingredients: 2 lbs. green summer squash, rinsed, cubed | ½ cup walnuts, crushed
3 garlic cloves, crushed | 10 sprigs parsley, minced | 2 tbsp. + 1 tbsp. vegetable oil

Directions: In a preheated pan with oil, add cubed squash and cook over high heat until soft. In a bowl, combine minced parsley, garlic, walnuts and 1 tbsp. oil. Mix well. Add the walnut mixture to the pan and mix well. Turn the heat off. Serve warm or cooled to your liking.

Fried Tofu

Preparation Time: 5 minutes | **Cooking Time:** 10 minutes | **Servings:** 4 | **Calories**: 76

Ingredients: 1 lb. tofu, cubed | 2 tomatoes, chopped | 1 chili pepper, chopped | ½ cup onion, chopped
2 garlic cloves, minced | 1 tbsp. olive oil | 1 tbsp. lime juice | 1 tsp ground chili | ½ tsp cumin
½ tsp oregano | salt, to taste

Directions: In a preheated pan with olive oil pan add fresh chili pepper, onions, garlic and fry stirring for 4 minutes. Season with ground chili, cumin, oregano, and salt. Cook, stirring, 30 seconds. Add tofu to the pan and lower the heat. Cook, stirring, for 5 minutes. Right before serving, top with lime juice. Serve with fresh tomatoes.

Keto Croque Monsieur

Preparation Time: 5 minutes | **Cooking Time:** 7 minutes | **Servings:** 2 | **Calories**: 479

Ingredients: 2 eggs | 25 g of grated cheese | 25 g of ham (1 large slice) | 40 ml of cream
40 ml of mascarpone | 30 g of butter | pepper and salt | basil leaves (optional), to garnish

Directions: Carefully crack eggs in a neat bowl, add some salt and pepper. Add the cream, mascarpone and grated cheese and stir together. Melt the butter over a medium heat. The butter must not turn brown. Once the butter has melted, set the heat to low. Add half of the omelette mixture to the frying pan and then immediately place the slice of ham on it. Now pour the rest of the omelette mixture over the ham and then immediately put a lid on it. Allow it to fry for 2-3 minutes over a low heat until the top is slightly firmer. Slide the omelette onto the lid to turn the omelette. Then put the omelette back in the frying pan to fry for another 1-2 minutes on the other side (still on low heat), then put the lid back on the pan. Don't let the omelette cook for too long! It does not matter if it is still liquid. Garnish with a few basil leaves if necessary.

Basil Stuffed Chicken

Preparation Time: 14 minutes | **Cooking Time:** 45 minutes | **Servings**: 2 | **Calories**: 362

Ingredients: 2 chicken breasts, bone-in, skin-on | 2 tablespoons cream cheese | black pepper, to taste 2 tablespoons mozzarella cheese, shredded | ¼ teaspoon garlic paste | 3 fresh basil leaves, chopped

Directions: At 375 degrees F, preheat your oven. Mix cream cheese with garlic paste, shredded cheese, black pepper, and basil in a bowl. Gently cut each of the chicken breast's skin from one side and stuff the cream cheese mixture inside. Place the prepared chicken in the baking sheet and bake them for 45 minutes in the preheated oven. Serve warm.

Coconut Leek Soup

Preparation Time: 5 minutes | **Cooking Time:** 30 minutes | **Servings:** 4 | **Calories**: 142

Ingredients: 1 leek, circled | 1 carrot, sliced | 3 celery stalks, sliced | ½ lemon, juiced | 2 cups water 1-½ cups coconut milk | 1 tsp curry | 3 tbsp. grated ginger root | ½ tsp salt | 2 tbsp. olive oil

Directions: Add the leeks, carrots, and celery to a pot with olive oil and some water. Let stew until the vegetables are soft. Add 1 ½ cup water and 1 ½ cup coconut milk and bring to boil. Cook for 2 minutes on low. Add lemon juice, ginger, curry, and salt and cook on low for 2 minutes.

Citric Cauliflower Rice

Preparation Time: 10 minutes | **Cooking Time:** 15 minutes | **Servings:** 4 | **Calories**: 200

Ingredients: 1 tablespoon ghee, melted | juice of 2 limes | a pinch of salt and black pepper 1 cup cauliflower rice | 1 and ½ cup veggie stock | 1 tablespoon cilantro, chopped

Directions: Heat up a pan with the ghee over medium-high heat, add the cauliflower rice, stir and cook for 5 minutes. Add lime juice, salt, pepper and stock, stir, bring to a simmer and cook for 10 minutes. Add cilantro, toss, divide between plates and serve as a side dish.

Taco Casserole

Preparation Time: 10 minutes | **Cooking Time:** 20 minutes | **Servings:** 8 | **Calories:** 367

Ingredients: ground turkey or beef (1.5 to 2 lb.) | taco seasoning (2 tbsp.) | cottage cheese (16 oz.) shredded cheddar cheese (8 oz.) | salsa (1 cup)

Directions: Heat the oven to reach 400° Fahrenheit. Combine the taco seasoning and ground meat in a casserole dish. Bake it for 20 minutes. Combine the salsa and both kinds of cheese. Set aside for now. Carefully transfer the casserole dish from the oven. Drain away the cooking juices from the meat. Break the meat into small pieces and mash with a potato masher or fork. Sprinkle with cheese. Bake in the oven for 15 to 20 more minutes until the top is browned.

Risotto with Mushrooms

Preparation Time: 15 minutes | **Cooking Time:** 25 minutes | **Servings:** 2 | **Calories:** 206

Ingredients: 2 tbsp olive oil | 2 minced garlic cloves | 1 small onion, finely diced | 1 tsp salt ½ tsp ground white pepper | 200 g chopped mushrooms | ¼ cup chopped oregano leaves 255 g "rice" of cauliflower | ¼ cup vegetable broth | 2 tbsp butter | ⅓ cup grated Parmesan

Directions: Sauté oil, garlic, onions, salt, and pepper, and sauté for 5-7 minutes until the onions become transparent. Add mushrooms and oregano, and cook for 5 minutes. Add cauliflower rice and vegetable broth, then reduce heat to medium. Cook the risotto, frequently stirring, for 10-15 minutes, until the cauliflower is soft. Remove from heat, and mix with butter and parmesan. Try and add more seasoning if you want.

Creamy Chicken Salad

Preparation Time: 10 minutes | **Cooking Time:** 30 minutes | **Servings:** 4 | **Calories:** 299.5

Ingredients: 1 lb. chicken breast | 2 avocado | 2 garlic cloves | 3 tsp minced lime juice | .33 cup onion
1 minced jalapeno pepper | minced salt | 1 tsp dash cilantro | pepper | dash

Directions: You will want to start this recipe off my prepping the stove to 400°F. As this warms up, get out your cooking sheet and line it with paper or foil. Next, it is time to get out the chicken. Go ahead and layer the chicken breast up with some olive oil before seasoning to your liking. When the chicken is all set, you will want to line them along the surface of your cooking sheet and pop it into the oven for about twenty minutes. By the end of twenty minutes, the chicken should be cooked through and can be taken out of the oven for chilling. Once cool enough to handle, you will want to either dice or shred your chicken, dependent upon how you like your chicken salad. Now that your chicken is all cooked, it is time to assemble your salad! You can begin this process by adding everything into a bowl and mashing down the avocado. Once your ingredients are mended to your liking, sprinkle some salt over the top and serve immediately.

Keto Wraps with Cream Cheese and Salmon

Preparation Time: 5 minutes | **Cooking Time:** 10 minutes | **Servings:** 2 | **Calories**: 237

Ingredients: 80 g of cream cheese | 1 tablespoon of dill or other fresh herbs | 30 g of smoked salmon
1 egg | 15 g of butter | pinch of cayenne pepper | pepper and salt

Directions: Beat the egg well in a bowl. With 1 egg, you can make two thin wraps in a small frying pan. Melt the butter over a medium heat in a small frying pan. Once the butter has melted, add half of the beaten egg to the pan. Move the pan back and forth so that the entire bottom is covered with a very thin layer of egg. Turn down the heat! Carefully loosen the egg on the edges with a silicone spatula and turn the wafer-thin omelette as soon as the egg is no longer dripping (about 45 seconds to 1 minute). You can do this by sliding it into a lid or plate and then sliding it back into the pan. Let the other side be cooked for about 30 seconds and then remove from the pan. The omelette must be nice and light yellow. Repeat for the rest of the beaten egg. Once the omelettes are ready, let them cool on a cutting board or plate and make the filling. Cut or cut the dill into small pieces and put in a bowl. Add the cream cheese and the salmon, cut into small pieces. Mix together. Add a tiny bit of cayenne pepper and mix well. Taste immediately and then season with salt and pepper. Spread a layer on the wrap and roll it up. Cut the wrap in half and keep in the fridge until you are ready to eat it.

Meat-Free Zoodles Stroganoff

Preparation Time: 20 minutes | **Cooking Time:** 12 minutes | **Servings:** 5 | **Calories**: 77

Ingredients: For Mushroom Sauce: 1-½ tbsp. butter | 1 large garlic clove, minced | ¼ cup cream
1-¼ c. fresh button mushrooms, sliced | ¼ c. homemade vegetable broth | salt & ground black pepper
For Zucchini Noodles: 3 large zucchinis, spiralized with blade C | ¼ c. fresh parsley leaves, chopped

Directions: For mushroom sauce: In a large skillet, melt the butter over medium heat and sauté the garlic for about 1 minute. Stir in the mushrooms and cook for about 6-8 minutes. Stir in the broth and cook for about 2 minutes, stirring continuously. Stir in the cream, salt and black pepper and cook for about 1 minute. Meanwhile, for the zucchini noodles: in a large pan of the boiling water, add the zucchini noodles and cook for about 2-3 minutes. With a slotted spoon, transfer the zucchini noodles into a colander and immediately rinse under cold running water. Drain the zucchini noodles well and transfer onto a large paper towel-lined plate to drain. Divide the zucchini noodles onto serving plates evenly. Remove the mushroom sauce from the heat and place over zucchini noodles evenly. Serve immediately with the garnishing of parsley.

Slow Cooker Chili

Preparation Time: 15 minutes | **Cooking Time:** 6 hours & 15 minutes | **Servings:** 6 | **Calories:** 137

Ingredients: 2-½ lbs ground beef | 1 red onion, diced | 5 cloves garlic, minced | 1-½ c celery, diced 6 ounces can tomato paste | 14.5 oz can diced tomatoes with green chilies | 14.5 oz can stewed tomatoes 4 tsp chili powder | 2 tsp ground cumin | 2 tsp salt | 1 tsp garlic powder | 1 tsp onion powder 3 tsp cayenne pepper | 1 tsp red pepper flakes

Directions: Cook ground beef in a large skillet. Add onion, garlic, and celery and cook until ground beef browned. Drain the fat from the beef . Place beef and vegetable mixture into the slow cooker set on a low setting. Add tomatoes and seasonings then stir to mix. Place the lid on the slow cooker and cook on low for 6 hours. Serve with cheese on top if desired. Adjust the red pepper to taste.

Indian Chicken Curry

Preparation Time: 20 minutes | **Cooking Time:** 40 minutes | **Servings:** 6 | **Calories:** 110

Ingredients: 3 tablespoons of olive oil, divided | 6 boneless, skinless chicken thighs 2 tablespoons of fresh garlic | 1 tablespoon of fresh ginger | 1 tablespoon of hot curry powder (here) ¾ cup of water | ¼ cup of coconut milk | 1 small sweet onion | 2 tablespoons of fresh cilantro

Directions: Place 2 tablespoons of oil over medium to high place in a large skillet. Add the chicken and roast for about 10 minutes until the thighs are browned all over. Remove the chicken on a plate with tongs and set aside. In the skillet, add the remaining 1 tablespoon of oil and sauté the onion, garlic and ginger for about 3 minutes or until softened. Remove the curry powder, water and milk from the coconut. Go back to the skillet with the chicken and bring the liquid to a boil. Reduce heat to low, cover the skillet and cook for 26 minutes or until the chicken is tender and the sauce is thick. Serve with cilantro on hand.

Weekend Dinner Stew

Preparation Time: 15 minutes | **Cooking Time:** 55 minutes | **Servings:** 6 | **Calories:** 293

Ingredients: 1-½ lb. grass-fed beef stew meat, trimmed and cubed into 1-inch size | 1 tbsp. paprika salt and freshly ground black pepper, to taste | 1 tbsp. olive oil | 1 cup homemade tomato puree 4 cups homemade beef broth | 2 cup zucchini, chopped | 2 celery ribs, sliced | 1 tsp. dried rosemary ½ cup carrots, peeled and sliced | 2 garlic cloves, minced | ½ tbsp. dried thyme | 1 tsp. dried parsley 1 tsp. onion powder | 1 tsp. garlic powder

Directions: In a large bowl, add the beef cubes, salt and black pepper and toss to coat well. In a large pan, heat the oil over medium-high heat and cook the beef cubes for about 4-5 minutes or until browned. Add the remaining ingredients and stir to combine. Increase the heat to high and bring to a boil. Reduce the heat to low and simmer, covered for about 40-50 minutes. Stir in the salt and black pepper and remove from the heat. Serve hot.

Persian Chicken

Preparation Time: 10 minutes | **Cooking Time:** 20 minutes | **Servings:** 6 | **Calories**: 303.8

Ingredients: ½ small sweet onion | ¼ cup freshly squeezed lemon juice | 1 tablespoon dried oregano 1/2 tbsp of sweet paprika | ½ tbsp of ground cumin | 6 boneless, skinless chicken thighs | ½ cup olive oil

Directions: Put the vegetables in a blender. Mix it well. Put the olive while the motor is running. In a sealable bag for the freezer, place the chicken thighs and put the mixture in the sealable bag. Refrigerate it for 2 hours, while turning it two times. Remove the marinade thighs and discard the additional marinade. Preheat to medium the barbecue. Grill the chicken, turning once or until the internal

Perfect Pan-Seared Scallops

Preparation Time: 10 minutes | **Cooking Time:** 4 minutes | **Servings:** 4 | **Calories:** 181

Ingredients: 1 lb scallops, rinse and pat dry | 1 tbsp olive oil | 2 tbsp butter | pepper | salt

Directions: Season scallops with pepper and salt. Heat butter and oil in a pan over medium heat. Add scallops and sear for 2 minutes then turn to other side and cook for 2 minutes more. Serve.

Low Carb Green Bean Casserole

Preparation Time: 15 minutes | **Cooking Time:** 60 minutes | **Servings:** 4 | **Calories:** 244

Ingredients: 2 tbsp butter | 1 small chopped onion | 2 minced garlic cloves | ½ cup chicken stock
226.8 g chopped mushrooms | ½ tsp salt | ½ tsp ground pepper | ½ cup of fat cream
½ tsp xanthan gum | 453.59 g green beans (with cut ends) | 56.7 g crushed cracklings

Directions: Preheat the oven to 190 degrees. Add oil, onion, and garlic to a non-stick pan over high heat. Fry until onion is transparent. Add mushrooms, salt, and pepper. Cook for 7 minutes until the mushrooms are tender. Add chicken stock and cream, and bring to a boil. Sprinkle with xanthan gum, mix and cook for 5 minutes. Add the string beans to the creamy mixture and pour it into the baking dish. Cover with foil and bake for 20 minutes. Remove the foil, sprinkle with greaves and bake for another 10-15 minutes.

Eye-Catching Veggies

Preparation Time: 51 minutes | **Cooking Time:** 20 minutes | **Servings:** 4 | **Calories**: 160

Ingredients: 6 scallions, sliced | 1 lb. fresh white mushrooms, sliced | 1 cup tomatoes, crushed
salt and freshly ground black pepper, to taste | 2 tbsp. feta cheese, crumbled | ¼ cup butter

Directions: In a large pan, melt the butter over medium-low heat and sauté the scallion for about 2 minutes. Add the mushrooms and sauté for about 5-7 minutes. Stir in the tomatoes and cook for about 8-10 minutes, stirring occasionally. Stir in the salt and black pepper and remove from the heat. Serve with the topping of feta.

Flavorful Shrimp Creole

Preparation Time: 10 minutes | **Cooking Time:** 1 hour 30 minutes | **Servings:** 8 | **Calories**: 208

Ingredients: 2 lbs shrimp, peeled | 3/4 cup green onions, chopped | 1 tsp garlic, minced | pepper
2-1/2 cups water | 1 tbsp hot sauce | 8 oz can tomato sauce, sugar-free | 8 oz can tomato paste
1/2 cup bell pepper, chopped | 3/4 cup celery, chopped | 1 cup onion, chopped | 2 tbsp olive oil | salt

Directions: Heat oil in a saucepan over medium heat. Add celery, onion, bell pepper, pepper, and salt and saute until onion is softened. Add tomato paste and cook for 5 minutes. Add hot sauce, tomato sauce, and water and cook for 1 hour. Add garlic and shrimp and cook for 15 minutes. Add green onions and cook for 2 minutes more. Serve and enjoy.

Creamy Scallops

Preparation Time: 10 minutes | **Cooking Time:** 10 minutes | **Servings:** 4 | **Calories:** 202

Ingredients: 1 lb scallops, rinse and pat dry | 1 tsp fresh parsley, chopped | 1/8 tsp cayenne pepper
2 tbsp white wine | 1/4 cup water | 3 tbsp heavy cream | 1 tsp garlic, minced | 1 tbsp butter, melted
1 tbsp olive oil | pepper | salt

Directions: Season scallops with pepper and salt. Heat butter and oil in a pan over medium heat. Add scallops and sear until browned from both the sides. Transfer scallops on a plate. Add garlic in the same pan and saute for 30 seconds. Add water, heavy cream, wine, cayenne pepper, and salt. Stir well and cook until sauce thickens. Return scallops to pan and stir well. Garnish with parsley and serve.

Mustard Glazed Salmon

Preparation Time: 10 minutes | **Cooking Time:** 20 minutes | **Servings:** 1 | **Calories**: 240

Ingredients: 1 big salmon fillet | black pepper and salt, to taste | 2 tablespoons mustard
1 tablespoon coconut oil | 1 tablespoon maple extract

Directions: Mix maple extract with mustard in a bowl. Massage salmon with salt and pepper and half of the mustard mix. Heat-up a pan to high heat, place salmon flesh side down and cook for 5 minutes. Rub salmon with the rest of the mixture, transfer to a baking dish, place in the oven at 425 degrees F and bake for 15 minutes. Serve with a tasty side salad. Enjoy!

Skillet Chicken with White Wine Sauce

Preparation Time: 5 minutes | **Cooking Time:** 30 minutes | **Servings:** 4 | **Calories**: 276

Ingredients: 4 boneless chicken thighs | 1 tsp. garlic powder | 1 tsp. dried thyme | 1 tbsp. olive oil
1 tbsp. butter | 1 yellow onion diced | 3 garlic cloves minced | 1 cup dry white wine | ½ cup heavy cream
fresh chopped parsley | salt and pepper

Directions: Heat your oil in a skillet. Season your chicken, add it to the skillet, and then cook it about 5-7 minutes. Flip the chicken and cook until looking golden brown. Remove the chicken to a plate. Add butter to the skillet. Then add onions and cook them until softened. Stir in garlic, salt and pepper, add the wine and cook for 4-5 minutes. Stir in the thyme and the heavy cream. Place the breasts back to the skillet and leave to simmer for 2-3 minutes. Top them with the parsley.

Stir Fry Kimchi and Pork Belly

Preparation Time: 10 minutes | **Cooking Time:** 18 minutes | **Servings:** 3 | **Calories:** 790

Ingredients: 300 g pork belly | 1 lb. kimchi | 1 tbsp. soy sauce | 1 tbsp. rice wine | 1 tbsp. sesame seeds
1 stalk green onion

Directions: Slice the pork as thin as possible and marinate it in soy sauce and rice wine for 8-10 minutes. Heat a pan. When very hot, add the pork belly and stir-fry until brown. Add the kimchi to the pan and stir-fry for 2 minutes to let the flavors completely mix. Turn off heat and slice the green onion. Top with sesame seeds.

Lemon Butter Sauce with Fish

Preparation Time: 10 minutes | **Cooking Time:** 10 minutes | **Servings:** 2 | **Calories:** 371

Ingredients: 150 g thin white fish fillets | 4 tbsps. butter | 2 tbsps. white flour | 2 tbsps. olive oil
1 tbsp. fresh lemon juice | salt and pepper | chopped parsley

Directions: Place the butter in a small skillet over medium heat. Melt it and leave it, just stirring it casually. After 3 mins, pour into a small bowl. Add lemon juice and season it, and set it aside. Dry the fish with paper towels, season it to taste, and sprinkle with flour. Heat oil in a skillet over high heat: when shimmering, add fish & cook around 2-3 mins. Remove to a plate & serve with sauce. Top with parsley.

Ribeye Steak with Shitake Mushrooms

Preparation Time: 15 minutes | **Cooking Time:** 10 minutes | **Servings:** 1 | **Calories**: 478

Ingredients: 6 ounces ribeye steak | 2 tbsp butter | 1 tsp olive oil | ½ cup shitake mushrooms, sliced
salt and black pepper, to taste

Directions: On a pan, heat the olive oil on medium heat. Rub the steak with salt and black pepper and cook about 4 minutes per side; set aside. Melt the butter in the pan and cook the shitakes for 4 minutes. Pour the butter and mushrooms over the steak to serve.

Chicken Tomato Bake

Preparation Time: 10 minutes | **Cooking Time:** 15 minutes | **Servings:** 4 | **Calories**: 242

Ingredients: 4 tablespoons pesto | 4 chicken breasts | 1 tablespoon olive oil | ½ lb. cherry tomatoes

Directions: At 450 degrees F, preheat your oven. Grease a roasting tray with olive oil. Place the chicken breasts in the roasting tray. Spread pesto on top and drizzle olive oil on top. Place the cherry tomatoes around the chicken. Bake the tomato-chicken for 15 minutes in the preheated oven. Serve warm.

Bacon Bleu Cheese Filled Eggs

Preparation Time: 10 minutes | **Cooking Time:** 90-120 minutes | **Servings:** 3 | **Calories**: 217

Ingredients: 8 eggs | ¼ cup crumbled Bleu cheese | 3 slices of cooked bacon | ¼ cup sour cream
1/3 cup mayo | ¼ tsp. pepper and dill | ½ tsp. salt | 1 tbsp. mustard | parsley

Directions: Hard boil your eggs and then cut them half. Place the yolks in a bowl. With a fork, mash the yolks, add the sour cream, mayo, Bleu cheese, mustard, and the seasoning and mix until creamy enough for your taste. Slice up the bacon to small pieces. Stir in the rest of the ingredients: and fill up the eggs.

Mexican Pork Stew

Preparation Time: 15 minutes | **Cooking Time:** 2 hours 10 minutes | **Servings:** 1 | **Calories**: 288

Ingredients: 3 tbsp. unsalted butter | 2-½ lb. boneless pork ribs, cut into ¾-inch cubes
1 large yellow onion, chopped | 4 garlic cloves, crushed | 1-½ cup homemade chicken broth
2 (10-oz.) cans sugar-free diced tomatoes | 1 cup canned roasted poblano chiles | 2 tsp. dried oregano
1 tsp. ground cumin | salt, to taste | ¼ cup fresh cilantro, chopped | 2 tbsp. fresh lime juice

Directions: In a large pan, melt the butter over medium-high heat and cook the pork, onions and garlic for about 5 minutes or until browned. Add the broth and scrape up the browned bits. Add the tomatoes, poblano chiles, oregano, cumin, and salt and bring to a boil. Reduce the heat to medium-low and simmer, covered for about 2 hours. Stir in the fresh cilantro and lime juice and remove from heat. Serve hot.

Hungarian Pork Stew

Preparation Time: 15 minutes | **Cooking Time:** 2 hours 20 minutes | **Servings:** 10 | **Calories**: 529

Ingredients: 3 tbsp. olive oil | 3½ lb. pork shoulder, cut into 4 portions | 1 tbsp. butter
2 medium onions, chopped | 16 oz. tomatoes, crushed | 5 garlic cloves, crushed | 1 tsp. hot paprika
2 Hungarian wax peppers, chopped | 3 tbsp. Hungarian sweet paprika | 1 tbsp. smoked paprika
½ tsp. caraway seeds | 1 bay leaf | 1 cup homemade chicken broth | 1 packet unflavored gelatin
2 tbsp. fresh lemon juice | pinch of xanthan gum | salt and freshly ground black pepper, to taste

Directions: In a heavy-bottomed pan, heat 1 tbsp. of oil over high heat and sear the pork for about 2-3 minutes or until browned. Transfer the pork onto a plate and cut into bite-sized pieces. In the same pan, heat 1 tbsp. of oil and butter over medium-low heat and sauté the onions for about 5-6 minutes. With a slotted spoon transfer the onion into a bowl. In the same pan, add the tomatoes and cook for about 3-4 minutes, without stirring. Meanwhile, in a small frying pan, heat the remaining oil over-low heat and sauté the garlic, wax peppers, all kinds of paprika and caraway seeds for about 20-30 seconds. Remove from the heat and set aside. In a small bowl, mix together the gelatin and broth. In the large pan, add the cooked pork, garlic mixture, gelatin mixture and bay leaf and bring to a gentle boil. Reduce the heat to low and simmer, covered for about 2 hours. Stir in the xanthan gum and simmer for about 3-5 minutes. Stir in the lemon juice, salt and black pepper and remove from the heat. Serve hot.

Broccoli Soup

Preparation Time: 12 minutes | **Cooking Time:** 35 minutes | **Servings:** 4 | **Calories**: 348

Ingredients: 2 cloves garlic | 1 medium white onion | 1 tbsp butter | 2 cups vegetable stock
1 cup heavy cream | salt and ground black pepper, to taste | ½ tsp paprika | 2 cups of water
1-½ cups broccoli, divided into florets | 1 cup cheddar cheese

Directions: Peel and mince garlic. Peel and chop the onion. Preheat pot on medium heat, add butter and melt it. Add garlic and onion and sauté for 5 minutes, stirring occasionally. Pour in water, vegetable stock, heavy cream, and add pepper, salt and paprika. Stir and bring to boil. Add broccoli and simmer for 25 minutes. After that, transfer soup mixture to a food processor and blend well. Grate cheddar cheese and add to a food processor, blend again. Serve soup hot.

Simple Tomato Soup

Preparation Time: 15 minutes | **Cooking Time:** 10 minutes | **Servings:** 6 | **Calories**: 397

Ingredients: 4 cups canned tomato soup | 2 tbsp apple cider vinegar | 1 tsp dried oregano |
4 tbsp butter | 2 tsp turmeric | 2 oz red hot sauce | salt and ground black pepper to taste | 4 tbsp olive oil
8 bacon strips, cooked and crumbled | 4 oz fresh basil leaves, chopped | 4 oz green onions, chopped

Directions: Pour tomato soup in the pot and preheat on medium heat. Bring to boil. Add vinegar, oregano, butter, turmeric, hot sauce, salt, black pepper, and olive oil. Stir well. Simmer the soup for 5 minutes. Serve soup topped with crumbled bacon, green onion, and basil.

Green Soup

Preparation Time: 12 minutes | **Cooking Time:** 15 minutes | **Servings:** 6 | **Calories**: 227

Ingredients: 2 cloves garlic | 1 white onion | 1 cauliflower head | 2 oz butter | 1 bay leaf, crushed
1 cup spinach leaves | ½ cup watercress | 4 cups vegetable stock | salt and ground black pepper, to taste
1 cup of coconut milk | ½ cup parsley, for serving

Directions: Peel and mince garlic. Peel and dice onion. Divide cauliflower into florets. Preheat pot on medium-high heat, add butter and melt it. Add onion and garlic, stir, and sauté for 4 minutes. Add cauliflower and bay leaf, stir and cook for 5 minutes. Add spinach and watercress, stir and cook for another 3 minutes. Pour in vegetable stock—season with salt and black pepper. Stir and bring to boil. Pour in coconut milk and stir well. Take off heat. Use an immersion blender to blend well. Top with parsley and serve hot.

Sausage and Peppers Soup

Preparation Time: 15 minutes | **Cooking Time:** 1 hour 15 minutes | **Servings:** 6 | **Calories**: 531

Ingredients: 1 tbsp avocado oil | 2 lbs pork sausage meat | salt and ground black pepper, to taste
1 green bell pepper, seeded and chopped | 5 oz canned jalapeños, chopped | 1 tsp Italian seasoning
5 oz canned tomatoes, chopped | 1-¼ cup spinach | 4 cups beef stock | 1 tbsp cumin | 1 tsp onion powder
1 tsp garlic powder | 1 tbsp chili powder

Directions: Preheat pot with avocado oil on medium heat. Put sausage meat in pot and brown for 3 minutes on all sides. Add salt, black pepper, and green bell pepper and continue to cook for 3 minutes. Add jalapeños and tomatoes, stir well and cook for 2 minutes more. Toss spinach and stir again close lid and cook for 7 minutes. Pour in beef stock, Italian seasoning, cumin, onion powder, chili powder, garlic powder, salt, and black pepper, stir well. Close lid again. Cook for 30 minutes. When time is up, uncover the pot and simmer for 15 minutes more. Serve hot.

Roasted Bell Peppers Soup

Preparation Time: 15 minutes | **Cooking Time:** 20 minutes | **Servings:** 6 | **Calories**: 180

Ingredients: 1 medium white onion | 2 cloves garlic | 2 celery stalks | 12 oz roasted bell peppers, seeded
2 tbsp olive oil | salt and ground black pepper, to taste | 1-quart chicken stock | 2/3 cup water
¼ cup Parmesan cheese, grated | ⅔ cup heavy cream

Directions: Peel and chop onion and garlic. Chop celery and bell pepper. Preheat pot with oil on medium heat. Put garlic, onion, celery, salt, and pepper in the pot, stir and sauté for 8 minutes. Pour in chicken stock and water. Add bell peppers and stir. Bring to boil, close lid, and simmer for 5 minutes. Reduce heat if needed. When time is up, blend soup using an immersion blender. Add cream and season with salt and pepper to taste. Take off heat. Serve hot with grated cheese.

Avocado Soup

Preparation Time: 12 minutes | **Cooking Time:** 15 minutes | **Servings:** 4 | **Calories:** 329

Ingredients: 2 tbsp butter | 2 scallions, chopped | 3 cups chicken stock | ⅔ cup heavy cream
2 avocados, pitted, peeled, and chopped | salt and ground black pepper, to taste

Directions: Preheat pot on medium heat, add butter and melt it. Toss scallions, stir, and sauté for 2 minutes. Pour in 2 ½ cups stock and bring to simmer—Cook for 3 minutes. Meanwhile, peel and chop avocados. Place avocado, ½ cup of stock, cream, salt, and pepper in a blender and blend well. Add avocado mixture to the pot and mix well. Cook for 2 min. Sprinkle with more salt & pepper, stir & serve.

Delicious Tomato Basil Soup

Preparation Time: 10 minutes | **Cooking Time:** 40 minutes | **Servings:** 4 | **Calories**: 225

Ingredients: ¼ cup olive oil | ½ cup heavy cream | 1 lb. tomatoes, fresh | 4 cup chicken broth, divided
4 cloves garlic, fresh | sea salt & pepper to taste

Directions: Preheat oven to 400° Fahrenheit and line a baking sheet with foil. Remove the cores from your tomatoes and place them on the baking sheet along with the cloves of garlic. Drizzle tomatoes and garlic with olive oil, salt, and pepper. Roast at 400° Fahrenheit for 30 minutes. Pull the tomatoes out of the oven and place into a blender, along with the juices that have dripped onto the pan during roasting. Add two cups of the chicken broth to the blender. Blend until smooth, then strain the mixture into a large saucepan or a pot. While the pan is on the stove, whisk the remaining two cups of broth and the cream into the soup. Simmer for about ten minutes. Season to taste, then serve hot!

Chicken Enchilada Soup

Preparation Time: 10 minutes | **Cooking Time:** 45 minutes | **Servings:** 4 | **Calories:** 420

Ingredients: ½ cup fresh cilantro, chopped | 1-¼ tsp. chili powder | 1 cup fresh tomatoes, diced
1 med. yellow onion, diced | 1 small red bell pepper, diced | 1 tbsp. cumin, ground | 1 tsp. dried oregano
1 tbsp. extra virgin olive oil | 1 tbsp. lime juice, fresh | 2 cloves garlic, minced | 2 lg. stalks celery, diced
4 cups chicken broth | 8 oz. chicken thighs, boneless & skinless, shredded | 8 oz. cream cheese, softened

Directions: In a pot over medium heat, warm olive oil. Once hot, add celery, red pepper, onion, and garlic. Cook for about 3 minutes or until shiny. Stir the tomatoes into the pot and let cook for another 2 minutes. Add seasonings to the pot, stir in chicken broth and bring to a boil. Once boiling, drop the heat down to low and allow to simmer for 20 minutes. Once simmered, add the cream cheese and allow the soup to return to a boil. Drop the heat once again and allow to simmer for another 20 minutes. Stir the shredded chicken into the soup along with the lime juice and the cilantro. Spoon into bowls & serve hot!

Buffalo Chicken Soup

Preparation Time: 20 minutes | **Cooking Time:** 20 minutes | **Servings:** 4 | **Calories**: 563

Ingredients: 4 med. stalks celery, diced | 2 med. carrots, diced | 4 chicken breasts, boneless & skinless
6 tbsp. butter | 1 qt. chicken broth | 2 oz. cream cheese | ½ cup heavy cream | ½ cup buffalo sauce
1 tsp. sea salt | ½ tsp. thyme, dried
For garnish: sour cream | green onions, thinly sliced | bleu cheese crumbles

Directions: Set a large pot to warm over medium heat with the olive oil in it. Cook celery and carrot until shiny and tender. Add chicken breasts to the pot and cover. Allow to cook about five to six minutes per side. Once the chicken has cooked and formed some caramelization on each side, remove it from the pot. Shred the chicken breasts and set aside. Pour the chicken broth into the pot with the carrots and celery, then stir in the cream, butter, and cream cheese. * Bring the pot to a boil, then add chicken back to the pot. Stir buffalo sauce into the mix and combine completely. Feel free to increase or decrease as desired. Add seasonings, stir, and drop the heat to low. Allow the soup to simmer for 15 to 20 minutes, or until all the flavors have fully combined. Serve hot with a garnish of sour cream, bleu cheese crumbles, and sliced green onion!

Cauliflower Curry Soup

Preparation Time: 5 minutes | **Cooking Time:** 40 minutes | **Servings:** 4 | **Calories**: 390.5

Ingredients: 1 large cauliflower, chopped | 4 tbsp. olive oil | ½ red onion, finely chopped
4 garlic cloves, minced | 1 tbsp. yellow curry paste | 1 inch piece ginger, grated | 1 tbsp. sesame oil
1 (12 oz. pack) extra firm tofu, drained, scrambled | 1 tsp. chili flakes | juice of 1 medium lime
4 cups vegetable broth | 1 tsp. low-sodium soy sauce | 1 cup full-fat coconut milk

Directions: Preheat the oven to 400°F and line a baking tray with parchment paper. Put the cauliflower florets on the baking tray and drizzle 2 tablespoons of olive oil over them, covering them evenly. Put the baking tray into the oven and bake for about 25-30 minutes, until the florets are golden brown. Put a large pot over medium heat and add the remaining 2 tablespoons of olive oil. Take the baking tray out of the oven and set it aside for a few minutes to let the cauliflower florets cool down. Add the onion and garlic to the pot and fry for about a minute, stirring occasionally. Add the curry paste to the pot along with the ginger, scrambled tofu, and chili flakes. Stir for another minute. Put the baked cauliflower florets into a blender or food processor, along with the vegetable broth, sesame oil, soy sauce, and coconut milk. Blend these ingredients until smooth, then transfer the mixture into the pot. Incorporate all the ingredients, stirring occasionally until the contents of the pot start to cook. Once the soup reaches the boiling point, bring the heat down to a simmer. Cover the pot and let the soup simmer for about 10 minutes, then take the pot off the heat and set it aside to cool for a few minutes. Enjoy!

Cabbage Garlic Soup

Preparation Time: 10 minutes | **Cooking Time:** 35 minutes | **Servings:** 4 | **Calories**: 127

Ingredients: 10 cloves of garlic | 1 cabbage | 5 onions | 2 carrots | 7 tbsp. olive oil | half chili pepper
salt and pepper | chives, chopped

Directions: Chop the garlic, onions and cabbage, heat the oil in a frying pan or wok and fry the vegetables for 10 minutes stirring all the time. Peel and cut the carrots into cubes and fry for 5 minutes with the other vegetables. Place all the vegetables to a saucepan and boil for 20 minutes. Sprinkle with the chopped fresh chives and you are free to serve.

Onion Soup

Preparation Time: 10 minutes | **Cooking Time:** 25 minutes | **Servings:** 6 | **Calories:** 290

Ingredients: 2 cups white onion, diced | 4 tablespoons butter | ½ cup white mushrooms, chopped
3 cups of water | 1 cup heavy cream | 1 teaspoon salt | 1 teaspoon chili flakes | 1 teaspoon garlic powder

Directions: Put butter in the saucepan and melt it. Add diced white onion, chili flakes, and garlic powder. Mix it up and saute for 10 minutes over the medium-low heat. Then add water, heavy cream, and chopped mushrooms. Close the lid. Cook the soup for 15 minutes more. Then blend the soup until you get the creamy texture. Ladle it in the bowls.

Pumpkin Almond Soup

Preparation Time: 10 minutes | **Cooking Time:** 50 minutes | **Servings:** 4 | **Calories:** 230

Ingredients: 5 oz. pumpkin, cubed | 1 onion, chopped | 7 tbsp. almond flour | 2 celery stalks, chopped
5 cups of vegetable broth | 7 tbsp. olive oil | 5 fresh basil leaves | herbes de Provence | salt and pepper

Directions: Heat the water in a saucepan and boil the pumpkin for 20 minutes until soft. Heat the oil in a frying pan or wok and fry the onions for about 5 minutes until clear. Spoon the almond flour and mix well and then add the celery and fry for 10 min. Add all the vegetables and vegetable broth to a saucepan with the pumpkin and boil for 15 min. Add the basil and spices and serve.

Coconut Apricots Soup

Preparation Time: 10 minutes | **Cooking Time:** 25 minutes | **Servings:** 4 | **Calories**: 129

Ingredients: 7 tbsp. coconut, shredded | 3 cups coconut milk | 15 oz. apricots, cubed | 1 cup water
3 tbsp. erythritol | a piece of ginger, not bigger than a hazelnut

Directions: Cut the ginger into small pieces and send into a pan with a cup of water and boil for 10 minutes. Pour the coconut milk and boil for 5 minutes, and then add the shredded coconut, apricots and erythritol. Boil the coconut soup for 10 minutes and then serve.

Tomatoes Coconut Cream Soup

Preparation Time: 10 minutes | **Cooking Time:** 25 minutes | **Servings:** 4 | **Calories:** 209

Ingredients: 4 tomatoes | 8 tbsp. coconut cream | 8 garlic cloves | 2 onions | 2 tbsp. garlic powder
4 tbsp. sesame seeds oil | salt and pepper

Directions: Cut the tomatoes into cubes and fry them with the coconut cream for 5 minutes stirring all the time. Add the tomatoes, garlic powder, some salt and ground pepper to a saucepan and boil for 10 minutes. Chop the onions with garlic and then combine with the soup and boil for 10 minutes to serve.

Pumpkin Coconut Soup

Preparation Time: 10 minutes | **Cooking Time:** 30 minutes | **Servings:** 4 | **Calories**: 149

Ingredients: 2 lb. pumpkin | 3 cups of water | 1 cup coconut milk | 2 tbsp. coconut cream | salt
1 tbsp. erythritol

Directions: Peel the pumpkin, remove the skin and seeds, and then cut into cubes and put into a pan. Pour the water and boil the pumpkin for 15 minutes until soft and tender. Blend the pumpkin using a blender or food processor until the homogenous mass. Pour the water and coconut milk, smashed pumpkin, coconut cream, erythritol and salt to a saucepan and then cook for 15 minutes and serve!

Cheesy Pesto Chicken

Preparation Time: 18 minutes | **Cooking Time:** 45 minutes | **Servings:** 4 | **Calories**: 309

Ingredients: 3 tablespoons basil pesto | 4 chicken breasts, sliced in 8 pieces | 1/2 teaspoons salt
8 oz mozzarella cheese, shredded | 1/4 teaspoons black pepper

Directions: At 350 degrees F, preheat your oven. Grease a baking dish with cooking spray. Place the 8 chicken pieces in the baking dish. Sprinkle black pepper and salt on top. Spread pesto on each of the chicken breasts then adds mozzarella cheese on top. Bake, the pesto chicken for 45 minutes in the preheated oven. Serve warm.

Pressure Cooker Crack Chicken

Preparation Time: 5 minutes | **Cooking Time:** 25 minutes | **Servings:** 8 | **Calories:** 437

Ingredients: 2 lbs. boneless chicken thighs | 2 slices bacon | 8 oz. cream cheese | 1 scallion sliced
½ cup shredded cheddar | 1-½ tsp. garlic and onion powder | 1 tsp. red pepper flakes and dried dill
salt and pepper | 2 tbsps. apple cider vinegar | 1 tbsp. dried chives

Directions: On pressure cooker, use sauté mode and wait for it to heat up. Add the bacon and cook until crispy. Then set aside on a plate. Add everything in the pot, except the cheddar cheese. On Manual high, pressure cooks them for 15 mins and then release it. On a large plate, shred the chicken and then return to the pot and the cheddar. Top with the bacon and scallion.

Slow Cooker Barbecue Ribs

Preparation Time: 15 minutes | **Cooking Time:** 4 hours | **Servings:** 2 | **Calories**: 956

Ingredients: 1lb. pork ribs | pink salt | freshly ground black pepper | ½ cup sugar-free barbecue sauce
1.25 oz. package dry rib-seasoning rub

Directions: With the crock insert in place, preheat your slow cooker to high. Generously season the pork ribs with pink salt, pepper, and dry rib-seasoning rub. Stand the ribs up along the walls of the slow-cooker insert, with the bonier side facing inward. Pour the barbecue sauce on both sides of the ribs, using just enough to coat. Cover, cook for 4 hours and serve.

Chicken with Lemon and Garlic

Preparation Time: 5 minutes | **Cooking Time:** 20 minutes | **Servings:** 4 | **Calories:** 279

Ingredients: 4 boneless chicken thighs | 2 garlic cloves minced | juice of 1 lemon | garlic powder
¼ tsp. smoked paprika | red chili flakes | 2 tsp. Italian seasoning | salt and pepper | 1 tbsp. heavy cream
fresh parsley | ¼ small onion | 1 tbsp. olive oil | 1-½ tbsp. butter

Directions: Season your chicken with all spices. In a skillet over medium heat, add the olive oil and cook for 5-6 mins on each side. Set aside on a plate. Heat the skillet again and add in the butter. Stir in onion and garlic and add your lemon juice. Season them with everything left. After that, stir in your heavy cream. Once the sauce has thickened up, add the chicken back to the pot. Serve it with lemon slices.

Bacon-Wrapped Chicken

Preparation Time: 18 minutes | **Cooking Time:** 30 minutes | **Servings:** 8 | **Calories:** 308

Ingredients: 6 chicken breasts, sliced cross-sectionally | 2 tablespoons poultry seasoning rub
½ lb. bacon strips, cut in half | 4 oz cheddar cheese, shredded

Directions: At 400 degrees F, preheat your oven. Grease a baking sheet with cooking spray. Rub the chicken breasts with seasoning rub, and place them in the baking sheet. Place the bacon strips on top and drizzle shredded cheddar cheese on top. Bake the chicken for 30 mins in the preheated oven. Serve warm.

Barbacoa Beef Roast

Preparation Time: 15 minutes | **Cooking Time:** 8 hours | **Servings:** 4 | **Calories**: 723

Ingredients: 1 lb. beef chuck roast | 4 chipotle peppers in adobo sauce | 6 oz. can green jalapeño chili
2 tablespoons apple cider vinegar | ½ cup beef broth

Directions: With the crock insert in place, preheat your slow cooker to low. Massage the beef chuck roast on both sides with pink salt and pepper. Put the roast in the slow cooker. Pulse the chipotle peppers and their adobo sauce, jalapeños, and apple cider vinegar in a blender. Add the beef broth and pulse a few more times. Pour the chili mixture over the top of the roast. Cover and cook on low within 8 hours, then shred the meat. Serve hot.

Beef & Broccoli Roast

Preparation Time: 15 minutes | **Cooking Time:** 4 hours 30 minutes | **Servings:** 2 | **Calories**: 803

Ingredients: 1 lb. beef chuck roast | ½ cup beef broth | ¼ cup soy sauce | 1 teaspoon toasted sesame oil
1 bag frozen broccoli (16 ounces)

Directions: With the crock insert in place, preheat your slow cooker to low. On a cutting board, season the chuck roast with pink salt and pepper, and slice the roast thin. Put the sliced beef in your slow cooker. Combine sesame oil and beef broth in a small bowl then pour over the beef. Cover and cook on low for 4 hours. Add the frozen broccoli and cook for 30 minutes more. If you need more liquid, add additional beef broth. Serve hot.

Cauliflower and Pumpkin Casserole

Preparation Time: 15 minutes | **Cooking Time:** 1 hour & 30 minutes | **Servings:** 4 | **Calories**: 83

Ingredients: 2 tbsp. olive oil | 1/4 medium yellow onion, minced | 3 cups frozen, thawed brown rice
6 cups chopped forage kale into small pieces (about 140 g) | 1 little clove garlic, minced
salt and freshly ground black pepper | 1/2 cup low sodium chicken broth | 1/3 cup grated Parmesan
2 cups of 1.5 cm diced pumpkin (about 230 g) | 2 cups of 1.5 cm diced zucchini (about 230 g)
2 tbsp. mayonnaise | 1 cup grated Swiss cheese | 1 cup panko flour | 1 large beaten egg | cooking spray

Directions: Preheat oven to 200°C. Heats the oil in a large non-stick skillet over medium heat. Add onions and cook, occasionally stirring, until browned and tender (about 5 minutes). Add the cabbage, garlic, and 1/2 teaspoon salt and 1/2 teaspoon pepper and cook until the cabbage is light (about 2 minutes). Put the stock and cook within 5 minutes, then put the squash, zucchini, and 1/2 teaspoon salt and mix well. Continuously cooking within 8 minutes. Remove from heat and add mayonnaise. In a bowl, combine cooked vegetables, brown rice, cheese, 1/2 cup flour, and large egg and mix well. Spray a 2-liter casserole with cooking spray. Put the mixture to the pan and cover with the remaining flour, 1/4 teaspoon salt and a few pinches of pepper. Bake until the squash and zucchini are tender and the top golden and crispy (about 35 minutes). Serve hot. Advance Preparation Tip: Freeze the casserole for up to 2 weeks. Cover with aluminum foil and heat at 180°C until warm (35 to 45 minutes).

Pesto Pork Chops

Preparation Time: 20 minutes | **Cooking Time:** 20 minutes | **Servings:** 3 | **Calories**: 366.5

Ingredients: 3 top-flood pork chops, boneless, fat | 8 tablespoons herb pesto | ½ cup bread crumbs
1 tablespoon olive oil

Directions: Preheat the oven to 360°F. Cover a foil baker's sheet; set aside. Rub 1 tbsp of pesto evenly across each pork chop on both sides. Every pork chop in the crumbs of bread is lightly dredged. Heat the oil in a medium-high heat large skillet. Brown the pork chops for about 6 minutes on each side. Place on the baking sheet the pork chops. Bake until the pork reaches 136°F in the center for about 10 minutes.

Mexican Casserole with Black Beans

Preparation Time: 20 minutes | **Cooking Time:** 20 minutes | **Servings:** 6 | **Calories**: 325

Ingredients: 2 cups of minced garlic cloves | 2 cups of Monterey Jack and cheddar | 3/4 cup of salsa
1-1/2 cups chopped red pepper | 2 teaspoons ground cumin | 2 cans black beans | 12 corn tortillas
3 chopped tomatoes | 1/2 cup of sliced black olives | 2 cups of chopped onion

Directions: Let the oven heat to 350°F. Place a large pot over medium heat. Pour the onion, garlic, pepper, cumin, salsa, and black beans in the pot — Cook the ingredients for 3 minutes, stirring frequently. Arrange the tortillas in the baking dish. Ensure they are well spaced and even overlapping the dish if necessary. Spread half of the bean's mixture on the tortillas. Sprinkle with the cheddar. Repeat the process across the tortillas until everything is well stuffed. Cover the baking dish with foil paper and place in the oven. Bake it for 15 minutes. Remove from the oven to cool down a bit. Garnish the casserole with olives and tomatoes

Cheesy Pinwheels with Chicken

Preparation Time: 10 minutes | **Cooking Time:** 30 minutes | **Servings:** 2 | **Calories**: 463

Ingredients: 2 tbsp. ghee | 1 garlic, minced | 1/3 pound chicken breasts, cubed | 1 tsp creole, seasoning
1/3 red onion, chopped | 1 tomato, chopped | ½ cup chicken stock | ¼ cup whipping cream | 5 eggs
½ cup mozzarella cheese, grated | ¼ cup fresh cilantro, chopped | salt and black pepper, to taste
4 ounces cream cheese | a pinch of garlic powder

Directions: Season the chicken with creole seasoning. Heat a pan at medium heat and warm 1 tbsp ghee. Put chicken and cook per side for 2 minutes; remove to a plate. Melt the rest of the ghee and stir in garlic and tomato; cook for 4 minutes. Return the chicken to the pan and pour in stock; cook for 15 minutes. Place in whipping cream, red onion, salt, mozzarella cheese, and black pepper; cook for 2 minutes. In a blender, mix the cream cheese with garlic powder, salt, eggs, and black pepper, and pulse well. Place the mixture into a lined baking sheet, and then bake for 10 minutes in the oven at 320°F. Allow the cheese sheet to cool down, place on a cutting board, roll, and slice into medium slices. Organize the slices on a serving plate and top with chicken mixture. Sprinkle with cilantro to serve.

Beef Skewers with Ranch Dressing

Preparation Time: 10 minutes | **Cooking Time:** 15 minutes | **Servings:** 4 | **Calories**: 230

Ingredients: 1 lb. sirloin steak, boneless, cubed | ¼ cup ranch dressing, divided | chopped scallions

Directions: Preheat the grill on medium heat to 400°F and thread the beef cubes on the skewers, about 4 to 5 cubes per skewer. Brush half of the ranch dressing on the skewers (all around) and place them on the grill grate to cook for 6 minutes. Turn the skewers once and cook further for 6 minutes. Brush the remaining ranch dressing on the meat and cook them for 1 more minute on each side. Plate, decorate with the scallions and serve with a mixed veggie salad, and extra ranch dressing.

Spicy Pork Patties

Preparation Time: 10 minutes | **Cooking Time:** 10 minutes | **Servings:** 2 | **Calories:** 234

Ingredients: 1/2 lb. ground pork | 1 tablespoon Cajun seasoning | 1 egg, lightly beaten | pepper | salt
1/2 cup almond flour

Directions: Add all ingredients into the large bowl and mix until well combined. Make two equal shapes of patties from the meat mixture. Select Air Fry mode. Set time to 10 minutes and temperature 360°F then press START. The air fryer display will prompt you to ADD FOOD once the temperature is reached then place patties in the air fryer basket. Serve and enjoy.

Italian Sausage Satay

Preparation Time: 15 minutes | **Cooking Time:** 25 minutes | **Servings:** 6 | **Calories**: 461

Ingredients: 6 links Italian sausage (4 ounces) | 2 tablespoons butter | 4 garlic cloves, minced ½ red onion, sliced | 1 yellow onion, sliced | 1 green bell pepper, sliced | 1 large red bell pepper, sliced 1 teaspoon dried oregano | 1 teaspoon dried basil | ¼ cup white wine

Directions: Place a large skillet over medium heat. Put the sausage on the hot skillet and cook until it is browned. Transfer the sausage to a plate and cut into slices. Add the butter in the skillet and heat to melt. Toss in the garlic, red onion, and yellow onion. Sauté for about 3 minutes, then add the green bell pepper, red bell pepper, oregano, basil, and white wine. Cook them until the onions are soft. Put the sausage back to the skillet and reduce the heat to low, then continue cooking covered for about 15 minutes until warmed through. Remove from the heat and serve hot.

Herb Pork Chops

Preparation Time: 10 minutes | **Cooking Time:** 15 minutes | **Servings:** 4 | **Calories:** 266

Ingredients: 4 pork chops | 2 teaspoons oregano | 2 teaspoons thyme | 2 teaspoons sage 1 teaspoon garlic powder | 1 teaspoon paprika | 1 teaspoon rosemary | pepper | salt

Directions: Spray pork chops with cooking spray. Mix together garlic powder, paprika, rosemary, oregano, thyme, sage, pepper, and salt and rub over pork chops. Select Air Fry mode. Set time to 15 minutes and temperature 360°F then press START. The air fryer display will prompt you to ADD FOOD once the temperature is reached then place pork chops in the air fryer basket. Turn pork chops halfway through. Serve and enjoy.

Spicy Parmesan Pork Chops

Preparation Time: 10 minutes | **Cooking Time:** 9 minutes | **Servings:** 2 | **Calories**: 359

Ingredients: 2 pork chops, boneless | 1 teaspoon paprika | 3 tablespoons parmesan cheese, grated 1/3 cup almond flour | 1 teaspoon Cajun seasoning | 1 teaspoon dried mixed herbs

Directions: In a shallow bowl, mix together parmesan cheese, almond flour, paprika, mixed herbs, and Cajun seasoning. Spray pork chops with cooking spray and coat with parmesan cheese. Select Air Fry mode. Set time to 9 minutes and temperature 350°F then press START. The air fryer display will prompt you to ADD FOOD once the temperature is reached then place breaded pork chops in the air fryer basket. Turn pork chops halfway through. Serve and enjoy.

Moist Pork Chops

Preparation Time: 10 minutes | **Cooking Time:** 14 minutes | **Servings:** 2 | **Calories**: 284

Ingredients: 2 pork chops | 1 tsp paprika | 1 teaspoon garlic powder |1 teaspoon olive oil | pepper | salt

Directions: Brush pork chops with olive oil and season with garlic powder, paprika, pepper, and salt. Select Air Fry mode. Set time to 14 minutes and temperature 360°F then press START. The air fryer display will prompt you to ADD FOOD once the temperature is reached then place pork chops in the air fryer basket. Turn pork chops halfway through. Serve and enjoy.

Air Fried Pork Bites

Preparation Time: 10 minutes | **Cooking Time:** 15 minutes | **Servings:** 4 | **Calories:** 524

Ingredients: 1 lb pork belly, cut into 1-inch cubes | 1 teaspoon soy sauce | pepper | salt

Directions: In a bowl, toss pork cubes with soy sauce, pepper, and salt. Select Air Fry mode. Set time to 15 minutes and temperature 400°F then press START. The air fryer display will prompt you to ADD FOOD once the temperature is reached then place pork cubes in the air fryer basket. Serve and enjoy.

Beef Kebabs

Preparation Time: 10 minutes | **Cooking Time:** 15 minutes | **Servings:** 4 | **Calories:** 223

Ingredients: 1 lb ground beef | 1/2 cup onion, minced | 1/4 teaspoon ground cinnamon
1/4 teaspoon ground cardamom | 1/2 teaspoon cayenne | 1/2 teaspoon turmeric | 1 teaspoon salt
1/2 tablespoon ginger paste | 1/2 tablespoon garlic paste | 1/4 cup cilantro, chopped

Directions: Add meat and remaining ingredients into the large bowl and mix until well combined. Make sausage shape kebabs. Select Bake mode. Set time to 15 minutes and temperature 350°F then press START. The air fryer display will prompt you to ADD FOOD once the temperature is reached then place kebabs in the air fryer basket. Serve and enjoy.

Steak Tips

Preparation Time: 10 minutes | **Cooking Time:** 5 minutes | **Servings:** 3 | **Calories**: 317

Ingredients: 1 lb. steak, cut into cubes | 1 tsp olive oil | 1 tsp Montreal steak seasoning | pepper | salt

Directions: In a bowl, add steak cubes and remaining ingredients and toss well. Select Air Fry mode. Set time to 5 minutes and temperature 400°F then press START. The air fryer display will prompt you to ADD FOOD once the temperature is reached then place steak cubes in the air fryer basket and serve.

Rosemary Beef Tips

Preparation Time: 10 minutes | **Cooking Time:** 12 minutes | **Servings:** 4 | **Calories:** 243

Ingredients: 1 lb. steak, cut into 1-inch cubes | 1 teaspoon paprika | 2 teaspoon onion powder
1 teaspoon garlic powder | 2 tbsp coconut aminos | 2 tsp rosemary, crushed | pepper | salt

Directions: Add meat and remaining ingredients into the mixing bowl and mix well and let it sit for 5 minutes. Select Air Fry mode. Set time to 12 minutes and temperature 380°F then press START. The air fryer display will prompt you to ADD FOOD once the temperature is reached then place steak cubes in the air fryer basket. Stir halfway through. Serve and enjoy.

Flavorful Burger Patties

Preparation Time: 10 minutes | **Cooking Time:** 15 minutes | **Servings:** 4 | **Calories:** 223

Ingredients: 1 lb. ground lamb | 1/4 teaspoon cayenne pepper | 1/4 cup fresh parsley, chopped
1/4 cup onion, minced | 1 tablespoon garlic, minced | 1/2 teaspoon ground allspice
1 teaspoon ground cinnamon | 1 teaspoon ground coriander | 1 teaspoon ground cumin
1/4 teaspoon pepper | 1 teaspoon kosher salt

Directions: Add all ingredients into the large bowl and mix until well combined. Make 4 patties from the meat mixture. Select Bake mode. Set time to 14 minutes and temperature 375°F then press START. The air fryer display will prompt you to ADD FOOD once the temperature is reached then place patties in the air fryer basket. Turn patties halfway through. Serve and enjoy.

Chicken & Cheese Filled Avocados

Preparation Time: 10 minutes | **Cooking Time:** 0 minutes | **Servings:** 2 | **Calories**: 518

Ingredients: 2 avocados | ¼ cup mayonnaise | 1 tsp dried thyme | 2 tbsp. cream cheese
1-½ cups chicken, cooked and shredded | salt and black pepper, to taste | ¼ tsp cayenne pepper
½ tsp onion powder | ½ tsp garlic powder | 1 tsp paprika | 2 tbsp. lemon juice

Directions: Halve the avocados and scoop the insides. Put the flesh in a bowl, then add in the chicken; stir in the remaining ingredients. Fill the avocado cups with chicken mixture and serve.

Meatballs

Preparation Time: 10 minutes | **Cooking Time:** 20 minutes | **Servings:** 4 | **Calories**: 235

Ingredients: 1 lb. ground lamb | 2 tablespoon fresh parsley, chopped | 1 tablespoon garlic, minced
1 egg, lightly beaten | 1/4 teaspoon red pepper flakes | 1 teaspoon ground cumin
2 teaspoon fresh oregano, chopped | 1/4 teaspoon pepper | 1 teaspoon kosher salt

Directions: Add all ingredients into the mixing bowl and mix until well combined. Make small meatballs from meat mixture. Select Bake mode. Set time to 20 minutes and temperature 400°F then press START. The air fryer display will prompt you to ADD FOOD once the temperature is reached then place meatballs in the air fryer basket. Serve and enjoy.

Paprika Chicken & Pancetta in a Skillet

Preparation Time: 20 minutes | **Cooking Time:** 10 minutes | **Servings:** 2 | **Calories**: 323

Ingredients: 1 tbsp. olive oil | 5 pancetta strips, chopped | 1/3 cup Dijon mustard | 1 onion, chopped
salt and black pepper, to taste | 1 cup chicken stock | 2 chicken breasts, skinless and boneless
¼ tsp sweet paprika | 2 tbsp. oregano, chopped

Directions: In a bowl, combine the paprika, black pepper, salt, and mustard. Sprinkle this mixture the chicken breasts and massage. Heat a skillet over medium heat, stir in the pancetta, cook until it browns, for about 3-4 minutes, and remove to a plate. To the pancetta fat, add olive oil and cook the chicken breasts for 2 minutes per side. Place in the stock, black pepper, pancetta, salt, and onion. Sprinkle with oregano and serve.

Winter Chicken with Vegetables

Preparation Time: 5 minutes | **Cooking Time:** 30 minutes | **Servings:** 2 | **Calories**: 483

Ingredients: 2 tbsp. olive oil | 2 cups whipping cream | 1 pound chicken breasts, chopped | 1 bay leaf
1 onion, chopped | 1 carrot, chopped | 2 cups chicken stock | salt and black pepper, to taste
1 turnip, chopped | 1 parsnip, chopped | 1 cup green beans, chopped | 2 tsp fresh thyme, chopped

Directions: Heat a pan at medium heat and warm the olive oil. Sauté the onion for 3 minutes, pour in the stock, carrot, turnip, parsnip, chicken, and bay leaf. Place to a boil, and simmer for 20 minutes. Add in the asparagus and cook for 7 minutes. Discard the bay leaf, stir in the whipping cream, adjust the seasoning, and scatter it with fresh thyme to serve.

Keto Spicy Pork with Kelp Noodles

Preparation Time: 5 minutes | **Cooking Time:** 15 minutes | **Servings:** 4 | **Calories**: 223

Ingredients: 1-1/2 pounds pork tenderloin (sliced thinly) | 12 ounces kelp noodles | 2 tbsp rice vinegar
1 piece medium cucumber (sliced) | 2 cloves garlic (minced) | 1 tbsp olive oil | 1 tsp coconut aminos
2 teaspoons sesame oil | salt & pepper (taste) | 1/2 teaspoon ginger, minced | 1/2 tsp red pepper flakes

Directions: In a skillet over medium heat, put in the olive oil. Sautee the garlic for a minute or two until fragrant. Put in the pork slices. Cook them until they are brown on all sides. Put in the cucumber, followed by the kelp noodles. Stir to mix. Put in the ginger, coconut aminos, sesame oil, vinegar, pepper flakes, pepper, and salt. Stir to mix well. Cover the skillet. Continue cooking for another 7 minutes. Take out from the heat. Transfer onto a platter. Serve while hot.

Lamb Shashlyk

Preparation Time: 10 minutes | **Cooking Time:** 10 minutes | **Servings:** 4 | **Calories**: 467

Ingredients: 1 pound ground lamb | ¼ tsp cinnamon | 1 egg | 1 grated onion | salt & black pepper, taste

Directions: Place all ingredients in a bowl. Mix with your hands to combine well. Divide the meat into 4 pieces. Shape all meat portions around previously-soaked skewers. Preheat grill to medium and grill the kebabs for about 5 minutes per side.

Pancetta & Cheese Stuffed Chicken

Preparation Time: 15 minutes | **Cooking Time:** 25 minutes | **Servings:** 2 | **Calories**: 643

Ingredients: 4 slices pancetta | 2 tbsp. olive oil | 2 chicken breasts | 1 garlic clove, minced
1 shallot, finely chopped | 2 tbsp. dried oregano | 4 oz. mascarpone cheese | 1 lemon, zested
salt and black pepper, to taste

Directions: Warm the oil in a small skillet, then sauté the garlic and shallots for 3 minutes. Stir in salt, black pepper, and lemon zest. Transfer to a bowl and let it cool. Stir in the mascarpone cheese and oregano. Score a pocket in each chicken's breast, fill the holes with the cheese mixture and cover it with the cut-out chicken. Wrap each breast with two pancetta slices and secure the ends with a toothpick. Set the chicken on a greased baking sheet and cook in the oven for 20 minutes at 380°F.

Chili Chicken Kebab with Garlic Dressing

Preparation Time: 7 minutes | **Cooking Time:** 10 minutes - **Servings:** 2-4 | **Calories**: 410

Ingredients: skewers | 2 tbsp. olive oil | 3 tbsp. soy sauce, sugar-free | 1 tbsp. ginger paste
2 tbsp. swerve brown sugar | chili pepper to taste | 2 chicken breasts, cut into cubes | ¼ cup warm water
For dressing | ½ cup Tahini | 1 tbsp. parsley, chopped | 1 garlic clove, minced | salt & black pepper, taste

Directions: To make the marinade: In a small bowl, place and mix the soy sauce, ginger paste, brown sugar, chili pepper, and olive oil. Put the chicken in a zipper bag, pour the marinade over, seal, and shake for an even coat. Marinate in the fridge for 2 hours. Preheat a grill to high heat. Thread the chicken on skewers and cook for 10 mins, with three to four turnings to be golden brown. Transfer to a plate. Mix the tahini, garlic, salt, parsley & warm water in a bowl. Serve the chicken skewers topped with tahini sauce.

Easy Baked Shrimp Scampi

Preparation Time: 10 minutes | **Cooking Time:** 10 minutes | **Servings:** 4 | **Calories:** 708

Ingredients: 2 lbs shrimp, peeled | 3/4 cup olive oil | 2 tsp dried oregano | 1 tbsp garlic, minced
1/2 cup fresh lemon juice | 1/4 cup butter, sliced | pepper | salt

Directions: Preheat the oven to 350°F. Add shrimp in a baking dish. In a bowl, whisk together lemon juice, oregano, garlic, oil, pepper, and salt and pour over shrimp. Add butter on top of shrimp. Bake in preheated oven for 10 minutes or until shrimp cooked. Serve and enjoy.

Delicious Blackened Shrimp

Preparation Time: 10 minutes | **Cooking Time:** 5 minutes | **Servings:** 4 | **Calories**: 252

Ingredients: 1-1/2 lbs shrimp, peeled | 1 tbsp garlic, minced | 1 tbsp olive oil | pepper | salt
1 tsp garlic powder | 1 tsp dried oregano | 1 tsp cumin | 1 tbsp paprika | 1 tbsp chili powder

Directions: In a mixing bowl, mix together garlic powder, oregano, cumin, paprika, chili powder, pepper, and salt. Add shrimp and mix until well coated. Set aside for 30 minutes. Heat oil in a pan over medium-high heat. Add shrimp and cook for 2 minutes. Turn shrimp and cook for 2 minutes more. Add garlic and cook for 30 seconds. Serve and enjoy.

Rosemary-Lemon Shrimps

Preparation Time: 3 minutes | **Cooking Time:** 8 minutes | **Servings:** 4 | **Calories**: 315

Ingredients: 5 tablespoons butter | ½ cup lemon juice, freshly squeezed | 1 tsp rosemary
1-½ lb. shrimps, peeled and deveined | ¼ cup coconut aminos

Directions: Put all ingredients in a large pan on a high fire. Boil for 8 mins or until shrimp is pink, serve

Boiled Garlic Clams

Preparation Time: 3 minutes | **Cooking Time:** 10 minutes | **Servings:** 6 | **Calories**: 159

Ingredients: 3 tbsp butter | 6 cloves of garlic | 50 small clams in the shell, scrubbed
½ cup fresh parsley, chopped | 4 tbsps. extra virgin olive oil

Directions: In a large pot placed on medium-high fire, heat the butter and olive oil for a min. Stir in the garlic & cook until fragrant and slightly browned. Stir in the clams, water, and parsley—season with salt & pepper to taste. Cover & cook for 5 mins or until clams have opened. Discard unopened clams and serve.

Five-Spice Steamed Tilapia

Preparation Time: 15 minutes | **Cooking Time:** 15 minutes | **Servings:** 4 | **Calories**: 201

Ingredients: 1 lb. tilapia fillets | 1 tsp. Chinese five-spice powder | 3 tablespoons coconut oil
3 scallions, sliced thinly

Directions: In a large saucepan, place a trivet and pour a cup of water into the pan. Bring to a boil. Place tilapia in a heatproof dish that fits inside a saucepan. Drizzle oil on tilapia. Season with salt, pepper, and Chinese five-spice powder. Garnish with scallions. Seal dish with foil. Place the dish on the trivet inside the saucepan—cover and steam for 15 minutes. Serve and enjoy.

Keto Chili-Covered Salmon with Spinach

Preparation Time: 5 minutes | **Cooking Time:** 20 minutes | **Servings:** 4 | **Calories**: 461

Ingredients: 1-½ pounds salmon, in pieces | 1 tbsp chili paste | 1 oz Parmesan cheese, grated finely
1 tablespoon chili paste | ½ cup sour cream | 1 pound fresh spinach | salt & freshly ground black pepper

Directions: Preheat oven to 400°F (205°C). Grease the baking dish with half of the olive oil, season the salmon with pepper and salt, and put in the baking dish, skin-side down. Combine Parmesan cheese, chili paste and sour cream. Then spread them on the salmon fillets. Bake for 20 minutes, or until the salmon flakes easily with a fork or it becomes opaque. Heat the remaining olive oil in a nonstick skillet, sauté the spinach until it's wilted, about a couple of minutes, and season with pepper and salt. Serve with the oven-baked salmon immediately.

Shrimp and Cauliflower Jambalaya

Preparation Time: 20 minutes | **Cooking Time:** 15 minutes | **Servings:** 4 | **Calories**: 314

Ingredients: 2 cloves garlic, peeled and minced | 1 head cauliflower, grated | 1 cup chopped tomatoes
8 oz. raw shrimp, peeled and deveined | 1 tbsp Cajun seasoning

Directions: On medium-high fire, heat a non-stick saucepan for 2 minutes. To a pan, add oil and swirl to coat bottom and sides. Heat oil for a minute. Add garlic and sauté for a minute. Stir in tomatoes and stir fry for 5 minutes. Add water and deglaze the pan. Add remaining ingredients. Season generously with pepper. Increase fire to high and stir fry for 3 mins. Lower fire to low, cover, and cook for 5 mins & serve.

Keto Egg Butter with Avocado and Smoked Salmon

Preparation Time: 5 minutes | **Cooking Time:** 15 minutes | **Servings:** 4 | **Calories**: 638

Ingredients: 4 eggs | ½ teaspoon sea salt | ¼ teaspoon ground black pepper | 2 avocados | 2 tbsp oil
5 oz butter, at room temperature | 4 ounces smoked salmon | 1 tablespoon fresh parsley, chopped finely

Directions: Put the eggs in a pot and cover them with cold water. Then put the pot on the stove without a lid and bring it to a boil. Lower the heat and let it simmer for 6 to 9 minutes. Then remove eggs from the water and put them in a bowl with cold water. Peel the eggs and cut them finely. Use a fork to mix the eggs and butter. Then season to taste with pepper, salt. Serve the egg butter with slices of smoked salmon, finely chopped parsley, and a side of diced avocado tossed in olive oil.

Keto Baked Salmon with Butter and Lemon Slices

Preparation Time: 10 minutes | **Cooking Time:** 25 minutes | **Servings:** 6 | **Calories**: 474

Ingredients: 1 tablespoon olive oil | 2 pounds salmon | 1 teaspoon sea salt | 7 ounces butter
freshly ground black pepper, to taste | 1 lemon

Directions: Start by preheating the oven to 425°F (220°C). In a large baking dish, spray it with olive oil. Then add the salmon, skin-side down. Season with salt and pepper. Cut the lemon into thin slices and place them on the upper side of the salmon. Cut the butter in thin slices and spread them on top of the lemon slices. Put the dish in the heated oven and bake on the middle rack for about 25 to 30 minutes, or until the salmon flakes easily with a fork. Melt the rest of the butter in a small saucepan until it bubbles. Then remove from heat and let cool a little. Consider adding some lemon juice on the melted cool butter. Serve the fish with the lemon butter.

Grilled Tuna Salad with Garlic Sauce

Preparation Time: 10 minutes | **Cooking Time:** 15 minutes | **Servings:** 4 | **Calories**: 397

Ingredients: garlic dressing | ⅔ cup keto-friendly mayonnaise | 2 tbsp water | 2 tsp garlic powder
salt and freshly ground black pepper, to taste | For tuna salad: 2 eggs | 8 ounces green asparagus
1 tablespoon olive oil | ¾ pound fresh tuna, in slices | 4 ounces leafy greens | 2 ounces cherry tomatoes
½ red onion | 2 tablespoons pumpkin seeds | salt and freshly ground black pepper, to taste

Directions: Mix the ingredients together for the garlic dressing. And set them aside. Put the eggs in boiling water for 8 to 10 mins. Cooling in cold water would facilitate the peeling. Slice the asparagus into lengths and rapidly fry them inside a hot pan with no oil or butter. Then set them aside. Rub the tuna with oil and fry or grill for 2 to 3 mins on each side. Season with salt and pepper. Put the leafy greens, asparagus, peeled eggs cut in halves, tomatoes and thinly sliced onion into a plate. Finally, cut the tuna into slices and spread the slices evenly over the salad. Pour the dressing on top and add pumpkin seeds.

Quick Fish Bowl

Preparation Time: 11 minutes | **Cooking Time:** 15 minutes | **Servings:** 2 | **Calories**: 321

Ingredients: 2 tilapia fillets | 1 tbsp. olive oil | 1 avocado | 1 tbsp. ghee butter | 1 tbsp. cumin powder
1 tbsp. paprika | 2 cups coleslaw cabbage, chopped | 1 tbsp. salsa sauce | Himalayan rock salt & pepper

Directions: Preheat the oven to 425°F. Line a baking sheet with the foil. Mash the avocado. Brush the tilapia fillets using olive oil, season with salt and spices. Place the fish onto the baking sheet, greased with the ghee butter. Bake for 15 minutes, then remove the fish from the heat and let it cool for 5 minutes. In a bowl, combine the coleslaw cabbage and the salsa sauce, toss gently. Add the mashed avocado, season with salt and pepper. Slice the fish and add to the bowl. Bake for 14-15 minutes. Serve hot

Salmon Cakes

Preparation Time: 10 minutes | **Cooking Time:** 10 minutes | **Servings:** 2 | **Calories**: 370

Ingredients: 6 oz. canned salmon | 1 large egg | 2 tbsp. pork rinds | 3 tbsp. keto mayo
1 tbsp. ghee butter | 1 tbsp. Dijon mustard | salt and ground black pepper, to taste

Directions: In a bowl, combine the salmon (drained), pork rinds, egg, and half of the mayo, season with salt and pepper. Mix well. With the salmon mixture, form the cakes. Heat the ghee butter in a skillet over medium-high heat. Place the salmon cakes in the skillet and cook for about 3 minutes per side. Moved to a paper towel to get rid of excess fat. In a small bowl, combine the remaining half of mayo and the Dijon mustard, mix well. Serve the salmon cakes with the mayo-mustard sauce

Tender Creamy Scallops

Preparation Time: 15 minutes | **Cooking Time:** 21 minutes | **Servings:** 2 | **Calories**: 765

Ingredients: 8 fresh sea scallops | 4 bacon slices | ½ cup grated Parmesan cheese | 1 cup heavy cream
2 tbsp. ghee butter | salt and black pepper, to taste

Directions: Heat the butter in a skillet at medium-high heat. Add the bacon and cook for 4-5 minutes each side (till crispy). Moved to a paper towel to remove the excess fat. Lower the heat to medium, sprinkle with more butter. Put the heavy cream and Parmesan cheese, season with salt and pepper. Reduce the heat to low and cook for 8-10 minutes, constantly stirring, until the sauce thickens. In another skillet, heat the ghee butter over medium-high heat. Add the scallops to the skillet, season with salt and pepper. Cook for 2 minutes per side until golden. Transfer the scallops to a paper towel. Top with the sauce and crumbled bacon

Beef Cheeseburger Casserole

Preparation Time: 5 minutes | **Cooking Time:** 25 minutes | **Servings:** 6 | **Calories**: 385

Ingredients: 2 lb ground beef | salt and black pepper to taste | 1 cup cauli rice | 14 oz can diced tomatoes | 1 cup shredded Colby jack cheese

Directions: Preheat the oven to 370°F and grease a baking dish with cooking spray. Put beef in a pot and season with salt and black pepper and cook over medium heat for 6 minutes until no longer pink. Drain the grease. Add cauli rice, tomatoes, and ¼ cup water. Stir and bring to boil covered for 5 minutes to thicken the sauce. Adjust taste with salt and black pepper. Spoon over the beef mixture into the baking dish and spread evenly. Sprinkle with cheese and bake in the oven for 15 minutes until cheese has melted and it's golden brown. Remove and cool for 4 minutes and serve with low carb crusted bread.

Fried Steak and Eggs

Preparation Time: 5 minutes | **Cooking Time:** 20 minutes | **Servings:** 2 | **Calories**: 548

Ingredients: 2 strip loin steaks | 4 large eggs | 1 teaspoon chopped fresh parsley | salt, to taste
freshly ground black pepper, to taste | 3 tablespoons extra-virgin olive oil, divided

Directions: Put the steaks in a bowl, then sprinkle with salt and black pepper. Toss to coat well. In a nonstick skillet, warm 2 tablespoons of olive oil over medium-high heat until shimmering. Add the well-coated steaks to the skillet and fry for 12 minutes or until the steaks are fried through. Toss the steaks halfway through the cooking time. Transfer the steaks to a platter and let stand for at least 10 minutes. Warm the remaining olive oil over medium-low heat in the skillet, then break the eggs in the skillet and fry for 4 minutes or until they reach your desired doneness. Transfer two fried eggs over each steak and top with parsley before serving.

Seasoned Pork Chops

Preparation Time: 10 minutes | **Cooking Time:** 15 minutes | **Servings:** 8 | **Calories**: 412

Ingredients: 2 garlic cloves, minced | freshly ground black pepper, to taste | 1 lime, juiced
1 tablespoon fresh basil, chopped | 1 tablespoon Old Bay seafood seasoning | ½ cup apple cider vinegar |
½ cup olive oil | 8 boneless pork chops, cut into ½ inch thick

Directions: Add the minced garlic, black pepper, lime juice, basil, seasoning, apple cider vinegar, and olive oil to a Ziploc bag. Place the pork chops in this bag and seal it. Shake it well to coat the pork and place it in the refrigerator for 6 hours. Continue flipping and shaking the bag every 1 hour. Meanwhile, preheat your outdoor grill over medium-high heat. Remove the pork chops from the Ziploc bag and discard its marinade. Grill all the marinated pork chops for 7 minutes per side until their internal temperature reaches 145°F (63°C). Serve warm on a plate.

Steak and Cheese Plate

Preparation Time: 5 minutes | **Cooking Time:** 10 minutes | **Servings:** 2 | **Calories**: 714

Ingredients: 1 green onion, chopped | 2 oz chopped lettuce | 2 beef steaks | ½ cup mayonnaise
2 oz of cheddar cheese, sliced | Seasoning: ¼ tsp salt |1/8 tsp ground black pepper | 3 tbsp avocado oil

Directions: Prepare the steak, and for this, season it with salt and black pepper. Take a medium skillet pan, place it over medium heat, add oil and when hot, add seasoned steaks and cook for 7 to 10 minutes until cooked to the desired level. When done, distribute steaks between two plates, add scallion, lettuce, and cheese slices. Drizzle with remaining oil and then serve with mayonnaise.

Smoky No-Meat Chili

Preparation Time: 10 minutes | **Cooking Time:** 20 minutes | **Servings:** 8 | **Calories**: 208

Ingredients: 400 g cauliflower, trimmed and roughly chopped | 400 g crushed tomatoes
400 g Quorn mince | 2 cloves garlic, minced | 1 small shallot, minced | 1 tbsp. vegan Worcestershire sauce
1 tbsp. cumin powder | 1 tbsp. paprika | 1 tsp liquid smoke | 3 tbsp. olive oil | salt and pepper, to taste

Directions: Put cauliflower in a food processor and pulse into a coarse texture. Heat olive oil in a pot. Sautee garlic and shallots until aromatic. Add Quorn and cauliflower. Sweat for a few minutes. Add all remaining ingredients. Cover the pot and simmer over low heat for 15-20 minutes. Season with salt and pepper to taste. Garnish with your choice of toppings.

Low-Carb Chinese Lo Mein

Preparation Time: 10 minutes | **Cooking Time:** 5 minutes | **Servings:** 6 | **Calories**: 101

Ingredients: 500 g shirataki noodles | 150 g shiitake mushrooms, sliced | 100 g red bell pepper, sliced
100 g red bell pepper, sliced | 1 small shallot, minced | 2 cloves garlic, minced | 1 tbsp. peanut oil
1 tbsp. white wine vinegar | 2 tbsp. low-sodium soy sauce | 2 tbsp. sesame oil | salt and pepper, to taste
70 g snow peas | 70 g baby corn

Directions: Prepare shirataki noodles according to package directions. Heat peanut oil in a wok. Add young corn and sauté for 1-2 minutes. Add shiitake, snow peas, and red bell pepper. Stir. Fry for 1-2 minutes. Add shallots and garlic. Sautee until aromatic. Toss in prepared shirataki noodles together with the white wine vinegar, soy sauce, and sesame oil. Season with salt and pepper as needed. Serve hot.

Broiled Sirloin Steak with Mustard Sauce

Preparation Time: 10 minutes | **Cooking Time:** 15 minutes | **Servings:** 4 | **Calories**: 506

Ingredients: 4 sirloin steaks | For Mustard Sauce: ¼ cup grainy mustard | 1 cup heavy whipping cream
1 teaspoon chopped fresh thyme | salt, to taste | freshly ground black pepper, to taste
2 tablespoons extra-virgin olive oil

Directions: Set the oven to 450°F. Put the steaks in a bowl, and sprinkle with salt and black pepper. Toss to coat well. Arrange the steaks on a baking sheet, and brush with olive oil on both sides. Bring the baking sheet in the preheated oven and broil for 15 minutes or until the steaks are medium-rare. Toss the steaks halfway through the cooking time. Meanwhile, mix the mustard and cream in a saucepan, then bring the mixture to a boil over medium heat to make the sauce. Once the sauce is boiling, lower the heat temperature, then simmer for 5 minutes or until the sauce reduces about one third. Turn off the heat and then mix in the thyme. Remove the steaks from the oven to four plates, and then pour the mustard sauce over the steaks. Let the steak stand for at least 10 minutes and serve warm.

Seitan Tex-Mex Casserole

Preparation Time: 5 minutes | **Cooking Time:** 35 minutes | **Servings:** 4 | **Calories**: 464

Ingredients: 2 tbsp. vegan butter | 1-½ lb. seitan | 3 tbsp. Tex-Mex seasoning | ½ cup tomatoes
2 tbsp. chopped jalapeño peppers | salt and black pepper, to taste | ½ cup shredded vegan cheese
1 tbsp. chopped fresh green onion to garnish | 1 cup sour cream for serving

Directions: Preheat the oven and grease a baking dish with cooking spray. Set aside. Melt the vegan butter in a medium skillet over medium heat and cook the seitan until brown, 10 minutes. Stir in the Tex-Mex seasoning, jalapeño peppers, and tomatoes; simmer for 5 minutes and adjust the taste with salt and black pepper. Transfer and level the mixture in the baking dish. Top with the vegan cheese and bake in the upper rack of the oven for 15 to 20 minutes or until the cheese melts and is golden brown. Remove the dish and garnish with the green onion. Serve the casserole with sour cream.

Baked Mushrooms with Creamy Brussels sprouts

Preparation Time: 8 minutes | **Cooking Time:** 2 hours 35 minutes | **Servings:** 4 | **Calories**: 492

Ingredients: For the mushrooms: 1 lb. whole white button mushrooms | salt and black pepper to taste
2 tsp dried thyme | 1 bay leaf | 5 black peppercorns | ½ cups vegetable broth | 2 garlic cloves, minced
1 ½ oz. fresh ginger, grated | 1 tbsp. coconut oil | 1 tbsp. smoked paprika | For the creamy Brussel sprouts: ½ lb. Brussel sprouts, halved | 1-½ cups cashew cream | salt and ground black pepper, to taste

Directions: For the mushroom roast: Preheat the oven to 200°F. Pour all the mushroom ingredients into a baking dish, stir well, and cover with foil. Bake in the oven until softened, 1 to 2 hours. Remove the dish, take off the foil, and use a slotted spoon to fetch the mushrooms onto serving plates. Set aside. For the creamy Brussel sprouts: pour the broth in the baking dish into a medium pot and add the Brussel sprouts. Add about ½ cup of water if needed and cook for 7 to 10 minutes or until softened. Stir in the cashew cream, adjust the taste with salt and black pepper, and simmer for 15 min. Serve the creamy Brussel sprouts with the mushrooms.

White Pizza Frittata

Preparation Time: 10 minutes | **Cooking Time:** 30 minutes | **Servings:** 8 | **Calories**: 301

Ingredients: 5 ounces mozzarella cheese | 9 ounces bag frozen spinach | 12 large eggs
4 tablespoons olive oil | 1 ounce pepperoni | ¼ teaspoon nutmeg | 1 teaspoon minced garlic
½ cup grated parmesan cheese | ½ cup fresh ricotta cheese | salt and pepper

Directions: Preheat oven to 375°F in the meantime you are getting things ready. Take the frozen spinach and microwave it for 3 minutes or until defrosted. Squeeze the spinach using your hands to drain the excess water. Take a large bowl, crack all the eggs into it, and add the spices and olive oil. Whisk them together until well blended. Add the spinach, parmesan cheese and ricotta cheese and make sure that the spinach is added in small pieces. Mix together all the ingredients to prepare a good mixture. Transfer the mixture to the skillet, sprinkle cheese at the top, and then add the pepperoni. Place in the preheated oven and bake for 30 minutes or until the time you are satisfied. Remove from the oven once baked properly and serve with a keto sauce you love.

Gluten-Free Puttanesca

Preparation Time: 5 minutes | **Cooking Time:** 5 minutes | **Servings:** 2 | **Calories**: 181

Ingredients: 2 medium-sized zucchinis | 2 tbsp. olive oil | 4 cloves garlic, minced | 1 tsp red chili flakes
1 shallot, minced | 1 can diced tomatoes, drained | 2 tbsp. capers | 10 pcs black olives, sliced | salt, pepper

Directions: Process the zucchini in a vegetable spiralizer. Set aside. Heat olive oil in a pan. Add shallots, garlic, and chili flakes. Sautee until aromatic. Add diced tomatoes, capers, and black olives. Bring to a simmer — season with salt and pepper. Turn off the heat and toss in spiralized zucchini.

Tempeh with Garlic Asparagus

Preparation Time: 10 minutes | **Cooking Time:** 18 minutes | **Servings:** 4 | **Calories**: 181

Ingredients: For the tempeh: 3 tbsp. vegan butter | 4 tempeh slices | salt and black pepper to taste
For the garlic buttered asparagus: 2 tbsp. olive oil | 2 garlic cloves, minced | 1 tbsp. dried parsley
1 lb. asparagus, trimmed and halved | salt and black pepper to taste | 1 small lemon, juiced

Directions: For the tempeh: Melt the vegan butter in a medium skillet over medium heat, season the tempeh with salt, black pepper and fry in the butter on both sides until brown and cooked through, 10 minutes. Transfer to a plate and set aside in a warmer for serving.
For the garlic asparagus: Heat the olive oil in a medium skillet over medium heat, and sauté the garlic until fragrant, 30 seconds. Stir in the asparagus, season with salt and black pepper, and cook until slightly softened with a bit of crunch, 5 minutes. Mix in the parsley, lemon juice, toss to coat well, and plate the asparagus. Serve the asparagus warm with the tempeh.

Tempeh Coconut Curry Bake

Preparation Time: 7 minutes | **Cooking Time:** 23 minutes | **Servings:** 4 | **Calories**: 417

Ingredients: 1 oz. plant butter, for greasing | 2-½ cups chopped tempeh | salt and black pepper
4 tbsp. plant butter | 2 tbsp. red curry paste | 1-½ cup coconut cream | ½ cup fresh parsley, chopped
15 oz. cauliflower, cut into florets

Directions: Preheat the oven to 400°F and grease a baking dish with 1 ounce of vegan butter. Arrange the tempeh in the baking dish, sprinkle with salt and black pepper, and top each tempeh with a slice of the remaining butter. In a bowl, mix the red curry paste with the coconut cream and parsley. Pour the mixture over the tempeh. Bake in the oven for 20 minutes or until the tempeh is cooked. While baking, season the cauliflower with salt, place in a microwave-safe bowl, and sprinkle with some water. Steam in the microwave for 3 mins or until the cauliflower is soft and tender. Remove the curry bake and serve.

Spicy Cheese with Tofu Balls

Preparation Time: 20 minutes | **Cooking Time:** 20 minutes | **Servings:** 4 | **Calories**: 259

Ingredients: For the spicy cheese: 1/3 cup vegan mayonnaise | ¼ cup pickled jalapenos
1 tsp paprika powder | 1 tbsp. mustard powder | 1 pinch cayenne pepper | 4 oz. grated tofu cheese
For the tofu balls: 1 tbsp. flax seed powder + 3 tbsp. water | 2-½ cup crumbled tofu | salt and black pepper | 2 tbsp. plant butter, for frying

Directions: Make the spicy cheese. In a bowl, mix the mayonnaise, jalapenos, paprika, mustard powder, cayenne powder, and cheddar cheese. Set aside. In another medium bowl, combine the flax seed powder with water and allow absorbing for 5 minutes. Add the flax egg to the cheese mixture, the crumbled tofu, salt, and black pepper, and combine well. Use your hands to form large meatballs out of the mix. Then, melt the vegan butter in a large skillet over medium heat and fry the tofu balls until cooked and browned on the outside. Serve the tofu balls with roasted cauliflower mash and mayonnaise.

Pimiento Tofu Balls

Preparation Time: 10 minutes | **Cooking Time:** 15 minutes | **Servings:** 4 | **Calories**: 254

Ingredients: ¼ cup chopped pimientos | 1/3 cup mayonnaise | 3 tbsp. cashew cream
1 tsp paprika powder | 1 pinch cayenne pepper | 1 tbsp. Dijon mustard | 4 oz. grated vegan cheese
1-½ lbs. tofu, pressed and crumbled | salt and black pepper, to taste | 2 tbsp. olive oil, for frying

Directions: In a large bowl, add all the ingredients except for the olive oil and with gloves on your hands, mix the ingredients until well combined. Form bite size balls from the mixture. Heat the olive oil in a medium non-stick skillet and fry the tofu balls in batches on both sides until brown and cooked through, 4 to 5 minutes on each side. Transfer the tofu balls to a serving plate and serve warm.

Mushroom Curry Pie

Preparation Time: 15 minutes | **Cooking Time:** 55 minutes | **Servings:** 4 | **Calories**: 548

Ingredients: For the Piecrust: 1 tbsp. flax seed powder + 3 tbsp. water | 1 tbsp. psyllium husk powder
¾ cup coconut flour | 4 tbsp. chia seeds | 4 tbsp. almond flour | 1 tbsp. psyllium husk powder
1 tsp baking powder | 1 pinch salt | 3 tbsp. olive oil | 4 tbsp. water
For the filling: 1 cup chopped cremini mushrooms | 1 cup vegan mayonnaise | 3 tbsp. + 9 tbsp. water
½ red bell pepper, finely chopped | 1 tsp turmeric powder | ½ tsp paprika powder | ½ tsp garlic powder
¼ tsp black pepper | ½ cup cashew cream | 1-¼ cups shredded tofu cheese

Directions: In two separate bowls, mix the different portions of flax seed powder with the respective quantity of water and set aside to absorb for 5 minutes. Preheat the oven to 350°F. Make the crust: When the flax egg is ready, pour the smaller quantity into a food processor, and add the coconut flour, chia seeds, almond flour, psyllium husk powder, baking powder, salt, olive oil, and water. Blend the ingredients until a ball forms out of the dough. Line a springform pan with an 8-inch diameter parchment paper and grease the pan with cooking spray. Spread the dough in the bottom of the pan and bake in the oven for 15 minutes. Make the filling: In a bowl, add the remaining flax egg, mushrooms, mayonnaise, water, bell pepper, turmeric, paprika, garlic powder, black pepper, cashew cream, and tofu cheese. Combine the mixture evenly and fill the piecrust. Bake further for 40 minutes or until the pie is golden brown. Remove, slice, and serve the pie with a chilled strawberry drink.

Avocado Coconut Pie

Preparation Time: 30 minutes | **Cooking Time:** 50 minutes | **Servings:** 4 | **Calories:** 680

Ingredients: For the Piecrust: 1 tbsp. flax seed powder + 3 tbsp. water | 4 tbsp. coconut flour
4 tbsp. chia seeds | ¾ cup almond flour | 1 tbsp. psyllium husk powder | 1 tsp baking powder
1 pinch salt | 3 tbsp. coconut oil | 4 tbsp. water | For the filling: 2 ripe avocados | 1 cup vegan mayonnaise
3 tbsp. flax seed powder + 9 tbsp. water | 2 tbsp. fresh parsley, finely chopped 1 jalapeno, finely chopped
½ tsp onion powder | ¼ tsp salt | ½ cup cashew cream | 1-¼ cups shredded tofu cheese

Directions: In 2 separate bowls, mix the different portions of flax seed powder with the respective quantity of water. Allow absorbing for 5 minutes. Preheat the oven to 350°F. In a food processor, add the coconut flour, chia seeds, almond flour, psyllium husk powder, baking powder, salt, coconut oil, water, and the smaller portion of the flax egg. Blend the ingredients until the resulting dough forms into a ball. Line a spring form pan with about 12-inch diameter of parchment paper and spread the dough in the pan. Bake for 10 to 15 minutes or until a light golden brown color is achieved. Meanwhile, cut the avocado into halves lengthwise, remove the pit, and chop the pulp. Put in a bowl and add the mayonnaise, remaining flax egg, parsley, jalapeno, onion powder, salt, cashew cream, and tofu cheese. Combine well. Remove the piecrust when ready and fill with the creamy mixture. Level the filling with a spatula and continue baking for 35 minutes or until lightly golden brown. When ready, take out. Cool before slicing and serving with a baby spinach salad.

Mushroom Lettuce Wraps

Preparation Time: 5 minutes | **Cooking Time:** 16 minutes | **Servings:** 4 | **Calories**: 439

Ingredients: 2 tbsp. vegan butter | 4 oz. baby Bella mushrooms, sliced | 1-½ lbs. tofu, crumbled
½ tsp salt | ¼ tsp black pepper | 1 iceberg lettuce, leaves extracted | 1 cup shredded vegan cheese
1 large tomato, sliced

Directions: Put the vegan butter in a skillet and melt over medium heat. Add the mushrooms and sauté until browned and tender, about 6 minutes. Transfer the mushrooms to a plate and set aside. Add the tofu to the skillet, season with salt and black pepper, and cook until brown, about 10 minutes. Turn the heat off. Spoon the tofu and mushrooms into the lettuce leaves, sprinkle with the vegan cheese, and share the tomato slices on top. Serve the burger immediately.

Kale and Mushroom Pierogis

Preparation Time: 15 minutes | **Cooking Time:** 30 minutes | **Servings:** 4 | **Calories**: 364

Ingredients: For the Stuffing: 2 tbsp. vegan butter | 2 garlic cloves, finely chopped | 2 oz. fresh kale
1 small red onion, finely chopped |3 oz. baby Bella mushrooms, sliced | ½ tsp salt | ¼ tsp black pepper
½ cup cashew cream | 2 oz. grated tofu cheese | For the Pierogi: 1 tbsp. flax seed powder + 3 tbsp. water
½ cup almond flour | 4 tbsp. coconut flour | ½ tsp salt | 1 tsp baking powder | 5 tbsp. vegan butter
1-½ cups shredded tofu cheese | olive oil for brushing

Directions: Put the vegan butter in a skillet and melt over medium heat, then add and sauté the garlic, red onion, mushrooms, and kale until the mushrooms brown. Season the mixture with salt and black pepper and reduce the heat to low. Stir in the cashew cream and tofu cheese and simmer for 1 minute. Turn the heat off and set the filling aside to cool. Make the pierogis: In a small bowl, mix the flax seed powder with water and allow sitting for 5 minutes. In a bowl, combine the almond flour, coconut flour, salt, and baking powder. Put a small pan over low heat, add, and melt the tofu cheese and vegan butter while stirring continuously until smooth batter forms. Turn the heat off. Pour the flax egg into the cream mixture, continue stirring, while adding the flour mixture until a firm dough forms. Mold the dough into four balls, place on a chopping board, and use a rolling pin to flatten each into ½ inch thin round pieces. Spread a generous amount of stuffing on one-half of each dough, then fold over the filling, and seal the dough with your fingers. Brush with olive oil, place on a baking sheet, and bake for 20 minutes or until the pierogis turn a golden brown color. Serve the pierogis with a lettuce tomato salad.

Tofu and Spinach Lasagna with Red Sauce

Preparation Time: 20 minutes | **Cooking Time:** 45 minutes | **Servings:** 4 | **Calories**: 767

Ingredients: 2 tbsp. vegan butter | 1 white onion, chopped | 1 garlic clove, minced | 1 tsp salt
2-½ cups crumbled tofu | 3 tbsp. tomato paste | ½ tbsp. dried oregano | ¼ tsp ground black pepper
½ cup water | 1 cup baby spinach | Keto pasta: flax egg: 8 tbsp. flax seed powder + 1-½ cups water
1-½ cup dairy-free cashew cream | 1 tsp salt | 5 tbsp. psyllium husk powder
Dairy-free Cheese topping : 2 cups coconut cream | 5 oz. shredded vegan mozzarella cheese
2 oz. grated tofu cheese | ½ tsp salt | ¼ tsp ground black pepper | ½ cup fresh parsley, finely chopped

Directions: Melt the vegan butter in a medium pot over medium heat. Then, add the white onion and garlic, and sauté until fragrant and soft, about 3 minutes. Stir in the tofu and cook until brown. Mix in the tomato paste, oregano, salt, and black pepper. Pour the water into the pot, stir, and simmer the ingredients until most of the liquid has evaporated. While cooking the sauce, make the lasagna sheets. Preheat the oven to 300°F and mix the flax seed powder with the water in a medium bowl to make flax egg. Allow sitting to thicken for 5 minutes. Combine the flax egg with the cashew cream and salt. Add the psyllium husk powder a bit at a time while whisking and allow the mixture to sit for a few more minutes. Line a baking sheet with parchment paper and spread the mixture in. Cover with another parchment paper and use a rolling pin to flatten the dough into the sheet. Bake the batter in the oven for 10 to 12 minutes, remove after, take off the parchment papers, and slice the pasta into sheets that fit your baking dish. In a bowl, combine the coconut cream and two-thirds of the mozzarella cheese. Fetch out 2 tablespoons of the mixture and reserve. Mix in the tofu cheese, salt, black pepper, and parsley. Set aside. Grease your baking dish with cooking spray, layer a single line of pasta in the dish, spread with some tomato sauce, 1/3 of the spinach, and ¼ of the coconut cream mixture. Season with salt and black pepper as desired. Repeat layering the ingredients twice in the same manner making sure to top the final layer with the coconut cream mixture and the reserved cashew cream. Bake in the oven for 30 minutes at 400 F or until the lasagna has a beautiful brown surface. Remove the dish; allow cooling for a few minutes, and slice. Serve the lasagna with a baby green salad.

Tempeh Garam Masala Bake

Preparation Time: 5 minutes | **Cooking Time:** 24 minutes | **Servings:** 4 | **Calories**: 286

Ingredients: 3 tbsp. vegan butter | 3 cups tempeh slices | salt | 2 tbsp. garam masala
1 green bell pepper, finely diced | 1-¼ cups coconut cream | 1 tbsp. fresh cilantro, finely chopped

Directions: Preheat the oven to 400°F. Place a skillet over medium heat, add, and melt the vegan butter. Meanwhile, season the tempeh with some salt. Fry the tempeh in the butter until browned on both sides, about 4 mins. Stir half of the garam masala into the tempeh until evenly mixed; turn the heat off. Transfer the tempeh with the spice into a baking dish. Then, in a small bowl, mix the green bell pepper, coconut cream, cilantro, and remaining garam masala. Pour the mixture over the tempeh and bake in the oven for 20 minutes or until golden brown on top. Garnish with cilantro and serve with some cauli rice.

Green Avocado Carbonara

Preparation Time: 15 minutes | **Cooking Time:** 15 minutes | **Servings:** 4 | **Calories**: 941

Ingredients: 8 tbsp. flax seed powder + 1 ½ cups water | 1 ½ cups dairy-free cashew cream | 1 tsp salt
5-½ tbsp. psyllium husk powder | Avocado sauce : 1 avocado, peeled & pitted |1-¾ cups coconut cream |
1 teaspoon onion powder | ½ teaspoon garlic powder | ¼ cup olive oil | ¼ teaspoon black pepper
¾ teaspoon sea salt | walnut parmesan or store-bought parmesan | juice of ½ lemon
For serving : 4 tbsp. toasted pecans | ½ cup freshly grated tofu cheese

Directions: Preheat the oven to 300°F. In a medium bowl, mix the flax seed powder with water and allow sitting to thicken for 5 minutes. Add the cashew cream, salt, and psyllium husk powder. Whisk until smooth batter forms. Line a baking sheet with parchment paper, pour in the batter and cover with another parchment paper. Use a rolling pin to flatten the dough into the sheet. Place in the oven and bake for 10 to 12 minutes. Remove the pasta after, take off the parchment papers and use a sharp knife to slice the pasta into thin strips lengthwise. Cut each piece into halves, pour into a bowl, and set aside. For the avocado sauce, in a blender, combine the avocado, coconut cream, lemon juice, onion powder, and garlic powder. Puree the ingredients until smooth. Pour the olive oil over the pasta and stir to coat properly. Pour the avocado sauce on top and mix. Then, season with salt, black pepper, and the soy cheese. Combine again. Divide the pasta into serving plates, garnish with extra soy cheese and pecans, and serve immediately.

Cashew Buttered Quesadillas with Leafy Greens

Preparation Time: 10 minutes | **Cooking Time:** 20 minutes | **Servings:** 4 | **Calories**: 224

Ingredients: Tortillas: 3 tbsp. flax seed powder + ½ cup water | ½ cup dairy-free cashew cream
1-½ tsp psyllium husk powder | 1 tbsp. coconut flour | ½ tsp salt
Filling: 1 tbsp. cashew butter, for frying | 5 oz. grated vegan cheese | 1 oz. leafy greens

Directions: Preheat the oven to 400°F. In a bowl, mix the flax seed powder with water and allow sitting to thicken for 5 minutes. After, whisk the cashew cream into the flax egg until the batter is smooth. In another bowl, combine the psyllium husk powder, coconut flour, and salt. Add the flour mixture to the flax egg batter and fold in until fully incorporated. Allow sitting for a few minutes. Then, line a baking sheet with parchment paper and pour in the mixture. Spread into the baking sheet using a spatula and bake in the upper rack of the oven for 5 to 7 minutes or until brown around the edges. Keep a watchful eye on the tortillas to prevent burning. Remove when ready and slice into 8 pieces. Set aside. For the filling, spoon a little cashew butter into a skillet and place a tortilla in the pan. Sprinkle with some vegan cheese, leafy greens, and cover with another tortilla. Brown each side of the quesadilla for 1 minute or until the cheese melts. Transfer to a plate. Repeat assembling the quesadillas using the remaining cashew butter. Serve immediately with avocado salad.

Zucchini Boats with Vegan Cheese

Preparation Time: 3 minutes | **Cooking Time:** 4 minutes | **Servings:** 2 | **Calories**: 721

Ingredients:1 medium-sized zucchini | 4 tbsp. vegan butter | 2 garlic cloves, minced | 1-½ oz. baby kale salt & black pepper (taste) | 2 tbsp. unsweetened tomato sauce | 1 cup vegan cheese | olive oil for drizzling

Directions: Preheat the oven to 375°F. Use a knife to slice the zucchini in halves and scoop out the pulp with a spoon into a plate. Keep the flesh. Grease a baking sheet with cooking spray and place the zucchini boats on top. Put the vegan butter in a skillet and melt over medium heat. Add and sauté the garlic until fragrant and slightly browned, about 4 minutes. Add the kale and the zucchini pulp. Cook until the kale wilts; season with salt and black pepper. Spoon the tomato sauce into the boats and spread to coat the bottom evenly. Then, spoon the kale mixture into the zucchinis and sprinkle with the cheese. Bake in the oven for 20 to 25 minutes or until the cheese has a beautiful golden color. Plate the zucchinis when ready, drizzle with olive oil, and season with salt and black pepper. Serve immediately.

Vegan Curry Bowls

Preparation Time: 5 minutes | **Cooking Time:** 15 minutes | **Servings:** 4 | **Calories**: 272

Ingredients: 400 g firm tofu, sliced into bite-sized pieces | 50 g pineapple chunks | 2 Roma tomatoes, diced | 1 small shallot, minced | 1 tbsp. ginger-garlic paste | 1 tbsp. curry powder
1/3 cup coconut milk | bunch of cilantro, chopped | 2 tbsp. olive oil | salt, to taste

Directions: Heat olive oil in a non-stick pan. Pan Fry tofu until brown on all sides. Set aside on paper towels to drain excess oil. Pour off oil from the pan, leaving about a tablespoon. Add shallots and ginger-garlic paste. Sautee until aromatic. Add curry powder and roast briefly. Add about half a cup of water and bring to a simmer. Add tofu, pineapples, and tomatoes. Simmer until sufficiently reduced. Add coconut milk and simmer until thick. Simmer with salt to taste. Garnish with chopped cilantro.

Rainbow Quinoa Salad

Preparation Time: 20 minutes | **Cooking Time:** 15 minutes | **Servings:** 1 | **Calories:** 605

Ingredients: 3 cups cooked quinoa | 1 can cooked chickpeas, depleted and flushed
4 oz spinach leaves, washed | 3 carrots, stripped and julienned | 10 spring onions, slashed
2 roasted red peppers, meagerly cut | 2 oz coriander leaves, washed and slashed | 4 tbsp. pumpkin seeds

Directions: Place all the fixings in a bowl and mix well until everything is disseminated equally. Present with your preferred salad dressing. NOTES : You need 250ml (1 cup) of uncooked quinoa to deliver 750ml (3 cups) cooked quinoa. Basically stew in salted water for around 15 minutes or until cooked, at that point channel. You can purchase roasted red peppers in containers at the jam segment with sundried tomatoes. Some avocado and additionally blue cheddar function admirably with this salad as well!

Caprese Casserole

Preparation Time: 5 minutes | **Cooking Time:** 20 minutes | **Servings:** 4 | **Calories**: 588

Ingredients: 1 cup cherry tomatoes, halved | 1 cup vegan mozzarella cheese, cut into small pieces
2 tbsp. basil pesto | 1 cup vegan mayonnaise | 2 oz. tofu cheese | salt and black pepper | 1 cup arugula
4 tbsp. olive oil

Directions: Preheat the oven to 350°F. In a baking dish, mix the cherry tomatoes, mozzarella, basil pesto, and mayonnaise, half of the tofu cheese, salt, and black pepper. Level the ingredients with a spatula and sprinkle the remaining tofu cheese on top. Bake for 20 minutes or until the top of the casserole is golden brown. Remove and allow cooling for a few minutes. Slice and dish into plates, top with some arugula and drizzle with olive oil. Serve.

Avocado Tissue

Preparation Time: 10 minutes | **Cooking Time:** 30 minutes | **Servings:** 1 | **Calories:** 533

Ingredients: 300 g macaroni | 1 garlic clove | 1 lime | 200 g avocado tissue, around | 2 avocados
30 g new coriander leaves | ¼ tsp) salt | 90 ml (3fl oz.) almond milk | 30 g breadcrumbs
120 g ground mozzarella [optional] | 90 g ground cheddar [optional]

Directions: Cook macaroni until still somewhat firm, as indicated by the directions on the bundle. Channel and put in a safe spot. Preheat the stove to 370°F/190°C/gas mark 5. Place the garlic, lime, avo, salt, coriander, and milk in a nourishment processor and mix until smooth. Place the macaroni and avocado blend in an ovenproof dish and mix until altogether blended. [If you're vegan, you can now basically eat this hot or cold. Or then again, use substitutes for the following steps.] Mix the mozzarella, cheddar, and breadcrumbs in a bowl and sprinkle over the pasta. Bake for 20 minutes or until seared, firm, and the cheddar has liquefied. NOTES : If you are vegan, exclude the cheddar and preparing in the broiler at last. On the other hand, there are cheddar and vegan-safe breadcrumbs that can be filled in for customary adaptations.

Chicken Pea and Butternut Burgers

Preparation Time: 40 minutes | **Cooking Time:** 20 minutes | **Servings:** 1 | **Calories:** 350

Ingredients: 1 red bean stew, finely cleaved | 2 cloves garlic, stripped and finely cleaved
2.5 cm (1 in) new ginger, stripped and finely cleaved | 3 tbsp. vegetable oil | 1 lb. cooked chickpeas
2 lbs. cooked butternut squash | 5 oz. flour | 1 tsp. ground cumin | 1 tsp ground coriander
3 tbsp. roasted peanuts | Handful coriander leaves, cleaved

Directions: Fry the bean stew, garlic, and ginger in a huge skillet with 15ml (1 tbsp.) oil for 1 moment. Add the chickpeas, butternut, cumin, coriander, peanuts, leaves, and flour to the container and mix well. At this point, the blend shouldn't be clingy to deal with. In the event that it includes more flour until it isn't any longer. Form 10 even-sized chunks of the blend at that point press them level so as to frame burger patties. In a huge skillet, heat the rest of the oil and fry the patties in bunches until caramelized on the two sides. Serve in a burger bun with your preferred fillings. Right now utilized spinach, red onion, yogurt, and cress.

Mushroom Zoodle Pasta

Preparation Time: 10 minutes | **Cooking Time:** 16 minutes | **Servings:** 4 | **Calories:** 421.6

Ingredients: 3 large zucchinis | ½ tsp. salt | 1 tbsp. coconut oil | 1 large green onion, diced
3 garlic cloves, minced | 5 cups oyster mushrooms, chopped | pinch each of nutmeg, onion powder, paprika powder, white pepper, and salt | 1 cup full-fat coconut milk | ½ cup vegan mozzarella
½ cup baby spinach leaves, chopped | ¼ cup fresh thyme, chopped | 1 tbsp. miso paste

Directions: In a large bowl, toss the zoodles or zucchini slices with half a teaspoon of salt and set aside. Put a large skillet, over medium heat and add the coconut oil. Add the onion and cook until translucent, for about 5 minutes while stirring occasionally. Stir in the minced garlic, chopped mushrooms, and remaining seasonings. Cook all ingredients in the skillet for about 3 minutes, stirring continuously. Reduce heat to medium-low and slowly incorporate the coconut milk, followed by the mozzarella. Cover the skillet and let the ingredients heat through for about 8 minutes, stirring occasionally. Drain any excess liquid from the salted zoodles by dabbing them with paper towels. Add the dry zoodles to the skillet with the chopped spinach and stir well until all ingredients are combined. Turn off the heat and top the mushroom zoodle pasta with the chopped thyme. Add more seasonings to taste, serve the pasta in a bowl, and enjoy!

Sweet Potatoes and Mud Beans Falafel

Preparation Time: 30 minutes | **Cooking Time:** 30 minutes | **Servings:** 1 | **Calories:** 393

Ingredients: 1 lb. cooked mung beans | 1 lb. cooked sweet potato, crushed | 4 cloves garlic, squashed
5 cm (2 in) new ginger, stripped and ground | 1 tsp ground cumin | 1 tsp ground turmeric
½ tsp red stew powder | 1 tsp ocean salt | 10 pecans, hacked into little pieces | 2 tbsp. sesame seeds
2 oz flour [optional] | 1 egg, whisked [optional]

Directions: Preheat the cooker to 375°F/190°C/gas mark 5. Place the beans, sweet potato, garlic, ginger, cumin, turmeric, stew, salt and pecans in an enormous bowl and mix until altogether joined. At this point the blend shouldn't be clingy to deal with. In the event that it is include more flour until it isn't any longer. Form 5cm (2in) balls with the blend and spot on preparing material on a heating plate. Glace the balls with whisked egg or a touch of oil. Sprinkle sesame seeds on top and prepare for 30 minutes or until seared. Best served warm with a salad and dressing.

Stuffed Zucchini

Preparation Time: 5 minutes | **Cooking Time:** 30 minutes | **Servings:** 2 | **Calories:** 359.5

Ingredients: 1 large zucchini | 2 tbsp. olive oil | ¼ cup green onion, chopped | 1 garlic clove, minced
1 cup fresh baby spinach leaves | handful of fresh rocket, chopped | sea salt and black pepper, to taste
¼ cup vegan cheese | pinch of dried parsley

Directions: Preheat the oven to 375°F and line a baking tray with parchment paper. Cut the zucchini in half lengthwise and scoop out most of the pulp. Mash the zucchini pulp in a small bowl with a masher and set it aside. Heat a large skillet over medium heat and add half of the olive oil. Add the zucchini pulp, chopped onion, and minced garlic to the skillet. Stir continuously, cooking the ingredients for up to 5 minutes before adding the baby spinach and rocket. Stir for a few seconds, season with salt and pepper to taste, and turn off the heat. Add the vegan cheese and stir well to ensure all ingredients are incorporated and the cheese has melted. Scoop the mixture into the zucchini halves and transfer them onto the baking tray. Cover the baking tray with aluminum foil and transfer it to the oven. Bake the stuffed zucchini halves for 25 minutes. Then, turn off the oven, uncover the baking tray, and put the uncovered zucchini halves back into the oven for a few more minutes. Serve the stuffed zucchini garnished with the remaining olive oil and some dried parsley. Serve and enjoy!

Tofu Cheese Nuggets & Zucchini Fries

Preparation Time: 5 minutes | **Cooking Time:** 18 minutes | **Servings:** 2 | **Calories:** 813.5

Ingredients: Tofu Cheese Nuggets: 1 (12 oz. pack) extra firm tofu, drained, cubed | 2 tbsp. water
½ cup smoked chipotle cream cheese | ½ cup almond flour | Zucchini Fries: 2 tsp. red chili flakes
½ cup almond flour | ¼ cup olive oil | 1 large zucchini, skinned

Directions: Preheat the oven to 400°F and line a baking tray with parchment paper. Put the cream cheese, ½ cup almond flour, and water into a large bowl and mix thoroughly until all the ingredients are combined. Add the tofu cubes to the bowl and coat all the cubes evenly. Transfer the coated tofu cubes onto one half of the baking tray and set it aside. Put the chili flakes and almond flour into a large bowl and mix until all ingredients are combined. Pour the olive oil into a medium-sized bowl and dip each zucchini stick into the oil. Make sure to cover all fries evenly. Put the zucchini fries in the bowl with the almond flour mixture and gently stir the fries around until they are all evenly covered. Transfer the zucchini fries onto the baking tray with the tofu nuggets and spread them out evenly. If the nuggets and fries don't fit on the baking tray together, bake them in two batches. Put the baking tray into the oven and bake the nuggets and fries for about 18 mins, or until golden-brown and crispy. Take the baking tray out of the oven and let the dish cool down for a min. Serve & enjoy with a light salad of greens as a side dish.

Quick Veggie Protein Bowl

Preparation Time: 5 minutes | **Cooking Time:** 13 minutes | **Servings:** 1 | **Calories**: 296

Ingredients: 4 oz. extra-firm tofu, drained | ¼ tsp. turmeric | ¼ tsp. cayenne pepper | ½ tsp. paprika
1 tbsp. coconut oil | 1 cup broccoli florets, diced | 1 cup Chinese kale, diced | ½ tsp. dried oregano
½ cup button mushrooms, diced | ¼ cup of fresh oregano, diced | Himalayan salt and ground black
pepper, to taste

Directions: Cut the tofu into tiny pieces and season with the turmeric and cayenne pepper. Warm a large skillet over medium heat and add ¾ of the coconut oil. Once oil is heated, add the tofu and cook it for about 5 minutes, stirring continuously. Transfer the cooked tofu to a medium-sized bowl and set it aside. Add the remaining coconut oil, diced broccoli florets, Chinese kale, button mushrooms, and the remaining herbs to the skillet. Season with the salt, pepper, and paprika to taste. Cook the vegetables for 6-8 minutes, stirring continuously. Turn off the heat and transfer the cooked veggies and tofu to the bowl. Garnish with the optional fresh oregano. Serve and enjoy!

Cauliflower Pizza Crust

Preparation Time: 50 minutes | **Cooking Time:** 30 minutes | **Servings:** 2 | **Calories**: 360.9

Ingredients: For Crust: 16 oz. cauliflower rice | 3 flax eggs | 2 tbsp. chia seeds | ½ cup almond flour
½ tsp. garlic powder | ½ tsp. dried basil | pinch of salt | 2 tsp. water
For Topping: ½ cup simple marinara sauce | 1 medium zucchini, sliced | | handful of fresh rocket
1 medium green bell pepper, pitted, cored, sliced | 1 cup button mushrooms, diced | ½ cup vegan cheese
sea salt & ground black pepper, to taste | 1 jalapeño pepper, pitted, cored, diced | pinch of cayenne pepper

Directions: Preheat the oven to 400°F and line a baking sheet with parchment paper. Transfer the cauliflower rice to a large saucepan and add enough water to cover the 'rice.' Bring the water to a soft boil over medium heat. Cover the saucepan, turn down the heat to medium-low, and allow the rice to simmer for about 5 minutes before draining the water off. This step can be skipped if store-bought cauliflower rice is used. Transfer the cauliflower rice onto a clean dish towel and close the cloth by holding the edges. Wring out any excess water by twisting the lower part of the towel that contains the rice. Once the cauliflower rice is completely drained, transfer the towel to the freezer for up to 15 minutes. Doing so will cool the rice. When the cauliflower rice has cooled completely, put it into a large bowl. Add the flax eggs, chia seeds, almond flour, garlic, dried basil, and salt. Combine all the ingredients into a firm, kneadable dough. If the dough is too firm, add the optional 2 tablespoons of water. Spread the dough over the entire surface of the baking dish. The uncooked crust should be about ¼-inch thick. Bake the crust in the oven for 25 minutes, then sprinkle some additional water on top and bake for another 5 minutes. The top of the crust will turn lightly golden. Take the baking tray out of the oven and allow the crust to cool for a few minutes. Spread the marinara sauce evenly over the golden crust. Do the same for the vegetables. Finally, garnish the pizza with the vegan cheese, optional jalapeño, and cayenne pepper. Season the pizza with salt and pepper and transfer it back into the oven for a few more minutes. Serve the pizza warm, garnished with a handful of fresh rocket, and enjoy!

Cheesecake Cups

Preparation Time: 10 minutes | **Cooking Time:** 4 minutes | **Servings:** 12 | **Calories**: 217

Ingredients: For Crust: ½ cup pumpkin seeds, raw | 6 tbsp. shredded coconut, unsweetened
3 tbsp. coconut oil | 2 tbsp. organic soy protein, vanilla flavor | ½ tsp. stevia powder | pinch of salt
For Filling: 6 tbsp. coconut oil | 6 tbsp. almond butter | 6 tbsp. coconut cream | 2 tbsp. lemon juice
2 tbsp. organic soy protein, vanilla flavor | pinch of salt | ¼ tsp. xanthan gum | ¼ tsp. stevia powder

Directions: Line a cupcake tin with 6 cupcake liners. Heat a small frying pan over medium-high heat. Toast the pumpkin seeds in the frying pan, stirring occasionally for about 4 minutes. Add the shredded coconut and stir thoroughly to toast everything evenly. Take the frying pan off the heat and allow the ingredients to cool down before transferring them into a food processor or blender. Pulse the pumpkin seeds and shredded coconut into small crumbs. Transfer the crumbs to a medium-sized bowl and add the remaining crust ingredients. Combine all ingredients into a thick dough and divide this mixture into six equal-sized balls. Put one ball into each of the cupcake liners, pressing and flattening the balls into a crust at the bottom of each cupcake liner. Transfer the tin into the freezer and prepare the filling. Heat a medium-sized saucepan over medium heat and add the coconut oil. Remove the saucepan from the heat once the coconut oil has melted. Put the melted coconut oil, almond butter, coconut cream, lemon juice, organic soy protein, and a pinch of salt to the (uncleaned) food processor or blender. Process these ingredients until well combined with a smooth and creamy texture. Add the optional xanthan gum and stevia. Xanthan gum will help thicken the cheesecake fat bombs, while the stevia will add a sweeter flavor. Use slightly more or less stevia to taste. Take the cupcake tin out of the freezer and top all crusts with filling. Make sure to divide the filling equally among the 6 cups with a tablespoon. Transfer the tin back into the fridge until the cups are firm. Serve the cheesecake cups at room temperature and enjoy!

Destroyed Rainbow Salad with Edamame

Preparation Time: 30 minutes | **Cooking Time:** 5 minutes | **Servings:** 1 | **Calories**: 419

Ingredients: 1-½ lb. solidified edamame | ½ red cabbage, ground | ½ cup dried salted peanuts
4 enormous carrots, stripped and ground | 12 spring onions, washed and finely cut | 4 tbsp. nectar
½ cup coriander, washed and finely slashed | 4 tbsp. oil | 4 tbsp. rice vinegar | 2 tbsp. soy sauce
1 tbsp. sesame oil | 1 tbsp. crisp ginger, finely ground | 1 tsp bean stew sauce | 1 garlic clove, squashed

Directions: Boil the solidified edamame for 5 minutes in salted water at that point channel. Put aside to cool while you prep different vegetables. Mix the cabbage, carrots, onions, coriander, peanuts, and edamame in a huge bowl. In a little bowl, combine the salad dressing fixings, for example, nectar, oils, vinegar, soy sauce, ginger, stew sauce, and garlic. Pour the dressing over the salad, give it a decent mix, and serve right away. NOTES: If you are gluten narrow-minded, please use tamari rather than soy sauce.

Sugar-Free Lemon Bars

Preparation Time: 15 minutes | **Cooking Time:** 45 minutes | **Servings:** 8 | **Calories**: 272

Ingredients: ½ cup butter, melted | 1-¾ cup almond flour, divided | 1 cup powdered erythritol, divided 3 medium-size lemons | 3 large eggs

Directions: Prepare the parchment paper and baking tray. Combine butter, 1 cup of almond flour, ¼ cup of erythritol, and salt. Stir well. Place the mix on the baking sheet, press a little and put it into the oven (preheated to 350°F). Cook for about 20 minutes. Then set aside to let it cool. Zest 1 lemon and juice all of the lemons in a bowl. Add the eggs, ¾ cup of erythritol, ¾ cup of almond flour, and salt. Stir together to create the filling. Pour it on top of the cake and cook for 25 minutes. Cut into small pieces and serve with lemon slices.

Creamy Hot Chocolate

Preparation Time: 5 minutes | **Cooking Time:** 5 minutes | **Servings:** 4 | **Calories**: 193

Ingredients: 6 oz. dark chocolate, chopped | ½ cup unsweetened almond milk | ½ cup heavy cream 1 tbsp. erythritol | ½ tsp vanilla extract

Directions: Combine the almond milk, erythritol, and cream in a small saucepan. Heat it (choose medium heat and cook for 1-2 minutes). Add vanilla extract and chocolate. Stir continuously until the chocolate melts. Pour into cups and serve.

Fatty Bombs with Cinnamon and Cardamom

Preparation Time: 10 minutes | **Cooking Time:** 35 minutes | **Servings:** 10 | **Calories:** 90

Ingredients: ½ cup unsweetened coconut, shredded | 3 oz unsalted butter | ½ tsp vanilla extract ¼ tsp ground green cinnamon | ¼ ground cardamom

Directions: Roast the unsweetened coconut (choose medium-high heat) until it begins to turn lightly brown. Combine the room-temperature butter, half of the shredded coconut, cinnamon, cardamom, and vanilla extract in a separate dish. Cool the mix in the fridge for about 5-10 minutes. Form small balls and cover them with the remaining shredded coconut. Cool the balls in the fridge for about 10-15 minutes.

Easy Peanut Butter Cups

Preparation Time: 10 minutes | **Cooking Time:** 1 hour 35 minutes | **Servings:** 12 | **Calories**: 200

Ingredients: 1/2 cup peanut butter | 1/4 cup butter | 3 oz. cacao butter, chopped 1/3 cup powdered swerve sweetener | 1/2 tsp vanilla extract | 4 oz. sugar free dark chocolate

Directions: Line a muffin tin with parchment paper or cupcake liners. Using low heat, melt the peanut butter, butter, and cacao butter in a saucepan. Stir them until completely combined. Add the vanilla and sweetener until there are no more lumps. Carefully place the mixture in the muffin cups. Refrigerate it until firm. Put chocolate in a bowl and set the bowl in boiling water. This is done to avoid direct contact with the heat. Stir the chocolate until completely melted. Take the muffin out of the fridge and drizzle in the chocolate on top. Put it back again in the fridge to firm it up. This should take 15 minutes to finish. Store and serve when needed.

Keto Frosty

Preparation Time: 45 minutes | **Cooking Time:** 0 minutes | **Servings:** 4 | **Calories**: 164

Ingredients: 1-½ cups heavy whipping cream | 2 tablespoons cocoa powder (unsweetened) 3 tablespoons swerve | 1 teaspoon pure vanilla extract | salt to taste

Directions: In a bowl, combine all the ingredients. Use a hand mixer and beat until you see stiff peaks forming. Place the mixture in a Ziploc bag. Freeze for 35 minutes. Serve in bowls or dishes.

Red Velvet Cupcakes

Preparation Time: 15 minutes | **Cooking Time:** 25 minutes | **Servings:** 8 | **Calories**: 377

Ingredients: For Cupcake batter: 2 cups of almond flour | 2 tablespoons of Dutch cocoa | 3 eggs 3 tbsp of butter | 1/3 cup of monk fruit/erythritol blend | 1/2 cup of sour cream | 1/3 cup of buttermilk 2 teaspoon of red food coloring | 1 teaspoon of baking powder | For Icing: 1/2 stick butter | 1 tsp vanilla 2 tablespoons of mascarpone cheese | 8 oz. of cream cheese | 1/4 cup of monk fruit sweetener

Directions: Using a large mixing bowl, add in the flour, cocoa, and baking powder then mix properly to combine. In another mixing bowl, add in the butter, sweetener, and eggs then beat properly with a stand mixer. Add in the sour cream, buttermilk, and red coloring then beat again to combine. Next, pour the egg mixture into the bowl containing the flour mixture then stir everything to combine. Place parchment paper on a multi-well muffin tin, pour in the batter, place the muffin tin into an oven and bake at 350 degrees F for about twenty-five to thirty minutes until an inserted toothpick comes out clean, set aside to cool. To make the icing, beat all its ingredients in a mixing bowl until the mixture becomes smooth. ice the cupcakes as desired then serve.

Delicious Coffee Ice Cream

Preparation Time: 10 minutes | **Cooking Time:** 5 minutes | **Servings:** 1 | **Calories:** 596

Ingredients: 6 ounces coconut cream, frozen into ice cubes | 1 ripe avocado, diced and frozen ½ cup coffee expresso | 2 tbsp. sweetener | 1 tsp vanilla extract | 1 tbsp. water | coffee beans

Directions: Take out the frozen coconut cubes and avocado from the fridge. Slightly melt them for 5-10 minutes. Add the sweetener, coffee expresso, and vanilla extract to the coconut-avocado mix and whisk with an immersion blender until it becomes creamy (for about 1 minute). Pour in the water and blend for 30 seconds. Top with coffee beans and enjoy!

Mocha Ice Cream

Preparation Time: 15 minutes | **Cooking Time:** 15 minutes | **Servings:** 2 | **Calories:** 246

Ingredients: 1 cup unsweetened coconut milk | ¼ cup heavy cream | ¼ teaspoon xanthan gum 2 tbsp granulated erythritol | 15 drops liquid stevia | 2 tbsp cacao powder | 1 tablespoon instant coffee

Directions: In a container, add the ingredients (except xanthan gum) and with an immersion blender, blend until well combined. Slowly, add the xanthan gum and blend until a slightly thicker mixture is formed. Transfer the mixture into ice cream maker and process according to manufacturer's instructions. Now, transfer the ice cream into an airtight container and freeze for at least 4–5 hours before serving.

Egg Custard

Preparation Time: 15 minutes | **Cooking Time:** 55 minutes | **Servings:** 8 | **Calories:** 77

Ingredients: 5 organic eggs | salt, as required | ½ cup Yacon syrup | 20 ounces unsweetened almond milk | ¼ teaspoon ground ginger | ¼ teaspoon ground cinnamon | ¼ teaspoon ground nutmeg | ¼ teaspoon ground cardamom | 1/8 teaspoon ground cloves | 1/8 teaspoon ground allspice

Directions: Preheat your oven to 325°F. Grease 8 small ramekins. In a bowl, add the eggs and salt and beat well. Arrange a sieve over a medium bowl. Through a sieve, strain the egg mixture into a bowl. Add the Yacon syrup in eggs and stir to combine. Add the almond milk and spices and beat until well combined. Transfer the mixture into prepared ramekins. Now, place ramekins in a large baking dish. Add hot water in the baking dish about 2-inch high around the ramekins. Place the baking dish in the oven and bake for about 30–40 minutes or until a toothpick inserted in the center comes out clean. Remove ramekins from the oven and set aside to cool. Refrigerate to chill before serving.

Vanilla Crème Brûlée

Preparation Time: 20 minutes | **Cooking Time:** 1 hour 20 minutes | **Servings:** 4 | **Calories:** 264

Ingredients: 2 cups heavy cream | 1 vanilla bean, halved with seeds scraped out | 4 organic egg yolks
1/3 teaspoon stevia powder | 1 tsp organic vanilla extract | pinch of salt | 4 tbsp granulated erythritol

Directions: Preheat your oven to 350°F. In a pan, add heavy cream over medium heat and cook until heated. Stir in the vanilla bean seeds and bring to a gentle boil. Reduce the heat to very low and cook, covered for about 20 minutes. Meanwhile, in a bowl, add the remaining ingredients (except erythritol) and beat until thick and pale mixture forms. Remove the heavy cream from heat and through a fine-mesh strainer, strain into a heat-proof bowl. Slowly, add the cream in egg yolk mixture beating continuously until well combined. Divide the mixture into 4 ramekins evenly. Arrange the ramekins into a large baking dish. In the baking dish, add hot water about half of the ramekins. Bake for about 30–35 minutes. Remove the pan from the oven and then let it cool slightly. Refrigerate the ramekins for at least 4 hours. Just before serving, sprinkle the ramekins with erythritol evenly. Holding a kitchen torch about 4–5-inches from the top, caramelize the erythritol for about 2 minutes. Set aside for 5 minutes before serving.

Lemon Soufflé

Preparation Time: 15 minutes | **Cooking Time:** 35 minutes | **Servings:** 4 | **Calories:** 130

Ingredients: 2 large organic eggs (whites and yolks separated) | ¼ cups granulated erythritol, divided
1 cup ricotta cheese | 1 tablespoon fresh lemon juice | 2 teaspoons lemon zest, grated
1 teaspoon poppy seeds | 1 teaspoon organic vanilla extract

Directions: Preheat your oven to 375°F. Grease 4 ramekins. Add egg whites and beat in a clean glass bowl until it has a foam like texture. Add 2 tablespoons of erythritol and beat the mixture until it is stiff. In another bowl, add ricotta cheese, egg yolks, and the remaining erythritol. until it is mixed thoroughly. Put the lemon juice and lemon zest in the bowl and mix well. Add the poppy seeds and vanilla extract and mix again. Add the whipped egg whites into the ricotta mixture and gently stir. Place the mixture into prepared ramekins evenly. Bake for about 20 minutes. Remove from oven and serve immediately.

Cottage Cheese Pudding

Preparation Time: 10 minutes | **Cooking Time:** 45 minutes | **Servings:** 6 | **Calories:** 226

Ingredients: For Pudding: 1 cup cottage cheese | ¾ cup heavy cream | 3 organic eggs | ¾ cup of water
½ cups granulated erythritol | 1 teaspoon organic vanilla extract
For Topping: 1/3 cup heavy whipping cream | 1/3 cup fresh raspberries

Directions: Preheat your oven to 350°F. Grease 6 (6-ounce) ramekins. Add all the ingredients (except cinnamon) and pulse in a blender until smooth. Transfer the mixture into prepared ramekins evenly. Now, place ramekins in a large baking dish. Add hot water in the baking dish, about 1-inch up sides of the ramekins. Bake for about 35 minutes. Serve warm with the topping o heavy whipping cream and raspberries.

Raspberry Mousse

Preparation Time: 10 minutes | **Cooking Time:** 10 minutes | **Servings:** 4 | **Calories:** 44

Ingredients: 2-½ cups fresh raspberries | 1/3 cups granulated erythritol | 1 teaspoon liquid stevia
1/3 cup unsweetened almond milk | 1 tablespoon fresh lemon juice | ¼ teaspoon salt

Directions: In a food processor, add all the listed ingredients and pulse until smooth. Transfer the mixture into serving glasses and refrigerate to chill before serving.

Keto Shake

Preparation Time: 15 minutes | **Cooking Time:** 0 minutes | **Servings:** 1 | **Calories**: 104

Ingredients: ¾ cup almond milk | ½ cup ice | 2 tablespoons almond butter | 1 tablespoon chia seeds
2 tablespoons cocoa powder (unsweetened) | 2 tablespoons swerve | 2 tablespoons hemp seeds
½ tablespoon vanilla extract | salt, to taste

Directions: Blend all the ingredients in a food processor. Chill in the refrigerator before serving.

Cream Cake

Preparation Time: 15 minutes | **Cooking Time:** 1 hour 5 minutes | **Servings:** 12 | **Calories**: 258

Ingredients: 2 cups almond flour | 2 teaspoons organic baking powder | ½ cup butter, chopped
2 ounces cream cheese, softened | 1 cup sour cream | 1 cups granulated erythritol
1 teaspoon organic vanilla extract | 4 large organic eggs | 1 tablespoon powdered erythritol

Directions: Preheat your oven to 350°F. Generously, grease a 9-inch Bundt pan. Add almond flour and baking powder in a large bowl and mix well. Set aside. In a microwave-safe bowl, add butter and cream cheese and microwave for about 30 seconds. Remove from microwave and stir well. Add sour cream, erythritol, and vanilla extract and mix until well combined. Add the cream mixture into the bowl of the flour mixture and mix until well combined. Add eggs and mix until well combined. Transfer the mixture into the prepared pan evenly. Bake for about 50 minutes or until a toothpick inserted in the center comes out clean. Remove from the oven and put onto a wire rack to cool for about 10 minutes. Carefully, invert the cake onto a wire rack to cool completely. Just before serving, dust the cake with powdered erythritol. Cut into 12 equal-sized slices and serve.

Keto Cheesecakes

Preparation Time: 25 minutes | **Cooking Time:** 15 minutes | **Servings:** 9 | **Calories**: 478.2

Ingredients: For the cheesecakes: 2 tablespoons butter | 1 tablespoon caramel syrup; sugar-free
3 tablespoons coffee | 8 ounces cream cheese | 1/3 cup swerve | 3 eggs
For the frosting: 8 ounces mascarpone cheese; soft | 3 tablespoons caramel syrup; sugar-free
2 tablespoons swerve | 3 tablespoons butter

Directions: In your blender, mix cream cheese with eggs, 2 tablespoons butter, coffee, 1 tablespoon caramel syrup, and 1/3 cup swerve and pulse very well. Spoon this into a cupcakes pan, introduce in the oven at 350 degrees F and bake for 15 minutes. Leave aside to cool down and then keep in the freezer for 3 hours. Meanwhile, in a bowl, mix 3 tablespoons butter with 3 tablespoons caramel syrup, 2 tablespoons swerve, and mascarpone cheese and blend well. Spoon this over cheesecakes and serve them.

Pumpkin and Cream Cheese Cup

Preparation Time: 10 minutes | **Cooking Time:** 12 minutes | **Servings:** 2 | **Calories**: 261

Ingredients: 4 tbsp almond flour | 1-1/3 tbsp coconut flour | 2 tbsp pumpkin puree | ½ of egg
2-2/3 tbsp cream cheese, softened | 2/3 tbsp butter, unsalted | ¼ tsp pumpkin spice
2/3 tsp baking powder | 2 tbsp erythritol sweetener

Directions: Turn on the oven, then set it to 350 degrees F and let it preheat. Take a medium bowl, place butter and 1 ½ tbsp sweetener in it, and then beat until fluffy. Beat in egg and then beat in pumpkin puree until well combined. Take a medium bowl, place flours in it, stir in pumpkin spice, baking powder until mixed, stir this mixture into the butter mixture and then distribute the mixture into two silicone muffin cups. Take a medium bowl, place cream cheese in it, and stir in remaining sweetener until well combined. Divide the cream cheese mixture into the silicone muffin cups, swirl the batter and cream cheese mixture by using a toothpick and then bake for 10 to 12 minutes until muffins have turned firm.

Chocolate Pudding Delight

Preparation Time: 52 minutes | **Cooking Time:** 0 minutes | **Servings:** 2 | **Calories:** 221.2

Ingredients: 1/2 teaspoon stevia powder | 2 tablespoons cocoa powder | 2 tablespoons water
1 tablespoon gelatin | 1 cup of coconut milk | 2 tablespoons maple syrup

Directions: Heat a pan with the coconut milk over medium heat; add stevia and cocoa powder and stir well. In a bowl, mix gelatin with water; stir well and add to the pan. Stir well, add maple syrup, whisk again, divide into ramekins and keep in the fridge for 45 minutes Serve cold.

Peanut Butter Fudge

Preparation Time: 2 hours 12 minutes | **Cooking Time:** 0 minutes | **Servings:** 12 | **Calories:** 85

Ingredients: 1 cup peanut butter; unsweetened | 1 cup of coconut oil | 1/4 cup almond milk
2 teaspoons vanilla stevia | a pinch of salt
For the topping: 2 tablespoons swerve | 1/4 cup cocoa powder | 2 tablespoons melted coconut oil

Directions: In a heatproof bowl, mix peanut butter with 1 cup coconut oil; stir and heat up in your microwave until it melts. Add a pinch of salt, almond milk, and stevia; stir well everything and pour into a lined loaf pan. Keep in the fridge for 2 hours and then slice it. In a bowl, mix 2 tbsp melted coconut with cocoa powder and swerve and stir very well. Drizzle the sauce over your peanut butter fudge and serve.

Keto Brownies

Preparation Time: 30 minutes | **Cooking Time:** 20 minutes | **Servings:** 12 | **Calories**: 183.7

Ingredients: 6 ounces coconut oil; melted | 4 ounces cream cheese | 5 tablespoons swerve | 6 eggs
2 teaspoons vanilla | 3 ounces of cocoa powder | 1/2 teaspoon baking powder

Directions: In a blender, mix eggs with coconut oil, cocoa powder, baking powder, vanilla, cream cheese, and swerve and stir using a mixer. Pour this into a lined baking dish, introduce in the oven at 350 degrees F and bake for 20 minutes. Slice into rectangle pieces when their cold and serve.

Cinnamon Streusel Egg Loaf

Preparation Time: 10 minutes | **Cooking Time:** 15 minutes | **Servings:** 2 | **Calories:** 152

Ingredients: 2 tbsp almond flour | 1 tbsp butter, softened | ½ tbsp grated butter, chilled | 1 egg
1 ounce cream cheese | Others: ½ tsp cinnamon, divided | 1 tbsp erythritol sweetener, divided
¼ tsp vanilla extract, unsweetened

Directions: Turn on the oven, then set it to 350 degrees F and let it preheat. Meanwhile, crack the egg in a small bowl, add cream cheese, softened butter, ¼ tsp cinnamon, ½ tbsp sweetener, and vanilla and whisk until well combined. Divide the egg batter between two silicone muffins and then bake for 7 minutes. Meanwhile, prepare the streusel and for this, place flour in a small bowl, add remaining ingredients and stir until well mixed. When egg loaves have baked, sprinkle streusel on top and then continue baking for 7 minutes. When done, remove loaves from the cups, let them cool for 5 minutes and then Serve and enjoy!

Keto Fat Bombs

Preparation Time: 30 minutes | **Cooking Time:** 0 minutes | **Servings:** 10 | **Calories:** 176

Ingredients: 8 tablespoons butter | ¼ cup swerve | ½ teaspoon vanilla extract | 2 cups almond flour
2/3 cup chocolate chips | salt. to taste

Directions: In a bowl, beat the butter until fluffy. Stir in the sugar, salt and vanilla. Mix well. Add the almond flour. Fold in the chocolate chips. Cover the bowl with cling wrap and refrigerate for 20 minutes. Create balls from the dough.

Snickerdoodle Muffins

Preparation Time: 10 minutes | **Cooking Time:** 12 minutes | **Servings:** 2 | **Calories:** 241

Ingredients: 6-2/3 tbsp coconut flour | 1 tbsp butter, unsalted, melted | 1-1/3 tbsp whipping cream
1 tbsp almond milk, unsweetened | ½ of egg | Others: 1-1/3 tbsp erythritol sweetener and more, topping
¼ tsp baking powder ¼ tsp ground cinnamon and more for topping | ¼ tsp vanilla extract, unsweetened

Directions: Turn on the oven, then set it to 350 degrees F and let it preheat. Meanwhile, take a medium bowl, place flour in it, add cinnamon, baking powder, and cinnamon and stir until combined. Take a separate bowl, place the half egg in it, add butter, sour cream, milk, and vanilla and whisk until blended. Whisk in flour mixture into incorporated and smooth batter comes together, divide the batter evenly between two silicon muffin cups and then sprinkle cinnamon and sweetener on top. Bake the muffins for 10 to 12 minutes until firm, and then the top has turned golden brown and then Serve and enjoy!

Sweet Cinnamon Muffins

Preparation Time: 5 minutes | **Cooking Time:** 2 minutes | **Servings:** 2 | **Calories:** 101

Ingredients: 4 tsp coconut flour | 2 tsp cinnamon |2 tsp erythritol sweetener | 1/16 tsp baking soda
2 eggs

Directions: Take a medium bowl, place all the ingredients in it, and whisk until well combined. Take two ramekins, grease them with oil, distribute the prepared batter in it and then microwave for 1 minute and 45 seconds until done. When done, take out muffin from the ramekin, cut in half, and serve.

Nutty Muffins

Preparation Time: 5 minutes | **Cooking Time:** 5 minutes | **Servings:** 2 | **Calories:** 131

Ingredients: 4 tsp coconut flour | 1/16 tsp baking soda | 1 tsp erythritol sweetener | 2 eggs
2 tsp almond butter, unsalted

Directions: Take a medium bowl, place all the ingredients in it, and whisk until well combined. Take two ramekins, grease them with oil, distribute the prepared batter in it and then microwave for 1 minute and 45 seconds until done. When done, take out muffin from the ramekin, cut in half, and serve.

Chocolate Mug Muffins

Preparation Time: 5 minutes | **Cooking Time:** 2 minutes | **Servings:** 4 | **Calories:** 208

Ingredients: 4 tbsps. almond flour | 1 tsp baking powder | 4 tbsp. granulated erythritol
2 tbsp. cocoa powder | ½ tsp vanilla extract | 2 pinches salt | 2 eggs beaten | 3 tbsp. butter, melted
1 tsp coconut oil, for greasing the mug | ½ oz. sugar-free dark chocolate, chopped

Directions: Mix the dry ingredients together in a separate bowl. Add the melted butter, beaten eggs, and chocolate to the bowl. Stir thoroughly. Divide your dough into 4 pieces. Put these pieces in the greased mugs and put them in the microwave. Cook for 1-1.5 minutes. Let them cool for 1 minute and serve.

Pumpkin Pie Mug Cake

Preparation Time: 5 minutes | **Cooking Time:** 2 minutes | **Servings:** 2 | **Calories:** 181

Ingredients: 2 tbsp coconut flour | 1 tsp sour cream | 2 tbsp whipping cream | 2 eggs
¼ cup pumpkin puree | Others: 2 tbsp erythritol sweetener | 1/3 tsp cinnamon | ¼ tsp baking soda

Directions: Take a small bowl, place cream in it, and then beat in sweetener until well combined. Cover the bowl, let it chill in the refrigerator for 30 minutes, then beat in eggs and pumpkin puree and stir in remaining ingredients until incorporated and smooth. Divide the batter between two coffee mugs greased with oil and then microwave for 2 minutes until thoroughly cooked. Serve.

Chocolate and Strawberry Crepe

Preparation Time: 5 minutes | **Cooking Time:** 5 minutes | **Servings:** 2 | **Calories:** 120

Ingredients: 1-1/3 tbsp coconut flour | 1 tsp of cocoa powder | ¼ tsp flaxseed | 1 egg
2-¾ tbsp coconut milk, unsweetened | 2 tsp avocado oil | 1/8 tsp baking powder | 2 oz strawberry, sliced

Directions: Take a medium bowl, place flour in it, and then stir in cocoa powder, baking powder, and flaxseed in it until mixed. Add egg and milk and then whisk until smooth. Take a medium skillet pan, place it over medium heat, add 1 tsp oil and when hot, pour in half of the batter, spread it evenly, and then cook for 1 minute per side until firm. Transfer crepe to a plate, add remaining oil and cook another crepe by using the remaining batter. When done, fill crepes with strawberries, fold them and serve.

Blackberry and Coconut Flour Cupcake

Preparation Time: 5 minutes | **Cooking Time:** 15 minutes | **Servings:** 2 | **Calories:** 420

Ingredients: 3-¼ tbsp coconut flour | 1/3 cup whipping cream | 1 tbsp cream cheese | 1-½ egg
1 ounce blackberry | 2-2/3 tbsp butter, unsalted, chopped | 5-1/3 tbsp erythritol sweetener
2/3 tsp baking powder | 1/3 tsp vanilla extract, unsweetened

Directions: Take a small bowl, place butter in it, add cream and them microwave for 30 to 60 seconds until it melts, stirring every 20 seconds. Then add cream cheese, cream, vanilla, and erythritol, whisk until smooth, whisk in coconut flour and baking powder until incorporated and then fold in berries. Distribute the mixture evenly between four muffin cups, then bake for 12 to 15 minutes until firm. Serve

Avocado Ice Pops

Preparation Time: 20 minutes | **Cooking Time:** 0 minutes | **Servings:** 10 | **Calories:** 176

Ingredients: 3 avocados | ¼ cup lime juice | 3 tablespoons swerve | ¾ cup coconut milk
1 tablespoon coconut oil | 1 cup keto friendly chocolate

Directions: Add all the ingredients except the oil and chocolate in a blender. Blend until smooth. Pour the mixture into the popsicle mold. Freeze overnight. In a bowl, mix oil and chocolate chips. Melt in the microwave. And then let cool. Dunk the avocado popsicles into the chocolate before serving.

Chocolate Milkshake

Preparation Time: 5 minutes | **Cooking Time:** 0 minutes | **Servings:** 1 | **Calories:** 303

Ingredients: 1/2 cup of full-fat coconut milk or heavy cream. | 1/2 medium and sliced avocado.
1-2 tablespoons of cacao powder | 1/2 teaspoon of vanilla extract | pink Himalayan salt to taste.
2-4 tablespoons of erythritol | 1/2 cup of ice | water as needed
Optional add-ins: MCT oil | hemp hearts | collagen peptides | mint extract or extract of choice

Directions: Using a food processor or a high-speed blender, add in all the ingredients on the list (aside from the ice) alongside your chosen add ins then blend until the mixture becomes creamy and smooth. pour the mixture into a serving cup, add in the ice then serve.

Raspberry and Coconut

Preparation Time: 15 minutes | **Cooking Time:** 0 minutes | **Servings:** 12 | **Calories:** 99.3

Ingredients: 1/4 cup swerve | 1/2 cup coconut oil | 1/2 cup raspberries; dried | 1/2 cup coconut butter
1/2 cup coconut; shredded

Directions: In your food processor, blend dried berries very well. Heat a pan with the butter over medium heat. Add oil, coconut and swerve; stir and cook for 5 minutes. Pour half of this into a lined baking pan and spread well. Add raspberry powder and also spread. Top with the rest of the butter mix, spread and keep in the fridge for a while cut into pieces and serve

Yogurt and Strawberry Bowl

Preparation Time: 5 minutes | **Cooking Time:** 0 minutes | **Servings:** 2 | **Calories**: 165

Ingredients: 3 oz mixed berries | 1 tbsp chopped almonds | 1 tbsp chopped walnuts | 4 oz yogurt

Directions: Divide yogurt between two bowls, top with berries, then sprinkle with almonds and walnuts.

Berries in Yogurt Cream

Preparation Time: 1 hour and 5 minutes | **Cooking Time:** 0 minutes | **Servings:** 2 | **Calories**: 245

Ingredients: 1 oz blackberries | 1 oz raspberry | 2 tbsp erythritol sweetener | 4 oz yogurt
4 oz whipping cream

Directions: Take a medium bowl, place yogurt in it, and then whisk in cream. Sprinkle sweetener over yogurt mixture, don't stir, cover the bowl with a lid, and then refrigerate for 1 hour. When ready to serve, stir the yogurt mixture, divide it evenly between two bowls, top with berries, and then Serve and enjoy!

Chocolate Spread with Hazelnuts

Preparation Time: 5 minutes | **Cooking Time:** 5 minutes | **Servings:** 6 | **Calories**: 271

Ingredients: 2 tbsp. cacao powder | 5 oz. hazelnuts, roasted and without shells | 1 oz. unsalted butter
¼ cup coconut oil

Directions: Whisk all the spread ingredients with a blender for as long as you want. Remember, the longer you blend, the smoother your spread.

Chocolate Truffles

Preparation Time: 10 minutes | **Cooking Time:** 10 minutes | **Servings:** 16 | **Calories**: 190

Ingredients: 9 oz. of sugar-free dark chocolate chips | 1/2 cup of heavy whipping cream or coconut milk
1 teaspoon of cinnamon or sugar-free vanilla | 2 tablespoons of cacao powder for dusting.

Directions: Place a saucepan over medium heat, add in the cream and the cinnamon or vanilla then heat for a few minutes until it starts to simmer. Place the chocolate in a mixing bowl, pour in the heated cream mixture then let sit for a few minutes until the chocolate dissolves, stir to combine. Place the mixture into the refrigerator to chill for about two hours. Once chilled form small balls out of the mixture then roll in the cacao powder, serve.

Quick and Simple Brownie

Preparation Time: 20 minutes | **Cooking Time:** 5 minutes | **Servings:** 2 | **Calories:** 100

Ingredients: 3 tbsp. Keto chocolate chips | 1 tbsp. unsweetened cacao powder | 2 tbsp. salted butter
2-¼ tbsp. powdered sugar

Directions: Combine 2 tbsp. of chocolate chips and butter, melt them in a microwave for 10-15 minutes. Add the remaining chocolate chips, stir and make a sauce. Add the cacao powder and powdered sugar to the sauce and whisk well until you have a dough. Place the dough on a baking sheet, form the Brownie. Put your Brownie into the oven (preheated to 350°F). Bake for 5 minutes.

Rich Chocolate Mousse

Preparation Time: 10 minutes | **Cooking Time:** 15 minutes | **Servings:** 3 | **Calories**: 269

Ingredients: ¼ cup low-fat coconut cream | 2 cups fat-free Greek-style yogurt, strained
4 tsp. powered cocoa, no added sugar | 2 tbsp. stevia/xylitol/bacon syrup | 1 tsp. natural vanilla extract

Directions: In a medium mixing bowl combine all the ingredients and mix well. Put individual serving bowls or glasses and refrigerate. Serve cold

Cute Peanut Balls

Preparation Time: 20 minutes | **Cooking Time:** 20 minutes | **Servings:** 18 | **Calories:** 194

Ingredients: 1 cup salted peanuts, chopped | 1 cup peanut butter | 1 cup powdered sweetener
8 oz keto chocolate chips

Directions: Combine the chopped peanuts, peanut butter, and sweetener in a separate dish. Stir well and make a dough. Divide it into 18 pieces and form small balls. Put them in the fridge for 10-15 minutes. Use a microwave to melt your chocolate chips. Plunge each ball into the melted chocolate. Return your balls in the fridge. Cool for about 20 minutes.

Coconut Bombs

Preparation Time: 30 minutes | **Cooking Time:** 15 minutes | **Servings:** 6 | **Calories**: 145

Ingredients: 4 oz. flaked coconut | ¼ cup coconut oil, melted | ¼ tsp. vanilla paste | 20 drops stevia

Directions: Preheat oven to 350°F. and line baking sheet with parchment paper. Spread over coconut flakes and put in the oven. Toast the flakes for 5-8 minutes until golden. Stir once to prevent burning. Transfer to a blender and pulse until smooth. Add the coconut oil, vanilla paste, and stevia. Stir to combine. Divide among 12 mini paper cases and put them in the freezer for 30 mins. Serve after it is firm.

Raspberry Cheesecake

Preparation Time: 10 minutes | **Cooking Time:** 25 minutes | **Servings:** 6 | **Calories:** 176

Ingredients: 2/3 cup coconut oil, melted | ½ cup cream cheese | 6 eggs | 3 tbsp. granulated sweetener
1 tsp. vanilla extract | ½ tsp. baking powder | ¾ cup raspberries

Directions: Preheat the oven to 350° F. Line a baking dish with parchment paper and set aside. In a bowl, beat together the coconut oil and cream cheese until smooth. Beat in eggs, then beat in the sweetener, vanilla, and baking powder until smooth. Spoon the batter into the baking dish and smooth out the top. Scatter the raspberries on top. Bake for 25 to 30 minutes or until the center is firm. Cool, slice, and serve.

Keto Chocolate Nut Clusters

Preparation Time: 5 minutes | **Cooking Time:** 10 minutes | **Servings:** 25 | **Calories**: 170

Ingredients: 9 oz. sugar-free dark chocolate chips | ¼ cup unrefined coconut oil | 2 cups salted mixed nuts

Directions: Line a rimmed baking sheet with parchment paper or a silicone baking mat. In a microwave-safe bowl, put a piece of the chocolate chips and coconut oil and microwave till the chocolate is melted. Use a spatula to mix. Let it cool handiest to some degree before using. Mix till everything of the nuts is overlaying inside the chocolate. Drop gigantic spoonful of the combo onto the prepared preparing sheet. Store scraps in the refrigerator for up to three weeks.

Cocoa Coconut Butter Fat Bombs

Preparation Time: 5 minutes | **Cooking Time:** 10 minutes | **Servings:** 12 | **Calories:** 297

Ingredients: 1 cup coconut oil | ½ cup unsalted butter | 6 tbsp. unsweetened cocoa powder
15 drops liquid stevia | ½ cup coconut butter

Directions: In a saucepan, put butter, coconut oil, cocoa powder, and stevia and cook over low heat, stirring frequently until melted. Melt coconut butter in another saucepan over low heat. Pour 2 tbsp. of cocoa mixture into each well of a 12-cup silicone mold. Add 1 tbsp. of melted coconut butter to each well. Put in the freezer until hardened, about 30 minutes. Serve.

Walnut Cakes

Preparation Time: 15 minutes | **Cooking Time:** 5 minutes | **Servings:** 2 | **Calories**: 162

Ingredients: 1 cup walnuts, ground | 10 oz. unsweetened dark chocolate | half cup coconut oil
7 tbsp. cocoa powder | 3 tbsp. erythritol | 5 tbsp. coconut butter | 1 tbsp. vanilla | salt

Directions: Melt the coconut oil in the microwave for 5 minutes and combine it with the cocoa powder, vanilla, erythritol and salt. Pour the mixture into the bowl and place in the fridge for around 10 minutes. Spoon half teaspoon of coconut butter and add the walnuts and then mix well. Spoon the mixture into paper muffin cups. Melt the dark chocolate on medium heat for around 5 min., stirring all the time. Cool the mixture and slowly pour it over the cakes. The cakes should be placed in the fridge for at least 2 hours.

Walnut Cookies

Preparation Time: 10 minutes | **Cooking Time:** 15 minutes | **Servings:** 16 | **Calories**: 340

Ingredients: 1/4 cup coconut flour | 8 tablespoon butter | 1/2 cup erythritol | 1 cup walnuts
1 teaspoon ground nutmeg | 1 teaspoon vanilla extract

Directions: Preheat oven to 325°F, and in the meantime take the baking sheet and line it with parchment paper. Grind the walnuts in a food processor and keep pulsing until they are well ground. Add the vanilla extract, erythritol, nutmeg and coconut floor to the ground walnuts in the food processer. Pulse again until all the ingredients are blended. Put butter in the food processer in the form of small pieces and pulse until you get a soft and smooth mixture. Make 16 balls on the baking sheet with the help of a cookie scooper and use your hands to press them to give them a cookie shape. Place in the preheated oven and bake for 15 minutes or until you find the cookies well baked. Remove from the oven once baked, set them aside for 15-20 minutes to cool. Sprinkle some additional nutmeg over the delicious walnut cookies if you like before you serve them.

Bounty Bars

Preparation Time: 20 minutes | **Cooking Time:** 0 minutes | **Servings:** 12 | **Calories**: 230

Ingredients: 1 cup coconut cream | 3 cups shredded unsweetened coconut | 5 oz. dark chocolate
1/4 c. extra virgin coconut oil | 1/2 tsp vanilla powder | 1/4 c. powdered erythritol | 1-1/2 oz. cocoa butter

Directions: Heat the oven at 350°F and toast the coconut in it for 5-6 minutes. Remove from the oven once toasted and set aside to cool. Take a bowl of medium size and add coconut oil, coconut cream, vanilla, erythritol and toasted coconut. Mix the ingredients well to prepare a smooth mixture. Make 12 bars of equal size with the help of your hands from the prepared mixture and adjust in the tray lined with parchment paper. Place the tray in the fridge for around one hour and in the meantime put the cocoa butter and dark chocolate in a glass bowl. Heat a cup of water in a saucepan over medium heat and place the bowl over it to melt the cocoa butter and the dark chocolate. Remove from the heat once melted properly, mix well until blended and set aside to cool. Take the coconut bars and coat them with dark chocolate mixture one by one using a wooden stick. Adjust on the tray lined with parchment paper and drizzle the remaining mixture over them. Refrigerate for around one hour before you serve the delicious bounty bars.

Keto Balls

Preparation Time: 15 minutes | **Cooking Time:** 4 minutes | **Servings:** 10 | **Calories**: 176

Ingredients: 2 eggs, beaten | 1 teaspoon coconut oil, melted | 9 oz coconut flour | cooking spray
5 oz Provolone cheese, shredded | 2 tbsp erythritol | 1 tsp baking powder | ¼ tsp ground coriander

Directions: Mix eggs with coconut oil, coconut flour, Provolone cheese, Erythritol, baking powder, and ground cinnamon. Make the balls and put them in the air fryer basket. Sprinkle the balls with cooking spray and cook at 400°F for 4 minutes.

Blueberry Lemon Cake

Preparation Time: 10 minutes | **Cooking Time:** 40 minutes | **Servings:** 4 | **Calories:** 274

Ingredients: For the Cake: 2/3 cup almond flour | 5 eggs | ⅓ cup almond milk, unsweetened
¼ cup erythritol | 2 tsp. vanilla extract | juice of 2 lemons | 1 tsp. lemon zest | ½ tsp. baking soda
pinch of salt | ½ cup fresh blueberries | 2 tbsp. butter, melted
For the Frosting: ½ cup heavy cream | juice of 1 lemon | 1/8 cup erythritol

Directions: Preheat the oven to 350°F. In a bowl, add the almond flour, eggs, and almond milk and mix well until smooth. Add the erythritol, a pinch of salt, baking soda, lemon zest, lemon juice, and vanilla extract. Mix and combine well. Fold in the blueberries. Use the butter to grease the spring form pans. Pour the batter into the greased pans. Put on a baking sheet for even baking. Put in the oven to bake until cooked through in the middle and slightly brown on the top, about 35 to 40 min. Let cool before removing from the pan. Mix the erythritol, lemon juice, and heavy cream. Mix well. Pour frosting on top. Serve.

Home Made Coconut Ice Cream

Preparation Time: 10 minutes | **Cooking Time:** 95 minutes | **Servings:** 4 | **Calories**: 182

Ingredients: 2 cups evaporated low-fat milk | ⅓ cup low-fat condensed milk | 1 tsp. dried coconut
1 cup low-fat coconut milk | ½ cup stevia/xylitol/bacon syrup | 2 scoops whey protein concentrate
2 tsp. sugar-free coconut extract

Directions: Put all of the ingredients in a mixing bowl and combine well. Heat the mixture over medium heat until it starts to bubble. Remove from heat and allow the mixture to cool down. Chill mixture for about an hour, then freeze in ice cream maker as outlined by the manufacturer's directions.

Berries with Coconut Cream

Preparation Time: 5 minutes | **Cooking Time:** 15 minutes | **Servings:** 2 | **Calories**: 200

Ingredients: 1 cup fat-free cream cheese | ¼ cup coconut chunks | ½ tsp. sugar-free coconut extract
½ cup mixed berries | 3 tsp. stevia/xylitol/yacon syrup

Directions: Beat cream cheese until fluffy. Put the coconut chunks and stevia inside a blender and puree. Combine using the Cream cheese and set in serving plates. Top with berries. Serve.

Raspberry Cream

Preparation Time: 10 minutes | **Cooking Time:** 20 minutes | **Servings:** 6 | **Calories:** 49.4

Ingredients: ½ cup raspberries | 1 tablespoon lime juice | 2 tablespoons water
3 tablespoons erythritol | ¼ teaspoon ground cinnamon

Directions: Blend the raspberries and mix with lime juice, water, Erythritol, and ground cinnamon.
Pour the mixture in the air fryer and cook at 345°F for 20 minutes.

Coconut Panna Cotta

Preparation Time: 5 minutes | **Cooking Time:** 20 minutes | **Servings:** 2 | **Calories**: 130

Ingredients: 2 cups skimmed milk | 1/2 cup water | 1 tsp. sugar-free coconut extract
1 envelope powdered grass-fed | organic gelatin | sugar-free | 2 scoops whey protein isolate
4 tbsp. stevia/xylitol/yacon syrup | ⅓ cup fresh raspberries | 2 tbsp. fresh mint

Directions: In a non-stick pan, pour the milk, stevia, water and coconut Extract. Bring to a boil. Slowly add the gelatin and stir well until the mixtures start to thicken. When ready, divide the mix among the small silicon cups. Refrigerate overnight to relax and hang up. Remove through the fridge and thoroughly turn each cup over ahead of a serving plate. Garnish with a raspberries and fresh mint, serve and revel in.

Lemon & Lime Sorbet

Preparation Time: 5 minutes | **Cooking Time:** 120 minutes | **Servings:** 2 | **Calories**: 150

Ingredients: 1 cup water | ¾ cup stevia/xylitol/yacon syrup | 1 cup fresh lemon juice | 2 scoops whey protein concentrate | 1/2 cup lime juice | 4 whole lemons cut in half; flesh removed

Directions: Put the lake, stevia, lemon and lime juice into a blender and puree. Transfer to a container and freeze for about a couple of hours. Remove from the freezer and puree once more using a blender. Transfer to an airtight container and return to freezer. Serve in lemon/orange cups and garnish with fresh mint.

Mint Pie

Preparation Time: 15 minutes | **Cooking Time:** 25 minutes | **Servings:** 2 | **Calories:** 313

Ingredients: 1 tablespoon instant coffee | 2 tablespoons almond butter, softened | 3 eggs, beaten
2 tablespoons erythritol | 1 teaspoon dried mint | 1 teaspoon spearmint, dried | cooking spray
4 teaspoons coconut flour

Directions: Spray the air fryer basket with cooking spray. Then mix all ingredients in the mixer bowl. When you get a smooth mixture, transfer it in the air fryer basket. Flatten it gently. Cook the pie at 365°F for 25 minutes.

Saffron Cookies

Preparation Time: 10 minutes | **Cooking Time:** 15 minutes | **Servings:** 12 | **Calories**: 106

Ingredients: 2 cups coconut flour | ½ cup Erythritol | ¼ cup coconut, melted | 1 egg, beaten
2 teaspoons saffron | 1 teaspoon vanilla extract

Directions: Mix all ingredients in the bowl and knead the dough. Make the cookies and put them in the air fryer basket in one layer. Cook the cookies at 355°F for 15 minutes.

Raspberry Jam

Preparation Time: 10 minutes | **Cooking Time:** 20 minutes | **Servings:** 12 | **Calories:** 28.6

Ingredients: ¼ cup erythritol | 7 oz raspberries | 1 tablespoon lime juice | ¼ cup of water

Directions: Put all ingredients in the air fryer and stir gently. Cook the jam at 350°F for 20 minutes. Stir the jam every 5 minutes to avoid burning.

Sage Muffins

Preparation Time: 10 minutes | **Cooking Time:** 20 minutes | **Servings:** 8 | **Calories**: 85

Ingredients: 3 tablespoons coconut oil, softened | 1 egg, beaten | ½ cup erythritol | ¼ cup almond flour
1 teaspoon dried sage | 3 tablespoons mascarpone | ½ teaspoon baking soda | cooking spray

Directions: Spray the muffin molds with cooking spray. Then mix all ingredients in the mixing bowl and stir until smooth. Pour the mixture in the muffin molds and transfer in the air fryer. Cook the muffins at 350°F for 20 minutes.

Pecan Tarts

Preparation Time: 10 minutes | **Cooking Time:** 10 minutes | **Servings:** 5 | **Calories**: 143

Ingredients: 3 pecans, chopped | ½ cup coconut flour | 1 egg, beaten | 1 tablespoon swerve
1 tablespoon coconut oil, softened | ½ teaspoon baking powder | cooking spray

Directions: Spray the air fryer basket with cooking spray. Then mix coconut flour with egg, coconut oil, swerve, and baking powder. When you get a smooth batter, pour it in the air fryer basket, flatten gently, and top with pecans. Cook the tart at 375°F for 10 minutes.

Vanilla Shortcake

Preparation Time: 15 minutes | **Cooking Time:** 30 minutes | **Servings:** 4 | **Calories**: 140

Ingredients: 3 eggs, beaten | ½ cup almond flour | ½ teaspoon baking powder | 2 teaspoons swerve
1 teaspoon vanilla extract | ½ cup coconut cream | cooking spray

Directions: Spray the air fryer basket with cooking spray. Then mix eggs with almond flour, baking powder, swerve, vanilla extract, and coconut cream. When the mixture is smooth, pour it in the air fryer basket and flatten gently with the help of the spatula. Cook the shortcake at 355°F for 30 minutes.

Coconut Hand Pies

Preparation Time: 20 minutes | **Cooking Time:** 26 minutes | **Servings:** 6 | **Calories**: 128

Ingredients: 8 oz coconut flour | 1 teaspoon vanilla extract | 2 tablespoons swerve | 2 eggs, beaten
1 tbsp almond butter, melted | 1 tablespoon almond meal | 2 tablespoons coconut shred | cooking spray

Directions: Mix coconut flour with vanilla extract, Swerve, eggs, almond butter, and almond meal. Knead the dough and roll it up. Cut the dough into squares and sprinkle with coconut shred. Fold the squares into the shape of pies and put in the air fryer basket. Sprinkle the pies with cooking spray and cook at 345°F for 13 minutes per side.

Milk Pie

Preparation Time: 10 minutes | **Cooking Time:** 20 minutes | **Servings:** 8 | **Calories**: 73

Ingredients: 3 tablespoons erythritol | 3 tablespoons butter, melted | ¼ cup organic almond milk
4 tablespoons coconut flour | ½ teaspoon baking powder | 2 eggs beaten

Directions: Put all ingredients in the mixer bowl and blend until smooth. Pour the mixture in the air fryer basket and cook at 365°F for 20 minutes.

Keto Hot Chocolate

Preparation Time: 10 minutes | **Cooking Time:** 7 minutes | **Servings:** 3 | **Calories**: 386

Ingredients: 1/4 teaspoon vanilla extract | 2 cups organic almond milk | 1 teaspoon coconut oil
1 tablespoon cocoa powder | 2 tablespoons erythritol

Directions: Mix all ingredients in the air fryer basket. Stir the mixture until smooth. Cook the dessert at 375°F for 7 minutes.

Cocoa Chia Pudding

Preparation Time: 40 minutes | **Cooking Time:** 10 minutes | **Servings:** 3 | **Calories**: 442

Ingredients: 3 tablespoons chia seeds | 2 cups coconut cream | 1 teaspoon of cocoa powder
1 teaspoon vanilla extract | 1 tablespoon erythritol

Directions: Pour the coconut cream in the air fryer. Add cocoa powder, vanilla extract, and Erythritol. Stir the liquid until smooth. Then cook it at 350°F for 10 minutes. Add chia seeds, carefully mix the dessert, and leave it to rest for 40 minutes.

Pumpkin Spices Muffins

Preparation Time: 15 minutes | **Cooking Time:** 10 minutes | **Servings:** 6 | **Calories**: 149

Ingredients: 1 cup coconut flour | 1 tablespoon pumpkin spices | ½ teaspoon baking powder
2 eggs, beaten | 2 tablespoons coconut oil | 2 tablespoons erythritol | 1 tablespoon coconut cream

Directions: Mix all ingredients in the mixing bowl. When the batter is smooth, pour it in the muffin molds and transfer in the air fryer basket. Cook the muffins at 365°F for 10 minutes.

Butter Cookies

Preparation Time: 15 minutes | **Cooking Time:** 10 minutes | **Servings:** 5 | **Calories**: 206

Ingredients: 4 tablespoons butter, softened | 4 teaspoons Splenda |1 egg, beaten | 1 cup coconut flour

Directions: In the mixing bowl, mix butter, Splenda, egg, and coconut flour. Knead the dough and make the balls (cookies). Put them in the air fryer and cook at 365°F for 10 minutes.

Mascarpone Brownies

Preparation Time: 10 minutes | **Cooking Time:** 25 minutes | **Servings:** 6 | **Calories**: 248

Ingredients: 6 tablespoons mascarpone | 3 eggs, beaten | 2 tbsp cocoa powder | 1 cup almond flour
3 tablespoons butter, softened | ¼ teaspoon baking soda | ¼ cup coconut cream | 3 tbsp erythritol

Directions: Mix all ingredients in the mixing bowl until smooth. Then line the air fryer basket with baking paper and pour the brownie batter inside. Cook the meal at 360°F for 25 minutes. Then cool the dessert little and cut into brownies.

Chia Balls

Preparation Time: 15 minutes | **Cooking Time:** 10 minutes | **Servings:** 4 | **Calories:** 126

Ingredients: 4 teaspoons chia seeds | 1 tablespoon coconut oil, softened | 1 tablespoon Erythritol
½ teaspoon vanilla extract | 1 tablespoon almond flour | 1 teaspoon almond flakes
1 egg, beaten | cooking spray

Directions: Spray the air fryer basket with cooking spray. Then mix all remaining ingredients in the mixing bowl and stir until homogenous. Make the balls from the mixture and put in the air fryer in one layer. Cook the chia balls at 365°F for 10 minutes.

Coconut Blueberries Ice Cream

Preparation Time: 15 minutes | **Cooking Time:** 0 minutes | **Servings:** 2 | **Calories:** 164

Ingredients: half cup fresh blueberries | 4 tbsp. shredded coconut | 1 cup unsweetened coconut milk
5 tbsp. coconut butter | 15 drops of stevia | 2 tbsp. vanilla

Directions: Pulse the blueberries, coconut milk, coconut butter, shredded coconut, stevia and vanilla using a blender. Spoon the mixture into the ice cream maker and process for 1 hour or according to manufacturer's instructions. Spoon the blueberries mixture into the silicone molds or an ice tray. Freeze the coconut and blueberries ice cream for overnight and then serve.

Cheesy Biscuits

Preparation Time: 20 minutes | **Cooking Time:** 20 minutes | **Servings:** 9 | **Calories:** 320

Ingredients: 4 eggs | 2 cups almond flour | 2-½ cups shredded cheddar cheese | 1/4 cup half-and-half
1 tablespoon baking powder

Directions: Preheat oven to 350°F and get the baking sheet ready by lining it with parchment paper. Take a large bowl and mix the baking powder and almond flour in that. Add cheddar cheese to the mixture and mix until well combined. Take a small bowl, add half and half and also crack the eggs into it. Mix well until fully blended. Add the eggs mixture to the flour mixture and keep whisking with the help of a spatula to prepare a smooth batter. Take portions of the batter using a scoop and put them on the baking sheet. Make sure that you take the portions in even sizes and flatten them a bit from the top. Place in the preheated oven and bake for 20 minutes or until the time you get a golden-brown look. Remove from the oven once baked and transfer to the wire rack to cool before serving.

Raspberries Mousse

Preparation Time: 5 minutes | **Cooking Time:** 15 minutes | **Servings:** 4 | **Calories:** 195

Ingredients: 1 cup fresh raspberries | half cup almond milk | 10 oz. coconut butter | 3 tbsp. erythritol 2 tbsp. vanilla

Directions: Boil the almond milk in a pan over low heat for 5 min. Combine the raspberries with the almond milk and pulse well using a blender. Use an electric hand mixer and beat together the raspberries mixture, coconut butter, erythritol and vanilla in a mixing bowl until the homogenous mass. Pour the raspberries mixture into the jars or glasses. Freeze the raspberries mixture for around 20 minutes and serve.

Dark Chocolate Raspberry Ice Cream

Preparation Time: 5 minutes | **Cooking Time:** 0 minutes | **Servings:** 2 | **Calories**: 104

Ingredients: 2 frozen bananas, sliced | ¼ cup fresh raspberries | 2 tablespoons cocoa powder, unsweetened | 2 tablespoons raspberry jelly

Directions: Place all the ingredients in a food processor, except for berries and pulse for 2 minutes until smooth. Distribute the ice cream mixture between two bowls, stir in berries until combined, and then serve immediately.

Peanut Butter and Honey Ice Cream

Preparation Time: 5 minutes | **Cooking Time:** 0 minutes | **Servings:** 2 | **Calories**: 190

Ingredients: 2-½ tablespoons peanut butter | 2 bananas frozen, sliced | 1-½ tablespoon honey

Directions: Place all the ingredients in a food processor and pulse for 2 minutes until smooth. Distribute the ice cream mixture between two bowls and then serve immediately.

Coconut Keto Vegan Ice Cream

Preparation Time: 5 minutes | **Cooking Time:** 1 hour and 20 minutes | **Servings:** 4 | **Calories**: 159

Ingredients: 15 oz. coconut cream | 5 oz. cocoa powder | half cup almond milk | shredded coconut 4 tbsp. powdered erythritol | vanilla

Directions: Place the coconut cream, cocoa powder, shredded coconut, erythritol and vanilla into a pot and heat gently for 10 minutes, stirring, warming up until dissolved. Use an electric hand mixer and whisk the almond milk and slowly pour the sweet coconut cream mixture, stirring all the time. Pour the almond-coconut mixture into the pot and heat gently for 10 minutes, stirring, warming up and then cool. Spoon the mixture into the ice cream maker and process for 1 hour or according to manufacturer's instructions and freeze for at least 3 hours.

Mango Ice Cream

Preparation Time: 5 minutes | **Cooking Time:** 0 minutes | **Servings:** 1 | **Calories**: 74

Ingredients: 2 frozen bananas, sliced | 1 cup diced frozen mango

Directions: Place all the ingredients in a food processor and pulse for 2 minutes until smooth. Distribute the ice cream mixture between two bowls and then serve immediately.

Blueberry Ice Cream

Preparation Time: 5 minutes | **Cooking Time:** 0 minutes | **Servings:** 2 | **Calories:** 68

Ingredients: 2 frozen bananas, sliced | ½ cup blueberries

Directions: Place all the ingredients in a food processor and pulse for 2 minutes until smooth. Distribute the ice cream mixture between two bowls and then serve immediately.

Coconut Pineapple Ice Cream

Preparation Time: 15 minutes | **Cooking Time:** 0 minutes | **Servings:** 4 | **Calories**: 154

Ingredients: 3 tsp. pure pineapple extract | 1 can pineapples | 1 cup unsweetened coconut milk
5 tbsp. coconut butter | 3 tbsp. erythritol | 2 tbsp. vanilla

Directions: Pulse the pineapple extract, coconut milk, coconut butter, erythritol and vanilla using a blender. Cut the canned pineapples into cubes and combine with the pineapple mixture. Spoon the mixture into the ice cream maker and process for 1 hour or according to manufacturer's instructions. Spoon the pineapples mixture into the silicone molds or an ice tray. Freeze the pineapples ice cream for overnight and then serve.

5-Ingredient Ice Cream

Preparation Time: 20 minutes | **Cooking Time:** 1 hour 10 minutes | **Servings:** 6 | **Calories**: 87

Ingredients: 1-½ cup full fat coconut milk | 1/3 cup natural peanut butter | 2 tbsp. vanilla extract
1/8 tsp stevia powder | a pinch of salt

Directions: Prior to starting this recipe, place a freezer-safe container in the freezer for at least 24 hours before to ensure that when the ice cream mixture is transferred no ice crystals are formed. Add all ingredients to a blender and blend until a smooth and creamy consistency is achieved. Chill this mixture by placing it in the refrigerator for 1 hour. Transfer the mixture to an ice-cream maker and churn for 10 minutes or until it achieves a soft serve consistency. Transfer the ice cream to the prepared freezer-safe container and freeze for at least one hour before serving. Can be served with caramel sauce

Wonderful Peanut Butter Mousse

Preparation Time: 2 to 5 minutes | **Cooking Time:** 0 minutes | **Servings:** 4 | **Calories**: 206

Ingredients: 4 tablespoons natural unsweetened peanut butter | ½ can coconut cream
1-½ teaspoons stevia

Directions: First of all, please check that you've all the ingredients obtainable. Now combine all ingredients & whip for one minute, until mixture forms peaks. Finally, chill for at least three hours or until a mousse texture is achieved.

Peanut Butter Mousse

Preparation Time: 50 minutes | **Cooking Time:** 0 minutes | **Servings:** 5 | **Calories**: 270

Ingredients: 3 tablespoons agave nectar | 14 ounces coconut milk, unsweetened, chilled
4 tablespoons creamy peanut butter, salted

Directions: Separate coconut milk and its solid, then add solid from coconut milk into the bowl and beat for 45 seconds until fluffy. Then beat in remaining ingredients until smooth, refrigerate for 45 minutes and serve.

No-Bake Coconut Chia Macaroons

Preparation Time: 2 hours | **Cooking Time:** 0 minutes | **Servings:** 6 | **Calories**: 129

Ingredients: 1 cup shredded coconut | 2 tbsp. chia seeds | ½ cup coconut cream | ½ cup erythritol

Directions: Combine all ingredients in a bowl. Mix until well combined. Chill the mixture for about half an hour. Once set, scoop the mixture into serving portions and roll into balls. Return to the chiller for another hour.

Lemon Bars

Preparation Time: 10 minutes | **Cooking Time:** 1 hour and 5 minutes | **Servings:** 5 | **Calories:** 159

Ingredients: 4 tbsp. lemon zest, minced | 8 oz. coconut butter | 4 tbsp. coconut cream
1 cup almond flour | half cup silken tofu | 4 tbsp. powdered erythritol | 4 tsp. baking soda | vanilla

Directions: Melt the coconut butter on medium heat for around 5 minutes, stirring all the time. Combine the coconut butter, half cup of the almond flour, silken tofu, 2 tsp. baking soda, vanilla and 2 tbsp. of the powdered erythritol in a mixing bowl, mashing with a fork until smooth. Spoon the mixture into the baking tray and bake for 30 minutes at 310/320 degrees Fahrenheit. Now let's start the filling by combining the lemon zest, coconut cream, remaining erythritol, baking soda and almond flour. Beat together the filling mixture, in a mixing bowl, using an electric hand mixer. Then, pour the lemon filling mixture onto the cooled almond crust and bake for 30 minutes at 320/330 degrees Fahrenheit. Then cool, cut into pieces and serve with the lemon slices on top and orange juice.

Almond Butter, Oat and Protein Energy Balls

Preparation Time: 1 hour 10 minutes | **Cooking Time:** 3 minutes | **Servings:** 4 | **Calories:** 200

Ingredients: 1 cup rolled oats | ½ cup honey | 2-½ scoops of vanilla protein powder | 1 cup almond butter | chia seeds for rolling

Directions: Take a skillet pan, place it over medium heat, add butter and honey, stir and cook for 2 minutes until warm. Transfer the mixture into a bowl, stir in protein powder until mixed, and then stir in oatmeal until combined. Shape the mixture into balls, roll them into chia seeds, then arrange them on a cookie sheet and refrigerate for 1 hour until firm. Serve straight away

Chocolate and Avocado Truffles

Preparation Time: 1 hour and 10 minutes | **Cooking Time: 1 minute** | **Servings:** 18 | **Calories:** 59

Ingredients: 1 medium avocado, ripe | 2 tablespoons cocoa powder | 10 ounces of dark chocolate chips

Directions: Scoop out the flesh from avocado, place it in a bowl, then mash with a fork until smooth, and stir in 1/2 cup chocolate chips. Place remaining chocolate chips in a heatproof bowl and microwave for 1 minute until chocolate has melted, stirring halfway. Add melted chocolate into avocado mixture, stir well until blended, and then refrigerate for 1 hour. Then shape the mixture into balls, 1 tablespoon of mixture per ball, and roll in cocoa powder until covered. Serve straight away.

Gluten-Free Nut-Free Red Velvet Cupcakes

Preparation Time: 20 minutes | **Cooking Time:** 50 minutes | **Servings:** 8 | **Calories:** 371.5

Ingredients: 2 tbsp. flax meal | 4 tbsp. cocoa powder | ½ cup of almond butter | 4 tbsp. ground flaxseed
½ cup unsweetened almond milk | 1 tbsp. granulated erythritol | 2 tbsp. apple cider vinegar
1 tsp baking powder | 1/2 tsp baking soda

Directions: Preheat your oven to 350 degrees F. Prepare a standard size muffin tin by lining it with paper liners. In a small bowl, whisk together almond butter, almond milk and apple cider vinegar until a smooth combined mixture is achieved. Stir in flax seeds and erythritol and set aside. In a large mixing bowl, sift together cocoa powder, flax meal, baking powder and baking soda. Mix to combine. Pour the wet mixture into the dry ingredients and stir until there are no lumps. Do not overmix. Divide the batter between the lined muffin wells. Ensure that each muffin is filled 3/4 of the way. Bake for 30 minutes or until the top of each muffin is firm to the touch. Remove from the oven and allow to cool in pan for 10 minutes. Remove the cupcakes from the pan and allow to cool completely. Serve.

Coconut Oil Cookies

Preparation Time: 10 minutes | **Cooking Time:** 10 minutes | **Servings:** 15 | **Calories**: 112

Ingredients: 3 cups oats | 2 cups coconut sugar | 1/2 cup cashew milk | 1/2 cups peanut butter
1 teaspoon vanilla extract, unsweetened | 1/4 cup cocoa powder | 1/2 cup liquid coconut oil | | 1/2 tsp salt

Directions: Take a saucepan, place it over medium heat, add all the ingredients except for oats and vanilla, stir until mixed, and then bring the mixture to boil. Simmer the mixture for 4 minutes, mixing frequently, then remove the pan from heat and stir in vanilla. Add oats, stir until well mixed and then scoop the mixture on a plate lined with wax paper. Serve straight away.

Almond Butter Cookies

Preparation Time: 35 minutes | **Cooking Time:** 5 minutes | **Servings:** 13 | **Calories**: 158

Ingredients: 1/4 cup sesame seeds | 1 cup rolled oats | 3 tablespoons sunflower seeds, roasted, unsalted
1/8 tsp sea salt | 1-1/2 tbsp coconut flour | 1/2 tsp vanilla extract, unsweetened | 1/2 cup coconut sugar
3 tablespoons coconut oil | 2 tablespoons almond milk, unsweetened | 1/3 cup almond butter, salted

Directions: Take a saucepan, place it over medium heat, pour in milk, stir in sugar and oil and bring the mixture to a low boil. Boil the mixture for 1 minute, then remove the pan from heat, and stir in remaining ingredients until incorporated and well combined. Drop the prepared mixture onto a baking sheet lined with wax paper, about 13 cookies, and let them stand for 25 mins until firm and set. Serve straight away.

Chocolate Cookies

Preparation Time: 40 minutes | **Cooking Time:** 5 minutes | **Servings:** 4 | **Calories**: 148

Ingredients: 1/2 cup coconut oil | 1 cup agave syrup | 1/2 cup cocoa powder | 1/2 teaspoon salt
2 cups peanuts, chopped | 1 cup peanut butter | 2 cups sunflower seeds

Directions: Take a small saucepan, place it over medium heat, add the first three ingredients, and cook for 3 minutes until melted. Boil the mixture for 1 minute, then remove the pan from heat and stir in salt and butter until smooth. Fold in nuts and seeds until combined, then drop the mixture in the form of molds onto the baking sheet lined with wax paper and refrigerate for 30 minutes. Serve straight away.

Pumpkin Cookies

Preparation Time: 20 minutes | **Cooking Time:** 20 minutes | **Servings:** 12 | **Calories:** 172

Ingredients: 3 tablespoons of water | 2 teaspoons of ground cinnamon | ½ teaspoon of baking powder
¼ cup of coconut oil | half a cup of brown erythritol | 1 tablespoon of flaxseed powder | ½ tsp sea salt
½ cup of pumpkin puree (unsweetened) | 1 teaspoon of vanilla extract | 2 cups of almond flour

Directions: Preheat your oven to 350°F. Line a cookie tray with pieces of parchment paper. Put baking powder, Almond flour and salt into a medium sized bowl, stir to combine. Use a spoon to break any uneven ball I'm the flour. Mix the flaxseed powder and three tablespoons of water to make "flax egg." Let sit for about five minutes. Put the coconut oil, pumpkin puree, vanilla extract and flax egg into a bowl, whisk until well combined and smooth. Add in the erythritol and stir until well combined. Add the pumpkin mix into the dry ingredients and stir until well mixed, the texture of the dough should be like that of regular cookie dough. Shape the dough into small round balls. If they do not come together, then add one tablespoon of Almond flour then stir, if it needs more, add another tablespoon. Do not pour in a huge amount of almond flour because you will put more than you need and your cookies will come out as though as stone. Set the dough aside to rest for 5 minutes. Grease your palms with some oil and roll the dough into balls, working with only two tablespoons of dough at a time. Place the dough balls on the pre-lined baking sheet and flatten them out using a fork. Bake for 20 minutes until they turn golden brown. Remove from the oven and allow to cool on the cookie tray for 20 minutes. Carefully move them to a cooling rack then serve once cooled.

Tantalizing Apple Pie Bites

Preparation Time: 20 minutes | **Cooking Time:** 0 minutes | **Servings:** 4 | **Calories**: 194

Ingredients: 1 cup chopped walnuts | ½ a cup of coconut oil | ¼ cup of ground flaxseed
½ ounce of frozen, dried apples | 1 teaspoon of vanilla extract | 1 teaspoon of cinnamon | liquid stevia

Directions: Melt the coconut oil until it is liquid. Take your blender and add walnuts, coconut oil, and process well. Add flaxseeds, vanilla, and Stevia. Keep processing until a fine mixture form. Stop and add crumbled dried apples. Process until your desired texture appears. Portion the mixture amongst muffin molds and allow them to chill.

Coconut Cacao Bites

Preparation Time: 1 hour 10 minutes | **Cooking Time:** 0 minutes | **Servings:** 20 | **Calories**: 120

Ingredients: 1-1/2 cups almond flour | 3 dates, pitted | 1-1/2 cups shredded coconut, unsweetened
1/4 teaspoons ground cinnamon | 2 tablespoons flaxseed meal | 1/16 teaspoon sea salt | 1/3 cup tahini
2 tablespoons vanilla protein powder | 1/4 cup cacao powder | 3 tablespoons hemp seeds
4 tablespoons coconut butter, melted

Directions: Place all the ingredients in a food processor and pulse for 5 minutes until the thick paste comes together. Drop the mixture in the form of balls on a baking sheet lined with parchment sheet, 2 tablespoons per ball and then freeze for 1 hour until firm to touch. Serve straight away.

Gingerbread Energy Bites

Preparation Time: 40 minutes | **Cooking Time:** 5 minutes | **Servings:** 14 | **Calories**: 111

Ingredients: 12 dates, pitted, chopped | 1 cup toasted pecans | 2 oz dark chocolate | ¼ teaspoon salt
¼ tsp cloves | 1 tsp ground ginger | 1 tbsp molasses | 1 teaspoon cinnamon ¼ teaspoon ground nutmeg

Directions: Place all the ingredients in a food processor, except for chocolate, pulse for 2 minutes until combined. Shape the mixture into 1-inch balls and place the balls on a cookie sheet lined with wax paper. Place chocolate in a heatproof bowl, microwave for 2 minutes until it has melted, stirring every 30 seconds. Pour the melted chocolate in a piping bag, drizzle it over prepared balls, refrigerate for 30 minutes until chocolate has hardened, and then serve.

Vegan Orange Muffins

Preparation Time: 15 minutes | **Cooking Time:** 0 minutes | **Servings:** 2 | **Calories**: 161

Ingredients: 2 tbsp. pure orange extract | 2 tsp. orange zest | 7 tbsp. coconut butter | 5 oz. coconut oil
5 oz. cocoa powder | 15 drops of stevia

Directions: In a bowl, combine the coconut butter, coconut oil, orange extract, orange zest, cocoa powder and stevia. Place all the ingredients into a food processor and blend until they have a smooth and creamy consistency. Spoon the mixture into paper muffin cups and place in the fridge for around 2 hours and then serve.

Vegan Compliant Protein Balls

Preparation Time: 20 minutes | **Cooking Time:** 0 minutes | **Servings:** 8 | **Calories**: 260

Ingredients: 1 cup of creamed coconut | 2 scoops of vegan sport chocolate protein
¼ cup of ground flax seed | ½ tsp vanilla extract | ½ a tsp of mint extract | 1-2 tbsp of cocoa powder

Directions: Take a large-sized bowl and melt the creamed coconut. Add the vanilla extract and stir well. Stir in flaxseed, protein powder and knead until the fine dough forms. Form 24 balls and allow the balls to chill for 10-15 minutes. Roll them up in some cocoa powder if you prefer and serve!

The Keto Lovers "Magical" Grain-Free Granola

Preparation Time: 10 minutes | **Cooking Time:** 75 minutes | **Servings:** 10 | **Calories**: 292

Ingredients: ½ a cup of raw sunflower seeds | ½ a cup of natural hemp hearts | ½ a cup of flaxseeds
¼ cup of chia seeds | 2 tablespoons of psyllium husk powder | 1 tablespoon of cinnamon | stevia
½ a teaspoon of baking powder | ½ a teaspoon of salt | 1 cup of water

Directions: Preheat your oven to 300 degrees Fahrenheit. Line up a baking sheet with parchment paper. Take your food processor and grind all the seeds. Add the dry ingredients and mix well. Stir in water until fully incorporated. Allow the mixture to sit for a while until it thickens up. Spread the mixture evenly on top of your baking sheet (giving a thickness of about ¼ inch). Bake for 45 minutes. Break apart the granola and keep baking for another 30 mins until the pieces are crunchy. Remove allow them to cool

Pumpkin Butter Nut Cup

Preparation Time: 135 minutes | **Cooking Time:** 0 minutes | **Servings:** 5 | **Calories**: 105

Ingredients: For Filing: ½ a cup of organic pumpkin puree | ½ a cup of almond butter
4 tbsp of organic coconut oil | ¼ tsp of organic ground nutmeg | ¼ tsp of organic ground ginger
1 tsp of organic ground cinnamon | 1/8 tsp of organic ground clove | 2 tsp of natural vanilla extract
For Topping : 1 cup of organic raw cacao powder | 1 cup of organic coconut oil

Directions: Take a medium-sized bowl and add all of the listed ingredients under pumpkin filling. Mix well until you have a creamy mixture. Take another bowl and add the topping mixture and mix well. Take a muffin cup and fill it up with 1/3 of the chocolate topping mix. Chill for 15 minutes. Add 1/3 of the pumpkin mix and layer out on top. Chill for 2 hours. Repeat until all the mixture has been used up

Unique Gingerbread Muffins

Preparation Time: 15 minutes | **Cooking Time:** 30 minutes | **Servings:** 12 | **Calories**: 158

Ingredients: 1 tablespoon of ground flaxseed | 6 tablespoon of coconut milk
1 tablespoon of apple cider vinegar | ½ a cup of peanut butter | 2-3 tablespoons of swerve
2 tablespoons of the gingerbread spice blend | 1 teaspoon of baking powder | 1 teaspoon of vanilla extract

Directions: Pre-heat your oven to a temperature of 350 degrees Fahrenheit. Take a bowl and add flaxseeds, sweetener, salt, vanilla, spices, and coconut milk. Keep it on the side for a while. Add peanut butter, baking powder and keep mixing until combined well. Stir in peanut butter and baking powder. Mix well. Spoon the mixture into muffin liners. Bake for 30 minutes. Allow them to cool and enjoy!

The Vegan Pumpkin Spicy Fat Bombs

Preparation Time: 100 minutes | **Cooking Time:** 0 minutes | **Servings:** 12 | **Calories**: 103

Ingredients: ¾ cup of pumpkin puree | ¼ cup of hemp seeds | ½ a cup of coconut oil | liquid stevia
2 teaspoons of pumpkin pie spice | 1 teaspoon of vanilla extract

Directions: Take a blender and add all of the ingredients. Blend them well and portion the mixture out into silicon molds. Allow them to chill and enjoy!

The Low Carb "Matcha" Bombs

Preparation Time: 100 minutes | **Cooking Time:** 0 minutes | **Servings:** 12 | **Calories**: 200

Ingredients: ¾ cup of hemp sees | ½ a cup of coconut oil | 2 tablespoons of coconut butter
1 teaspoon of matcha powder | 2 tablespoons of vanilla extract | ½ a tsp of mint extract liquid stevia

Directions: Take your blender and add hemp seeds, matcha, coconut oil, mint extract and Stevia Blend well and divide the mixture into silicone molds. Melt the coconut butter and drizzle them on top of your cups. Allow the cups to chill and serve!

The No-Bake Keto Cheese Cake

Preparation Time: 120 minutes | **Cooking Time:** 0 minutes | **Servings:** 4 | **Calories**: 182

Ingredients: For Crust: 2 tablespoons of ground flaxseed | 2 tablespoon of desiccated coconut
1 teaspoon of cinnamon | For Filling: 4 ounces of vegan cream cheese | 1 cup of soaked cashews
½ a cup of frozen blueberries | 2 tablespoons of coconut oil | 1 tablespoon of lemon juice
1 teaspoon of vanilla extract | liquid stevia

Directions: Take a container and mix all of the crust ingredients. Mix them well and flatten them at the bottom to prepare the crust. Take a blender and mix all of the filling ingredients and blend until smooth. Distribute the filling on top of your coat and chill it in your freezer for about 2 hours. Enjoy!

Raspberry Chocolate Cups

Preparation Time: 60 minutes | **Cooking Time:** 0 minutes | **Servings:** 12 | **Calories**: 158

Ingredients: ½ a cup of cacao butter | ½ a cup of coconut manna | 1 teaspoon of vanilla extract
4 tablespoons of powdered coconut milk | 3 tablespoons of granulated sugar substitute
¼ cup of dried and crushed frozen raspberries

Directions: Melt cacao butter and add coconut manna. Stir in vanilla extract. Take another dish and add coconut powder and sugar substitute. Stir the coconut mix into the cacao butter, 1 tablespoon at a time, making sure to keep mixing after each addition. Add the crushed dried raspberries. Mix well and portion it out into muffin tins. Chill for 60 minutes and enjoy it!

Exuberant Pumpkin Fudge

Preparation Time: 120 minutes | **Cooking Time:** 0 minutes | **Servings:** 25 | **Calories**: 120

Ingredients: 1 and a ¾ cup of coconut butter | 1 cup of pumpkin puree
1 teaspoon of ground cinnamon | ¼ teaspoon of ground nutmeg | 1 tablespoon of coconut oil

Directions: Take an 8x8 inch square baking pan and line it with aluminum foil to start with. Take a spoon of the coconut butter and add into a heated pan; let the butter melt over low heat. Toss in the spices and pumpkin and keep stirring it until a grainy texture has formed. Pour in the coconut oil and keep stirring it vigorously in order to make sure that everything is combined nicely. Scoop up the mixture into the previously prepared baking pan and distribute evenly. Place a piece of wax paper over the top of the mixture and press on the upper side to make evenly straighten up the topside. Remove the wax paper and throw it away. Place the mixture in your fridge and let it cool for about 1-2 hours. Take it out and cut it into slices, then eat

Lemon Fudge

Preparation Time: 5 minutes | **Cooking Time:** 0 minutes | **Servings:** 24 | **Calories:** 247

Ingredients: one cup of macadamia nut butter | fifteen drops of monk fruit extract
a quarter cup of coconut oil | one cup of desiccated coconut (unsweetened)
twenty-five drops of lemon essential oil | one teaspoon of vanilla extract

Directions: Line a loaf pan with pieces of parchment paper. Put all the ingredients into a food processor and process until well combined and smooth. Taste and add lemon essential oil or monk fruit extract if needed. Pour the blend mix into the loaf pan and refrigerate for 1-3 hours or until firm. Cut into cubes and serve immediately. Leftovers can be refrigerated for as long as 5 days. Note: To store the fudge, gently arrange them in a plastic airtight container, because if they are put in a jar, removing them will be very tricky because they can get really soft at room temperature.

Peanut Butter Jelly Cups

Preparation Time: 15 minutes | **Cooking Time:** 0 minutes | **Servings:** 12 | **Calories:** 221

Ingredients: peanut butter and jelly layer | half a piece of banana (sliced) | one cup of coconut oil a quarter cup of unsweetened berries or chia jam | half a cup of peanut butter | chocolate layer | a quarter cup of maple syrup | one teaspoon of sea salt | a quarter cup of cocoa powder

Directions: Put the coconut oil, maple syrup and cocaine powder into a bowl and whisk until well combined. Line a couple of muffin pans with paper cups. Scoop a small amount of the chocolate mixture into the muffin pan and refrigerate for 15 minutes. When the chocolate mix is firm, add a scoop of peanut butter, then top with jelly and banana slices. Pour another layer of chocolate over the banana slices, then freeze until solid.

Keto Vegan Granola Bars

Preparation Time: 10 minutes | **Cooking Time:** 60 minutes | **Servings:** 6 | **Calories:** 262

Ingredients : Toppings : 25 g of dark chocolate | 1 tablespoon of coconut oil | ¼ tablespoon cinnamon ½ teaspoon of peanut butter nut base | 4 tablespoons of coconut oil | 2 tablespoons of sweetener 1/4 cup of sliced pecans + ½ tablespoon extra | ¼ cup of dried strawberries, cranberries and blueberries ¼ cup of sliced almonds + 1 tablespoon extra | 4 tablespoons of peanut butter | 1 tablespoon of chia seeds ¼ tablespoon of vanilla extract | ¼ cup of pumpkin seeds | ¼ cup of shredded coconut (unsweetened) ¼ cup of sliced walnuts + one tablespoon extra | ¼ cup of flaxseed flour | 1 teaspoon of collagen

Note: all the extras are for decorating the top of the bars, do not add to the main recipe.

Directions: Put the collagen, sweetener, cinnamon, peanut butter, vanilla extract and two tablespoons of coconut oil into a medium sized mixing bowl. Stir until well combined. Put into the microwave for 1-2 minutes, removing once to stir then microwave for another minute, then set aside. Throw in all the nuts and seeds to the mixture and stir until well combined and nuts are fully coated. Line a baking dish with parchment paper. Pour mixture onto the baking dish and freeze for 20 minutes. Remove the refrigerated nut base and spread the toppings and spread the extras over it. Freeze for another hour then cut into bars and serve.

Vegan Fudge Revel Bars

Preparation Time: 1 hour | **Cooking Time:** 0 minutes | **Servings:** 12 | **Calories:** 160

Ingredients: 1 cup almond flour | ¾ cup erythritol | ¾ cup peanut butter | 1 tbsp. vanilla extract ½ cup sugar-free chocolate chips | 2 tbsp. margarine

Directions: Mix together almond butter, coconut flour, erythritol, and vanilla extract in a bowl until well combined. Press the mixture into a rectangular silicon mold and freeze for an hour to set. Melt the chocolate chips with the margarine for 1-2 minutes in the microwave. Pour melted chocolate on top of the mold and chill for another hour to set. Slice for serving.

Avocado Lassi

Preparation Time: 5 minutes | **Cooking Time:** 0 minutes | **Servings:** 3 | **Calories:** 305

Ingredients: 1 avocado | 1 cup coconut milk | 2 cups ice cubes | 2 tbsp. erythritol ½ tsp powdered cardamom | 1 tbsp. vanilla extract

Directions: Combine all ingredients in a bowl. Mix until well combined. Press the mixture into a rectangular silicon mold and freeze for an hour to set. Slice for serving.

No-Bake Coconut Chia Macaroons

Preparation Time: 2 hours | **Cooking Time:** 0 minutes | **Servings:** 6 | **Calories:** 129

Ingredients: 1 cup shredded coconut | 2 tbsp. chia seeds | ½ cup coconut cream | ½ cup erythritol

Directions: Combine all ingredients in a bowl. Mix until well combined. Chill the mixture for about half an hour. Once set, scoop the mixture into serving portions and roll into balls. Return to the chiller for another hour.

Vegan Banana Bread

Preparation Time: 10 minutes | **Cooking Time:** 1 hour | **Servings:** 12 | **Calories:** 192

Ingredients: 2 cups almond flour | ¼ cup coconut flour | 1 tbsp. baking powder | 4 flax eggs
1 tbsp. cinnamon powder | ¼ tsp salt | ¼cup chopped pecans | ½ cup coconut oil | ½ cup erythritol
¼ cup almond milk | 1 tbsp. banana extract

Directions: Preheat oven to 350°F. Combine all ingredients in a blender and process until smooth. Scrape the batter into a loaf pan lined with parchment. Top with chopped pecans. Bake for 50-60 minutes. Allow to cool before slicing.

Very White Chocolate Peanut Butter Bites

Preparation Time: 110 minutes | **Cooking Time:** 0 minutes | **Servings:** 8 | **Calories**: 77

Ingredients: ½ a cup of cacao butter | ½ a cup of salted peanut butter | 3 tablespoons of stevia
4 tablespoons of powdered coconut milk | 2 teaspoon of vanilla extract

Directions: Set your double boiler on low heat. Melt the cacao butter and peanut butter together and stir in vanilla extract. Take another bowl and add powdered coconut powder and Stevia. Stir one tablespoon at a time of the mixture into the vanilla extract mixture. Portion the mixture into silicone molds or lined up muffin tins and chill them for 90 minutes. Remove and enjoy it!

Chocolate Peanut Butter Cookies

Preparation Time: 20 minutes | **Cooking Time:** 10 minutes | **Servings:** 14 | **Calories:** 179

Ingredients: ½ cup peanut butter, melted | 3 tbsp. coconut oil | 2 cups almond flour | ½ teaspoon salt
½ cup vegan semi-sweet chocolate chips | ½ cup erythritol | ½ cup coconut milk | 1 tsp vanilla extract
½ teaspoon baking soda

Directions: Stir together peanut butter, coconut oil, vanilla extract erythritol, and coconut milk in a bowl. In a separate bowl, whisk together baking soda, flour, and salt. Stir the dry mixture into the wet mixture. Fold the chocolate chips in. Shape dough into cookies and arrange on a baking tray lined with parchment paper. Bake for 10 minutes at 375°F.

30 DAYS MEAL PLAN

Day	Breakfast	Lunch	Dinner	Dessert
1	Chia Breakfast Bowl	Spicy Pork Patties	Eye-Catching Veggies	Berries in Yogurt Cream
2	Baked Apples	Keto Meatballs	Green Soup	Egg Custard
3	Banana Pancakes	Creamy Scallops	Caprese Casserole	Cream Cake
4	Bacon & Cheese Frittata	Rainbow Quinoa Salad	Pressure Cooker Crack Chicken	Easy Peanut Butter Cups
5	Berry Chocolate Breakfast Bowl	Roasted Leg of Lamb	Low Carb Green Bean Casserole	Raspberry and Coconut
6	Coconut Crepes	Keto Sloppy Joes	Avocado Soup	Keto Brownies
7	Avocado Tofu Scramble	Vegan Curry Bowls	Slow Cooker Barbecue Ribs	Delicious Coffee Ice Cream
8	Vegan Breakfast Hash	Lamb Chops and Herb Butter	Simple Tomato Soup	Avocado Ice Pops
9	Cinnamon Muffins	Five Spice Steamed Tilapia	Easy Baked Shrimp Scampi	Raspberry Mousse
10	Keto Mushroom Sausage Skillet	Spicy Keto Chicken Wings	Beef & Broccoli Roast	Chocolate Spread with Hazelnuts
11	Keto Low Carb Crepe	Mushroom Lettuce Wraps	Chicken with Lemon and Garlic	Lemon Fudge
12	Keto Chewy Chaffle	Shrimp & Bell Pepper Stir-Fry	Risotto with Mushrooms	Yogurt and Strawberry Bowl
13	Yogurt Waffles	Buttered Cod	Persian Chicken	Chocolate Truffles
14	Eggplant Omelet	Rib Roast	Salmon Cakes	Pecan Tarts

15	Bacon & Avocado Omelet	Chicken Quesadilla	Buffalo Chicken Soup	Sweet Cinnamon Muffin
16	Savory Keto Pancake	Italian Sausage Satay	Pimiento Tofu Balls	Coconut Panna Cotta
17	Keto Parmesan Frittata	Lamb Chops and Herb Butter	Kale Mushroom Soup	Keto Brownies
18	Keto Porridge	Garlic Pork Loin	Stuffed Zucchini	Chia Balls
19	Herbed Eggs Mix	Mexican Pork Stew	Vegan Bolognese	Milk Pie
20	Vegan Breakfast Sausages	Spicy Keto Chicken Wings	Quick Protein Veggie Bowl	Lemon & Lime Sorbet
21	Breakfast Skillet	Beef with Bell Peppers	Turkey Meatballs	Lemon Bars
22	Spinach and Eggs Mix	Green Avocado Carbonara	Steamed Mustard Salmon	Mango Ice Cream
23	Quick Breakfast Yogurt	Chicken and Rice Congee	Korean Cucumber Salad	Yogurt and Strawberry Bowl
24	Keto Choco Oats	Salmon Teriyaki	Eggplant Rolls	Walnut Cake
25	Chai Waffles	Pesto Flavored Steak	Boiled Garlic Clams	Coconut Bombs
26	Keto Fruit Cereal	Garlic Pork Loin	Easy Meatballs	Chocolate Cookies
27	Overnight Oat Bowl	Lamb Chops and Herb Butter	Cauliflower Pizza Crust	5 Ingredients Ice Cream
28	Matcha Avocado Pancakes	Broccoli and Chicken Casserole	Pumpkin Almond Soup	Tantalizing Apple Pie Bites
29	Breakfast Granola	Chicken Nuggets	Keto Pizza Crust	Mint Pie
30	Apple Avocado Coconut Smoothie	Braised Lamb Shanks	Roast Beef and Mozzarella Plate	Gingerbread Energy Bites

Conclusion

Hopefully, this book can help you feel more comfortable about the keto diet. With this book, you can make healthy food for yourself and your friends who are also undergoing the keto diet. With 600 recipes, you'll never run out of delicious meals to prepare.

This guidebook's information can help a person move forward from deciding to try keto to taking concrete steps in their diet and achieve real results.

There are many benefits to starting the keto diet beyond just losing weight. Keto can also help people improve their heart health by reducing bad fats and forcing the body to work through fats it has stored, possibly in dangerous places like arteries. It can also help people with epilepsy reduce seizures by switching the brain onto ketone power.

Keto can also help women with PCOS regain their health by promoting weight loss and balancing their hormones, which can cause the condition. It can even help clear up acne in some people by reducing blood sugar, improving skin conditions.

Keeping keto long-term can seem difficult, but it is not so difficult once they are acclimated to the keto lifestyle. Planning out meals and snacks can help people keep up keto longer because it takes some of the work and thinking out of dieting. A person can simply grab what they need and go.

Thanks again and stay healthy!

Made in the USA
Las Vegas, NV
22 June 2024

91350989R00087